ONE SMALL CORNER

A HISTORY OF
BRADFORD DIOCESE

ASTRID HANSEN

In grateful memory of
the Rt. Revd. William Johnston
Archdeacon of Bradford 1965 - 1976

For his inspiration and friendship and his urging
that I should write a book, though neither of us
could have guessed that it would be this one!

The Diocese of Bradford and the author are most grateful to
Watmoughs Financial Print Limited, and in particular John
Barrett, for their support and helpful advice in the production
of this book, and to Arts, Museums and Libraries Division of
the City of Bradford Metropolitan District Council for their
financial contribution.

Published by
The Bradford Diocesan Board
of Finance
Stott Hill, Bradford
West Yorkshire BD1 4ET

ISBN 0 902279 08 4

Printed in Great Britain by
Watmoughs Financial Print Limited
Hillam Road, Bradford
West Yorkshire BD2 1QN

Front cover: Kettlewell
Frontispiece: Bradford Cathedral
Back cover: Aerial view of Cathedral

CONTENTS

FOREWORD
TO THE HISTORY OF THE
DIOCESE OF BRADFORD

When I first came to the Diocese of Bradford I was both pleased and interested to discover that the diocese was keen to record its first seventy five years. Even though we are a young diocese it is important that our history is told for future generations. There are great advantages of writing from a near perspective and I, for one, have always very much enjoyed modern history because of its immediate connection to the present. It gives sense to what is going on now and reminds us that we are part of a history which is unfolding.

I like the thought of the person who said that strictly speaking there is no history only biography. I am very grateful to Astrid for the way in which she has brought alive the people who have played a significant role in the diocese and with humour and candour has made judicious assessment of their contribution to the ebb and flow of diocesan life.

In a period in which change has been so rapid it has been vital that she has placed all this within the social context of the contrasts between urban and rural life, which are so marked in our diocese. This makes the point firmly that the church does not exist for its own perpetuation but shares in God's purpose for his world of which it is but a small part.

The research for this study will have been at times trying and at other times rewarding. But I hope too that it has also been an enjoyable undertaking and I commend it warmly to all who are interested in the Diocese of Bradford and hope that those who read it find it as interesting and informative as I have done.

+David Bradford

The Right Reverend David J. Smith
Bishop of Bradford.

INTRODUCTION

The writing of this history was prompted by the former Bishop of Bradford, the Rt. Revd. Robert (Roy) Williamson, who, looking ahead in 1990 to the 75th anniversary of the diocese in 1994, realised that it might still be possible to record first-hand reminiscences from people who had associations with its founding and early days. In determining the length, and to some extent the style, of the book, I was partly guided by the number of people the bishop and members of Bishop's Council suggested might be contacted - a number which grew like a chain reaction once I started! The length and breadth of my interview with Bishop Williamson himself gave some guidance on the degree of detail expected.

I am grateful to the many people who have been helpful and encouraging, but must record particular thanks to these:

Bishop Robert Williamson for entrusting me with the project;

The Ven. David Rogers for helping me to get started, by suggesting lines of approach and basic sources, as well as for a great deal of detailed information;

The Revd. Dr. Stanley Bennett for early encouragement and suggestions of topics that might be included;

Mr. G.A. Newby, historian and journalist, for the lesson that the first rule in writing is "apply seat of pants to seat of chair," and for his comments as the work progressed;

The Ven. David Rogers and Mr. Leslie Perowne for their patient vetting of the whole text for errors of fact, grammar and spelling;

Mr. Malcolm Halliday, Mr. Alex McLelland and their staff at the diocesan office; the diocesan registrar, Mr. Jeremy Mackrell, and his secretary Mrs Ann Carter;

Miss Jean Myers at Bishopscroft; Professor S.J.K. Baker and Miss Connie Priestley at the cathedral for making their archive material available;

The staff of the West Yorkshire Archive Service;

The staff of Bradford Central Library and Keighley Library for their many trips to the innermost recesses to bring me old copies of Crockford's and Who's Who, and material from their files; Mr John Triffitt, Principal Officer Libraries and Resources, and Miss Elvira Willmott, Specialist Librarian Local Studies, whose enthusiastic reaction to the manuscript helped to ensure support for the publication by Bradford Metropolitan District Council;

All those, listed under 'sources', who allowed me to interview them, or responded with long letters, and were so generous with their time and information, and those who kindly loaned photographs and drawings - if I have succeeded at all in bringing this story to life, it is very much thanks to them;

Those parishes which responded to my questionnaire, particularly those who supplied parish histories, centenary booklets and guide books - I read them all and even if a particular parish is not mentioned by name, the background information has influenced the account;

My son Phil for teaching a rather slow pupil to use a word processor, and the Revd. Ron Jackson for converting the resultant disc into the form required by the printer; most of all my husband John, for his unfailing encouragement over the past three years, even putting up with having our holidays determined by where there was someone I needed to see.

In a history of this sort, there are a number of possible approaches. It could be presented strictly chronologically, by topic, by area, even parish by parish. I opted for a chronological framework, with occasional forays backwards or forwards in time in order to cover a specific topic as a unit, rather than fragmented throughout the story. I hope I have managed to bring alive some of the key personalities involved, without producing nothing but a string of potted biographies. As I learned more about some of the remarkable men and women of the early years, I found myself reluctant to leave their personal stories and move on.

I hope too to have set events in the life of the Church of England in this area in a perspective of local and national history. It was impossible to mention every aspect of church work undertaken during the past three quarters of a century, every organisation that has come and gone, even every parish. To produce something both readable (I hope) and affordable, it has been necessary to select rather ruthlessly from a great deal of information and to resist a number of fascinating diversions. With the illustrations too, on some topics it has been much more difficult than I anticipated to get hold of pictures of suitable quality to be reproduced, and in other instances there has been an embarrassment of riches. With places, I have tried to represent different parts of the diocese and with people I have looked for activities rather than formal portraits where possible. I suspect that no two people would have made exactly the same choices and I can only apologise to those whose chosen field of church work or whose favourite spot has been omitted. I have visited every church in the diocese and I have not even managed to work in my personal favourite, little Eldroth as I first saw it, light dappling through its ancient east window on to the bluebell coloured carpet, and a whole story in itself.

Astrid Hansen.

Members of Bishop's Council at Parcevall Hall, 1990

Left to Right – front:
Archdeacon David Shreeve, Canon Peter Hutchinson,
Mrs. Nan Kershaw, Bishop Robert Williamson, Canon Bruce
Grainger, Mr. Tony Hesselwood

middle:
Mr. Nigel Cottam, Mr. Jim Heaton, Mrs Elaine Appelbee,
Rev. Patrick Foreman, Mrs. Joan Simms, Mrs. Janet Bower,
Provost John Richardson, Rev. Colin Spivey, Mrs Astrid Hansen,
Bishop David Evans

back:
Rev. Nigel Kinsella, Mr. Alex McLelland, Rev. John Poole,
Rev. Malcolm Goldsmith, Mr. Malcolm Halliday,
Archdeacon Brian Smith, Rev. John Tidy, Mr. Chris Wright

Archdeacon Shreeve is wearing a 'Committed to Caring' T-shirt –
he ran in local marathons to raise funds.

CHAPTER 1

ALL OUR WORKS BEGUN

The "war to end all wars" was twelve months over; the dashing Prince of Wales was twenty five and a popular hero; the forty year old vicar of St. Werburgh's was making his mark on Derby and beginning his association with the Labour Movement; a son of the 103rd Bishop of Worcester was Archdeacon of Plymouth, when on 25 November 1919, H.M. King George V made the Order in Council which founded the Diocese of Bradford. This date has the best claim to be the birth-date of the diocese, though there are other contenders.

The Bishoprics of Bradford and Coventry Act received Royal Assent on 6 February 1918, the bishop was appointed by Letters Patent on 9 January 1920, consecrated on February 2nd and enthroned on 17 February 1920.

The fourth bishop, the Right Revd. Michael Parker, felt there were grounds for regarding the enthronement of the first bishop as the true beginning of the diocese's existence, and the programme he master-minded for the jubilee of the diocese spanned nine months in 1969-1970, not tied to any of these specific dates and going on to culminate with Petertide celebrations.

There is a precedent for the Anglican Church in Bradford to be a little ambivalent about its anniversaries. In June 1908 there was a celebration of the anniversary of Bradford parish church and at a Civic Reception in St. George's Hall, the Lord Mayor enquired if they had settled the problem whether it was the 400th or 450th anniversary they were marking. In fact the third known church on the site was completed in 1458 but tower and transepts added later, the tower being completed in 1508. On that same occasion, the Lord Mayor, Alderman J.E. Fawcett, reminded the gathering that the advowson held by the Simeon Trustees had been purchased from his grandfather in 1826 by the Revd. Charles Simeon and he hoped "they would all remember that it was not freehold and that the advowees only held it for a period of 500 years."

There is some excuse for the assumption that Ripon, the mother diocese of most of Bradford, is itself of ancient foundation, with its venerable cathedral and traditions going back to St. Wilfrid. Ripon also claims England's first recorded Royal Charter giving it city status in the year 886. In fact Ripon was a see only for a short time in the 7th century and soon merged with York, later coming under the Diocese of Chester. The new Ripon Diocese was formed in 1836, consisting of the greater part of the West Riding, part of the North Riding and part of Lancashire. As the 19th century drew on, growth and movement of population gave the Church of England cause to look again at diocesan boundaries and areas all over the country.

Initially there was extreme parliamentary reluctance to sanction the creation of new dioceses, some of it for entirely honourable reasons. Dr. Owen Chadwick, in a lecture on the occasion of the centenary of St. Albans Diocese in 1977 referred to the view that what was needed was "more front line troops, not more staff officers." However, for those bishops who embraced the 'new' style of episcopacy pioneered by Samuel Wilberforce and were keen to move out of their palaces and be out and about throughout their dioceses, some of the existing areas and populations were impossibly large.

To take Confirmations as just one example of the difference in style, again described by Dr. Chadwick, many bishops had confirmed only in the largest centres, sometimes 1,000 children at a time, by raising their hands in the pulpit over the heads of the entire assembly. Now bishops went into little country churches and prayed over the head of each individual child. It was far better, but work for one man turned into work for four. In Bradford, in 1991, Killington, one of the tiniest parishes in the furthest north of the diocese, was the scene of the Confirmation of eleven candidates by the Bishop of Bradford, the Right Revd. Robert Williamson. This ancient church up among the Cumbrian hills had an electoral roll of 28, with a village population of just over 100, and this was in fact the first Confirmation in this church by a Bishop of Bradford since it became part of the diocese in 1951, although the annual list of Confirmations always includes many of the dales churches.

Back in the 19th century, as this style of pastoral care gained momentum, the Church of England addressed the problem in the best way open to it by reviving the office of Bishops Suffragan in 1870. In many cases, this office was combined with that of Archdeacon. Canon Gordon Hewitt, in his "History of the Diocese of Chelmsford", suggests that it was easy to assume that their pastoral ministry derived from their episcopal office and thus their role as archdeacons began to be thought of as one of administration and inspection of buildings. This of course did not happen in Bradford, which never became a suffragan see, although its archdeacons have from time to time been more closely associated with terriers, slates and drains than with more pastoral aspects.

Fortunately, parliamentary opinion began to modify and in 1888 Wakefield Diocese was formed from three parishes out of York Diocese and a slice off the southern end of Ripon. Population growth in the industrial West Riding in the latter half of the 19th century was phenomenal and proposals for even further subdivision were not long in following, but the shape and composition of the new see were not settled lightly.

In 1909 the fourteenth Viscount Mountgarret offered £5,000 towards the formation of a See of Bradford. He had close connections with the city. His mother was the only child of Mr. Thomas Rawson of Nidd Hall, Lord of the Manor of Bradford and formerly the occupant of the Manor Hall in Kirkgate. In due course Lord Mountgarret became Lord of the Manor. He was the founder

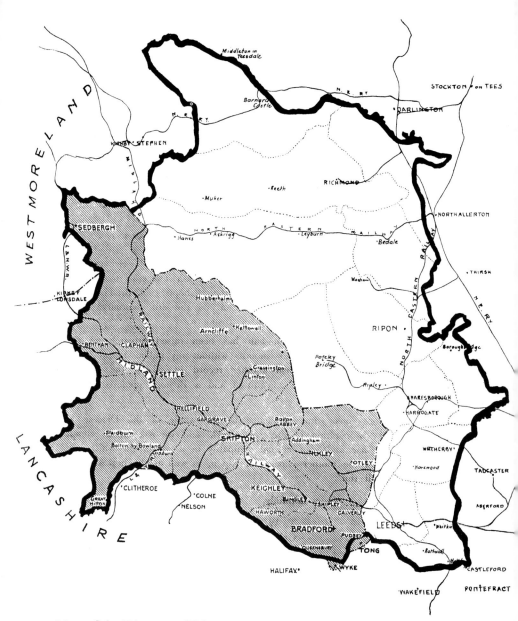

**Map of the Diocese of Ripon,
showing the portion allocated to the
Diocese of Bradford by shaded lines.**

of St. Chad's Manningham, commemorated by a plaque inside that church. The foundation stone was laid by Viscountess Mountgarret in February 1912, during the Viscount's illness. Lord Mountgarret's sister the Honourable Frances Sarah Whittuck, (née Butler), paid for the building of St. Clement's Church, Barkerend Road, in 1892, in memory of their mother.

The retirement of Archbishop W.D. Maclagan of York in 1909, followed by that of Bishop W. Boyd Carpenter of Ripon in 1911, brought the matter of the see to a temporary halt and Lord Mountgarret himself died in October 1912, the very year in which Ripon diocesan conference appointed a committee to produce a scheme for the subdivision of the See of Ripon. Among the possibilities considered by them were sees based on Leeds, on Leeds and Bradford together, and on Ripon's Craven Archdeaconry alone, which included the city of Bradford but would have made rather a small diocese. Proposals to include Leeds in the new diocese were discarded at an early stage, the Diocese of Ripon being unwilling to part with its major city and the bulk of its population. Removal of Leeds would not have solved the problem of transport and communication between Ripon and its Craven Archdeaconry. Removal of Leeds in addition to Bradford would have left a barely viable unit of small towns and scattered villages.

In 1916, the Revd. F.T. Woods, Vicar of Bradford, and Mr. George Ackroyd of Harden Hall near Bingley produced a scheme comprising the Craven Archdeaconry (made up of the four Craven Deaneries and the Deaneries of Clapham and Bradford) and Otley Deanery except for those parishes which had an over-riding natural affinity towards Leeds, namely Arthington, Bramhope, Horsforth, Poole, Stainburn, Weeton and Woodside. This would give approximately 150 parishes, a population of 600,000 in 880 square miles, and just short of 200 clergy. The Diocese of Ripon would be left with 220 parishes, 587,000 people in 1,300 square miles, and 300 clergy.

Dr. Woods, who was by this time Bishop of Peterborough, commended this plan to the diocesan conference in January 1917, supported by the ex Lord Mayor of Bradford Alderman Tom Howarth J.P., the Dean of Ripon, the current Vicar of Bradford Dr. Guy Warman and the Bishop of Ripon. Dr. Woods described this scheme, out of all the many which had been considered, as "very definitely and emphatically the survival of the fittest."

Dr. Warman, writing later in The Church Family newspaper, expressed gratitude to the churchmen of Leeds for forgoing their long-cherished desire, and notably to the Vicar of Leeds, Canon Samuel Bickersteth, for his hearty co-operation in the formation of the best possible plan for the diocese and the Church.

The scheme was received with great enthusiasm by conference, and the Bishop of Ripon, Dr. Drury, was asked to nominate a bishopric committee with himself as president. The vice-presidents were Lord Masham, Lady Powell, the Bishops Suffragan of Richmond and Knaresborough, the Dean of Ripon, the Archdeacons of Craven and Richmond, Colonel Greenwood and Messrs G. Ackroyd, J. Bairstow, R.J. Foster, H.E. Kemp and J.W. Morkill. The honorary

Holy Trinity Parish Church, Skipton

secretaries were Dr. Warman and a man whose name was to become almost synonymous with the Diocese of Bradford, the Bradford solicitor Mr. Frederick A.T. Mossman. The honorary treasurers were Messrs T. Howarth and A.T. Parkinson, but Mr. Parkinson was incapacitated by illness and Mr. Howarth engaged in London on War Service until the final stages, so most of this responsibility fell on Mr. Mossman, Mr. Ackroyd, and later Mr. F.D. Moore. The list of members ranged from Wyke to Sedbergh, Slaidburn to Otley, and many parishes in between, as well as members from the rest of the parent diocese.

The committee's work was divided between three subcommittees - General Purposes, chaired by the Very Revd. Dr. Charles Mansfield Owen , Dean of Ripon; Finance, chaired by Mr. George Ackroyd, and Boundaries, chaired by the Archdeacon of Craven, the Ven. Henry Lucas Cook.

There was early discussion about the choice of cathedral and even the name of the new see, with a minority in favour of a Bishopric of Craven with Skipton Parish Church as its cathedral. The mother diocese however, with its Ripon/Leeds dichotomy, had experience of the difficulties involved in having bishop and cathedral in a country market town in the north, and its main centre of population a large city at the opposite end of the diocese. In the city of Bradford itself, the 19th century All Saints' Church in Little Horton Green was also mentioned as a possible cathedral. This is an elegant building of light coloured stone, with a tall, slim spire, visible for miles around. This church offered accommodation for 900 - 1,000 people.

However, the final choice was the most obvious one, of Bradford's ancient parish church, dedicated to St. Peter and situated on the church hill in the very heart of the city. The committee could scarcely have anticipated the late 20th century drawback of the extreme shortage of car parking space in the vicinity of the cathedral and diocesan office.

The Yorkshire Post commented approvingly on the decision: "The Committee are thus following the example set by the great Bishopric builders of the English Church and also the tendency of modern times in making the home of the new See the greatest, and indeed the only, city of the diocese. As, 900 years ago, Bishoprics were moved from the villages of Elmham and Crediton to the cities of Norwich and Exeter, so now the Rural Deanery of Bradford, with more than half the population of the new diocese, will find its Bishop and its Cathedral within easy reach of them all. The claims of other parts of the diocese have been carefully considered. Country parts of the new diocese must and will be carefully tended. The ancient district of Craven will have its name perpetuated in the honourable office of its Archdeacon."

Archdeacon Cook opted to remain as Archdeacon of Craven in the new diocese and to be a Canon of Bradford instead of Ripon. Thus, although not the first Archdeacon of Craven, he became the first in the Diocese of Bradford. No Archdeaconry of Bradford at this time existed, so that, although the Venerable David Rogers (Archdeacon of Craven 1977 - 1986) lamented that he was often referred to as 'the other archdeacon', his was in fact the more venerable office.

Archdeacon Henry Lucas Cook, first Archdeacon of Craven in Bradford Diocese.

From Henry Lucas Cook onwards, the Archdeacons of Craven (less enthusiastic at being called the Craven Archdeacons) have appreciated the importance of their special charge to the people of the northern dales, but possibly none more so than the Ven. Arthur Sephton (1956 - 1972) described by a former diocesan secretary as the formidable Rector of Holy Trinity, Skipton. Certainly he was a fair and square, middle-of-the-road 1662 Matins Anglican of the old school and a renowned trainer of curates. Little that happened in Craven escaped his notice and the archdeaconry was run almost as a see within a see.

It is worth noting that although the first Bradford Diocesan Conference was held in Bradford, the second, in October 1920, was in Skipton and the fourth in Ilkley, so conscious steps were taken from the very beginning to make the work of the diocese inclusive.

The diocese is about 65 miles long from north-west to south-east and about 25 miles wide at its widest part, though Bishop Blunt's much quoted description of it as 'a banana on a tilt' gives only a very approximate idea of its shape - a considerably distorted banana might be nearer the mark! Although the cathedral city is well to the south of the diocese, a map such as that in the early Diocesan Year Books reveals that this presents nothing like the access problem that there was with Ripon. In the early years of the century, for movement of goods and for individual travel for business or pleasure, the railway was king, and Bradford was well served, mainly by the L.M.S. Railway Company. A railway line ran from beyond Howgill in the north, via Sedbergh, Thornton-in-Lonsdale, Ingleton, Clapham, Giggleswick, where it joined that from Hawes Junction, Horton-in-Ribblesdale, Stainforth, Langcliffe, Settle, on to Long Preston, Hellifield where the line from Lancaster comes in via Gisburn, through Gargrave down to Skipton. From the north-east came the line from Grassington, from the west the other Lancashire line via Kelbrook, Earby and Thornton-in-Craven. From Skipton, lines ran down Wharfedale and Airedale with branches for the Worth Valley, Denholme and Queensbury. Bradford, Calverley, Horton and Bowling Deaneries presented a veritable spider's web of rails.

The chief cash crop of the northern dales was wool and Bradford was the wool centre of the world, so that Craven wool and its buyers and sellers all found their way to the Bradford Wool Exchange. The diocese could almost be seen as built round the railway from Sedbergh to Bradford and its feeder lines, and early Year Books make no assumptions about private motor cars but list the rail and tram routes to the churches. It is fair to say that for no parish was access to or from Bradford more difficult than it had been to or from Ripon, and for most of them it was outstandingly better.

But wherever a man-made boundary is drawn, someone will always wish they were just the other side of it. Up to the end of the 19th century, the term 'diocese' meant little other than the area under the jurisdiction of a bishop, and the notion that individual parishes might have something in common other than coming under that same jurisdiction - some sort of family feeling, of belonging together is something that was just beginning to be expressed around the time Bradford Diocese came into being. The growth of synodical government and lay involvement in Church structures have contributed to this new meaning.

But all that is of the future. There was other work for the bishopric committee beside naming the new diocese and choosing its cathedral. There was a little matter of paying for it. The requirements of the Ecclesiastical Commissioners were that an endowment be raised, sufficient to produce £2,500 per annum plus a further sum for a residence. Money would also be needed for preliminary legal expenses and for adaption of the parish church. £300 p.a. was allocated from Ripon Diocese, leaving the committee to raise a capital sum of some £52,000.

The committee was determined not to be bound by tradition but to found a bishopric appropriate for the 20th century. They commented that bishops of older dioceses had large incomes, lived in ancient castles or palaces and dispensed much hospitality. An entirely false and fatal appearance of opulence was thereby created, which the committee considered detrimental to the recognition of the bishop as a real father-in-God.

They proposed that the £2,500 p.a. should be divided into two parts - £1,500 for the bishop's personal emolument and £1,000 for his official and diocesan expenses. In this way his real income would be clearly seen and understood. Their bishop should not live in a palace, but in a house of modest dimensions.

However, the Ecclesiastical Commissioners held out little hope for Bradford's novel proposal. Only a bill prepared along traditional lines would be introduced as a government measure. During the war the government had a monopoly of parliamentary time and would certainly not use it to introduce a Church Bill which might be regarded as contentious. Persistence with the proposal would mean waiting until after the war. The committee no doubt recollected the difficult passage matters of Church reform had suffered before the war, due both to party bitterness and general congestion of business. It had taken Sheffield six years to get its bill through, even after raising the endowment.

The new Diocese of Coventry was also on the point of coming to fruition and the Bishop of Worcester had resisted the removal of contentious clauses from his bill as strenuously as the Bishop of Ripon had for Bradford, with as little success. If they would agree to a traditional bill, the Home Secretary Sir John Cave had undertaken personally to introduce and pilot a joint bill for Bradford and Coventry through the House of Commons. Dr. Drury urged the committee not to lose the present unique opportunity of having the bill passed and hoped that arrangements for the division of the income might be made later when the bishopric was constituted.

Reluctantly the committee accepted the advice, although Mr. Ackroyd, while not withdrawing his support for the new diocese, resigned from the chairmanship of the finance committee in protest. Though Bradford failed to make official history with its new-style bishopric, what it actually achieved, as will be seen, under its first and subsequent bishops, was very close to the ideal at which the committee was aiming.

The Bishoprics of Bradford and Coventry Act was passed by the House of Commons during an air-raid in 1917, when local legend has it that opponents took to the shelter while those in favour braved the threat of bombing and remained for the vote. It was steered through the House of Lords by the Archbishop of Canterbury, Randall Davidson, who gave a personal assurance that Bradford's endowment would be raised without loss of time. When he spoke, the fund stood at £70!

The Act received Royal Assent on 6 Feb. 1918. On Thursday 13 June 1918, a Day of Thanksgiving for the passing of the Act was held, with the order of events as shown on the hand bill.

Mr. F.D. Moore of Burley-in-Wharfedale took Mr. Ackroyd's place as chairman of the finance committee and in October 1919 was able to report that the required funds had been handed to the Ecclesiastical Commissioners. Two records were thus set up - in securing the Act before the endowment was obtained, and in the speed of collecting the amount required. Translate £52,000 in 1918 into today's terms to appreciate the magnitude of the task.

Bishopric of Bradford.

DAY OF THANKSGIVING
(For the Passing of the Bishopric Act).

THURSDAY, JUNE 13TH, 1918,

BRADFORD PARISH CHURCH

7-30 a.m. Celebration of the Holy Communion.
11-0 a.m. Choral Celebration of the Holy Communion and Sermon by The LORD BISHOP OF RIPON
8-0 p.m. Thanksgiving Service and Sermon by The RIGHT REVD. BISHOP BOYD CARPENTER.

N.B.—The offertories will be given to the Bishopric Fund. It is hoped that as many as possible will communicate at one or other of the Celebrations.

3-0 p.m. PUBLIC MEETING IN THE

COUNCIL CHAMBER of the TOWN HALL,

Chairman :
The RIGHT HON. THE LORD MAYOR.

Speakers :
The LORD BISHOP OF RIPON.
The RIGHT REVD. BISHOP BOYD CARPENTER.
The DEAN OF RIPON.
F. D. MOORE, Esq., J.P., and others.

F. S. GUY WARMAN,
FREDK. A. T. MOSSMAN, } Hon. Secs.

S. F. SEWELL, PRINTER BRADFORD.

CHAPTER 2

LABOR OMNIA VINCIT

With parliamentary approval for the formation of the new diocese, there remained some details to be finalised by the boundaries committee. The consent of Wakefield Diocese was obtained and the parishes of Wyke, Tong and Tong Street added to make a more logical southern boundary in view of the relationship of these areas to the city of Bradford. The addition of Horsforth and Woodside was considered, but opposed by parishioners who felt they were more closely involved with Leeds, and in this they were supported by the Rural Dean of Otley.

Another addition came later, in 1925, when the tiny parishes of Firbank in Westmorland and Howgill in Yorkshire, beautifully set at the foot of the Howgill Fells, became a united benefice. Firbank was in the Diocese of Carlisle and Howgill in Bradford. Since the population of Howgill exceeded that of Firbank by some half dozen or so, the united benefice was allocated to Bradford even though the vicarage was in Firbank. Similarly, Killington, also in Westmorland, an ancient church which had been the private chapel of Killington Hall up to 1586, was merged into a united benefice with Sedbergh in 1951 and thus also transferred to Bradford Diocese. Further changes made a united benefice of Firbank, Howgill and Killington in 1977 and local government reorganisation put them all in Cumbria!

People in this corner of the diocese look to Kendal as their main town and for many of them, particularly in those villages that had never even been in Ripon Diocese, Bradford must have seemed remote. The opening of the M6 motorway has emphasised the accessibility of Kendal and also Lancaster. The Sedbergh, Howgill and Cautley Parish Magazine of November 1919 says: "It is perhaps true that we, in the northern part of this deanery, may feel that we are as remote as ever from the centre of diocesan activities, and that we shall not benefit in the least from the change. It would certainly have been better if, in addition to Bradford, a diocese of Lancaster had been created and we had been attached to it - it will certainly come about one day. Still, even though our geographical situation is remote, we shall belong to a compact and workable see, and we may hope that renewed and increased vigour may be shown in every parish of the new diocese."

Even with these reservations there was commitment to the work of Bradford Diocese from its north-western extremities right from the start, and the then

Churches in the Bradford Diocese

Deaneries	**Churches in Bradford Centre not shown**
1 Airedale	Bradford St Augustine
2 Bowling & Horton	Bradford St Clement
3 Calverley	Bradford St Columba
4 Otley	Bradford St Oswald
5 Bowland	Frizinghall
6 Ewecross	Girlington
7 Skipton	Manningham St Chad
8 South Craven	Manningham St Mary
	Manningham St Paul

Vicar of Sedbergh, Revd. A.H. Walker, was secretary of the committee for training of the ministry. Ewecross Deanery was fully represented on the new diocesan board of finance, two of its lay members being from Sedbergh School and Preparatory School, and another, Mr. H. Macpherson, from Cautley. Mr.Macpherson's daughter Marguerite recalled seeing notes in his motoring diary referring to meetings in Bradford, with the reminder to "pick up Archdeacon in Skipton". Years later, Marguerite was to marry a young curate in the Diocese of Ripon who was to become a much loved and respected Archdeacon of Bradford, the Venerable William Johnston, before he joined the considerable list of bishops to have been supplied by this little diocese.

Important though the work of the boundaries committee was, back in 1918, with £70 in hand, upwards of £50,000 required, the brunt of the work now fell to the finance committee. The Lord Lieutenant of the West Riding, The Earl of Harewood, and many members of the bishopric committee, had been opposed to launching a public appeal while the nation was at war. Members from the city of Bradford, including Mr. Mossman, urged that fund raising begin as soon as possible, pointing out that Coventry was going ahead with its collection. They argued too that the war, with its demand for uniforms, had been extremely profitable for the textile trade and there had never been so much 'spare' money around. Now, by 1918, with wool in short supply and various restrictions applying, trade was just beginning to fall off. Mr. Mossman, in a letter to the Dean of Ripon, gave his opinion that anxious times were coming - labour troubles seemed inevitable after the war and "men who would support us now will very soon be disposed to be cautious and to husband their resources - there is a tide in the affairs of men....." There were too in early 1918 a Lord Mayor and Deputy Lord Mayor who were strong churchmen and were prepared personally to go round and collect.

Even before Dr. Drury felt able to 'go public', the chairman of the finance committee, Mr. F.D. Moore, and his team were privately printing and delivering circulars. Day by day Mr. Moore, Mr. Mossman and Dr. Warman visited the offices of Bradford appealing for subscriptions. Lord Harewood's objections were overcome by the decision to invest all money raised in War Bonds, to be cashed only after the war, thus helping the war effort as well as the new diocese. A letter from the Governor of the Bank of England urged investment in National War Bonds, as suggested by the Chancellor of the Exchequer, as a patriotic duty, and also looking at it purely as an investment, commended it. An interesting glimpse of war-time conditions is given by the printed message at the top of the page: "Need for saving paper explains small size of this letter." Much of the surviving correspondence from this time is on small or flimsy paper, even from those who might normally have used something quite opulent, perhaps embossed with a crest.

At the fifth meeting of the bishopric committee, 16 March 1918, Dr. Drury asked that their gratitude be recorded to the Home Secretary and the Archbishop of Canterbury for the unprecedented rapidity with which the Act of Parliament had been passed, and said he hoped the committee would proceed at once to

21

Dean Charles Mansfield Owen

Dr. Guy Warman

collect funds. Mr. Ackroyd and other members of the finance committee were also involved in the work and there was tremendous help at the Ripon end from the Dean, the Very Revd. Charles Mansfield Owen. Of him, the Yorkshire Observer columnist Clericus wrote: "Dr. Owen is best described as being everything which one would naturally expect a Dean not to be. There is nothing about him of that pompous starchiness, coupled with an inefficiency begotten of detachment from mundane concerns, which is traditionally associated with a deanery. For vivacity, wit, humility, humanity and the genius of getting on with his work, the Dean of Ripon is supreme. His ready smile and repartee disarm criticism and his unaffectedness makes him a persona grata with all. In business he is a 'hustler' in the best sense, and his soft answer invariably turneth away wrath."

Mr. Moore, as well as giving so much of his time, launched the fund with an amazing £5,000 (1994 equivalent approx. £90,000).

Much of 1918 was devoted to fund raising by sending out circulars and lists of subscribers, following up by personal contact. Some responses were marvellous, such as Miss Cross of Coney Garth, Ripon, who sent £1000 with the promise of a further £500 when the fund reached £35,000. Some apologised for their inability to do more – Lord Masham regretted that heavy duties, coupled with the fact that much of his investment was in enemy and conquered countries, meant he must curtail expenditure, but sent £1,000.

Bradford businesses and Bradford businessmen rallied round, though not all responses were good enough for the indefatigable Mr. Mossman and some of his comments to Dean Owen were quite sharp: "Mr.... has contributed £10. Having regard to the amount which this gentleman has received from Bradford Corporation for his land, I think he might very well be expected to make this up to £1,000." "£250 is not enough. The three brothers ought to give at least £500 each." At the same time, he sent warm messages of thanks to those whose offerings were of the nature of the widow's mite, such as the cheque for £1-5-6d from Darlington with the message that "My extremely poor parish gave a collection yesterday to the Bradford Bishopric fund as a symbol of sympathy." Former residents in the area of the new diocese were tracked down all over the country and circularised, among them Anna Delius who sent £30 from Worthing. The Bishop of Ripon even wrote to the Duke of Devonshire in Toronto.

The level of activity involved on top of their normal duties took its toll on the principal workers. Several of the dean's letters begin "My Dear Mossman, Cheer up", but it was the dean himself who succumbed in August 1918 to an attack of shingles and was ordered to rest - "The Doctors say I have been doing too much. It's all very hard for me to bear as I like work better than any other occupation." A quiet rest at Bainbridge had to be cut short when the shingles led to eczema and the need for a course of treatment at Harrogate.

Meanwhile, Messrs Moore and Mossman and Dr. Warman soldiered on. A donation of £50 from a Member of Parliament came with the comment that his personal sympathies were more with the hard-pressed clergy than with new bishoprics. This was a question the bishopric committee must have wrestled with. They would have had to face the whole issue of how much the way they had chosen was in fact the best way of forwarding the Gospel message in their part of the world, and how much a matter of civic pride. Having made their choice, they must have been heartened by some of the other letters coming in e.g. from a Sheffield vicar: "The general shape of the new diocese is singularly like the new one at Sheffield and although the bulk of the population comes, as in our case, at the southern extremity, I do not think this is altogether a loss. What we have experienced during the last four years of the value of a new diocese makes me realise how much the church in Bradford and throughout the Craven district stands to gain by this new venture." From Woodhouse, Leeds: "I congratulate you heartily. I will do everything in my power to help what I regard as a real bit of Church Reform, badly, sadly and even madly overdue." Dean Owen himself contrasted his experiences in Birmingham when it was part of Worcester Diocese and afterwards, when the benefits were both material and spiritual, with new churches being built, increased Confirmations and communicants, and the clergy heartened in their work.

Meetings held throughout the area of the new diocese included a Drawing Room Meeting at Mrs. Farrer's home at Ingleborough Hall and a Garden Meeting at Myddleton Lodge, Ilkley. The Dean of Ripon and the Vicar of Bradford spoke at these and other gatherings. Support for the scheme was forthcoming, but some of Craven's churchmen still regretted the decision to base the see on the city of Bradford and Mr. Morkill, a Skipton representative on the bishopric committee, held out no hope of contributions from Craven magnates for this reason. At the other end of the financial scale, the parish of Chapel-le-Dale protested that Bradford had nothing to do with them, nor they with Bradford. They were hardly able to keep their church going and their vicar lived in penury. Nevertheless they sent five shillings.

In September 1919 Mr. Mossman was writing to Dean Owen, "I am afraid that the Craven churchmen imagine that the Bishop of Bradford will be no more to them than the Bishop of Ripon, inasmuch as they believe that the whole of his time will be spent at Bradford. It will be up to the new Bishop to prove the contrary." To put the geographical problem in perspective, a map of the dioceses of England shows few with a cathedral city in anything like a central position, and many at least as close to one of their boundaries as is Bradford.

To involve all the parishes, those designated for the new diocese and those to remain in Ripon, who would also benefit from the reduced size of that diocese, Sunday 8 December 1918 was designated Bishopric Sunday, the expectation being that all collections on that day should be sent to the fund. It was hoped too that the publicity of this special day might encourage parishes to undertake some local fund-raising. Articles explaining the history of the Bradford Bishopric Movement appeared in the Bradford Argus, Yorkshire Post and Yorkshire Observer in the week leading up to it, and a list of nine concise reasons for supporting the new bishopric was provided for the parishes. The Bolton-by-Bolland church magazine for December 1918 is an example of the way in which these were presented to parishioners, and the vicar's letter is reproduced in full, for this and for its illuminating references to the impact World War I had even in remote and peaceful villages.

My Dear Friends,

My letter this month must be short, because I wish to place before you some reasons why we should all - so far as in our power - support the proposal for the new Bishopric of Bradford, on behalf of which Collections will be made in every Church in the Diocese on Sunday, December 8th. The thought uppermost in all our minds at present is a feeling of deep thankfulness that an Armistice has been signed suspending hostilities. The Armistice, we all hope and believe will lead to a just and lasting peace, but before peace can be signed many months will probably elapse and many difficulties will arise. Tremendous difficulties, too, will arise in our own country, you can see them and think them out for yourselves. Let us pray then, that the electors may be guided wisely on December 14th and that a strong Government may be returned, able and anxious to deal with the problems that face the country in the work of reconstruction. We were all grieved to hear that Private Charles Geldard, Devon Light Infantry, lost his life on October 23rd. He received a very severe shell wound and died the same day. We are also sorry to hear of Private Richard Brotherton's illness, but hope he may now pull through. A very successful Whist Drive and Dance was held in the School on Friday, November 15th, to provide Christmas Parcels for our Bolton soldiers and Bolton widows and fatherless children. On Sunday, December 29th, at the afternoon service instead of a Sermon, the Choir will sing Christmas Carols and there will be a Collection for Sir Arthur Pearson's Fund for helping blinded soldiers and sailors.

Yours very truly,

C.C. Brodhurst.

BISHOPRIC OF BRADFORD

Reasons for Supporting the Movement:

1. The Spiritual Needs of the Church will be greater than ever after the War, and it must not miss the opportunity for want of organisation.

2. The Diocese of Ripon by reason of its unwieldy size, its inconvenient geographical position, and its large population, is far too great an undertaking for one Diocesan Bishop to manage.

3. The Success of this Scheme will bring aid to the remaining portion of the mother See as well as to Bradford and Craven. As the Bishop of Ripon said in a recent speech: "this is not a Bradford matter merely; it is a Diocesan matter." We confidently look for help from all classes and from all parts of the mother Diocese. From all classes because the interests of all who seek the well-being of the Church are equally concerned, and from all parts because the separation of the new See will set free much of the energy and time of the Bishop of Ripon for the benefit of the portion which will remain under his supervision.

4. The Population of the Diocese of Ripon is now one-and-a-quarter millions, spread over an area of about two thousand two hundred square miles. The new Bradford Diocese will contain two fifths of this area, with more than half the rapidly increasing population.

5. A Diocese of this enormous size and population, forming a large and expanding part of Yorkshire in which new religious and social problems are constantly arising, is a sphere of such grave responsibility before God that it is our bounden duty to make it as efficient as possible without delay.

6. The Scheme has been formulated at the request and with full co-operation of the Bishop of Ripon, who has allocated in perpetuity the sum of £300 per annum from the mother See to form part of the Endowment of the Diocese of Bradford.

7. The City of Bradford with its vigorous civic and commercial life (the centre of Worsted Trade), its ancient and noble Parish Church, and its growing population of nearly three hundred thousand, has been selected as the Cathedral City and the Seat of the Bishop of the new Diocese.

8. The Inspiring Effects upon Church life which have followed upon the formation of the Dioceses of Liverpool, Newcastle, Birmingham and Sheffield, have exceeded the most sanguine anticipations of those concerned.

9. Although the present time of national stress is not the most propitious to seek donations for a Bishopric, yet it is of the utmost importance that the Bishop should be at work and ready to deal with the problems which will arise immediately after the War, and as the Ecclesiastical Commissioners have agreed to accept the amount required to constitute the Bishopric in War Bonds, donations will be paid to the Treasury and the National Cause thereby promoted.

10. The New Bishopric will be founded on lines in accordance with modern thought. The Bishop will not live in a Palace, but in a Residence of the annual value of £150 or thereabouts. The total Income belonging to the new See will be £2,500 per annum, including the £300 allocated from the mother Diocese.

It proposed to divide the Income into two parts, of which one shall be paid to the Bishop for his personal use, and the other applied towards the payment of his official expenses.

The response was in general excellent and within a few days Mr. Mossman was sending out receipts and thanks. St. Mary Magdalene's, described as the "Highest church in the town" did particularly well with £116, a sum many churches would be pleased with as a Sunday's collection even in the '90s. Some of course laid themselves open to Mossman reprimands. One urban church divided its collection between the bishopric fund and the Bradford Hospital Fund and was reminded that the poorer churches stood to benefit most from the new arrangement, and furthermore it was the only church in the diocese to decide on such a division of its collection. The missing half arrived next day! The bankers to the bishopric fund, London Joint City and Midland Bank Ltd., did not escape a frosty note in which their attention was drawn to the fact that "the pass book shows an overdraft of £7,000 plus, instead of a balance of £1,800 plus, since at least eight items are wrongly entered."

As so often happens with appeals, the last £10,000 was the hardest to raise. A 'Half-Crown Fund' was initiated for small subscribers, parishes taking half-crown cards to fill up and cheques for amounts such as £12-10-0d (100 half-crowns) came in. Free Churchmen too contributed readily and substantially to the fund, a foretaste of interdenominational co-operation in all sorts of ways in the years to come.

Almost every letter Mr. Mossman wrote at this time, whatever its prime reason, had the appeal included, or a suggestion of names the recipient might care to approach. A general practitioner was thanked for his cheque, with the rider "if you can influence any of your patients to do likewise, I shall be very much obliged." He also proved himself a tough negotiator with Ripon Diocesan Board of Finance and secured for the new diocese 7/16 of its accumulated funds, a better deal than many of the new dioceses achieved.

To the record achievements of the embryo diocese, the Yorkshire Observer noted that a third should be added, namely the incredibly small amount taken up in expenses: "Almost £52,000 was raised by an expenditure of only £306 on stationery, printing and postage. The Bill was prepared and carried through Parliament without any legal charges whatever. Mr. Frederick A.T. Mossman, the Hon. Secretary, is to be heartily congratulated on such a satisfactory state of things."

On 28 October 1919, Dr. Warman preached at a Thanksgiving Service in Bradford Parish Church, but he was no longer Vicar of Bradford. Just ten days earlier, he had been consecrated as Bishop of Truro. This echoed the situation when Dr. Woods presented the bishopric proposals after becoming Bishop of Peterborough. In his sermon, Dr. Warman made to the people of the new diocese a parting plea for unity - between nations, classes, and within the Church of England. "A school of thought is one thing, and valuable," he said, "a Party is another, and an abominable symbol of death." In his forward-looking remarks he touched also on re-union with Christians outside the Church of England. The Yorkshire Observer's 'Observatory' column commented: "Bradford - it would be difficult to find a city wherein the quality of enlightened tolerance is more widespread." This tolerance was to face many severe tests in the decades ahead.

Frederic Sumpter Guy Warman was brought up in the evangelical tradition, but was himself of a more liberal mind. He accepted that the Church of England embraced a wide range, but was firm about its limits and believed that the central ground must be built up. The Church Times questioned the suitability of his appointment to Truro, which had a definite high church tradition and where he was to be dean as well as bishop, but conceded that he was welcomed by congregations of the most diverse views and in Bradford he recognised the right of English churchmen to a large amount of independence of thought and difference of view.

Dr. Warman was Bishop of Truro for four years and in 1923 became the second Bishop of Chelmsford and in 1929 Bishop of Manchester. His three years in Bradford were among the most active and dramatic in the history of that parish and his role in the formation of the diocese invaluable.

The key workers for the bishopric had of course more than one ball in the air and as well as explaining the scheme, defining boundaries and raising the endowment, there was also the matter of the see house. Of one thing everyone was sure - no palace for this bishop. The proposal was that a residence be provided for the bishop in or near Bradford with the following accommodation, or thereabouts:

Ground Floor.

Chapel, Dining Room of good size, Drawing Room of good size, Study, Chaplain's Room, Morning or Waiting Room, Cloak Room and Lavatories.

Bedrooms.

Seven Bedrooms, one Dressing Room, Two Bathrooms and two Lavatories, Three Bedrooms for Domestics.

Kitchen etc.

Kitchen and Scullery etc. Sewing Room or Servants' Hall, Outside Lavatory.

Garden not larger than can be kept in order at moderate expense.

If this sounds rather more than a modest house, it must be borne in mind that a diocesan bishop's home was also his office, and he would be called upon to provide hospitality ranging in quantity and style from ordination retreats to visits by archbishops and royalty.

At a very early stage, Lady Powell of Horton Old Hall, as well as making a large donation to the bishopric fund, offered her other property, Horton Hall, on a repairing lease for 21 years at £10 p.a. The committee reluctantly felt they must decline the generous offer, as the house was not altogether suitable and they hoped at that stage to purchase outright a property close to their promulgated ideal. Mr. Mossman actively sought out suitable houses, and as the requirements became known, estate agents and homeowners approached him with their proposals.

The Manningham/Frizinghall district of Bradford seems to have been the area of choice, convenient for the city but equally well placed for heading out to Keighley and the rest of Craven. At that time both Manningham and Frizinghall had well served railway stations. Among the houses considered were Bolton Royd (Manningham Lane), Aireville (Frizinghall), 6 Clifton Villas, Shipley Grange, Shipley Fields Hall and a whole group of "Oaks" - Oakbank, Oakleigh, Oakwell, and perhaps the likeliest contender Oaklands in Oak Avenue, which was bigger than the committee's ideal model. Mr. Mossman wrote to Mr. Ackroyd, "I do not think there is the least prospect of our persuading the Ecclesiastical Commissioners, Bishop, Dean and other powers that be to agree to anything smaller. Dr. Warman and I both feel the house opposite called Oak Bank would be suitable. Col. Wade offered me this for £3,000 and I induced the Bishop to go and see it, but his report was 'quite impossible.'"

Oaklands was eventually rejected as having too much land, being difficult to adapt and having rather grandiose marble pillars which might give the wrong impression. Not even Mr. Mossman's initiative in proposing that as the pillars were sham, the marble effect could be painted over, and the billiard room or conservatory converted into a chapel, managed to carry the day.

One Bradfordian had a novel suggestion of his own. He had two adjoining houses and he urged the Bishopric Committee to buy both, one for the bishop to live in, while the other "would do admirably for Confirmations and other diocesan work." He also indicated that a generous donation to the fund would be forthcoming if his houses were bought. Neither the houses nor the suggestions were considered appropriate, but the decision seems to have been received without ill-feeling as he and his wife appear among the list of donors, and a copy of the "Bishop's Messenger" a few years later refers to the Mothers' Union spending a delightful day at the country house to which the gentleman eventually moved, being entertained by his wife and local M.U. members.

Although the decision to centre the see on Bradford was taken in 1917, and an amendment in favour of Skipton moved by Mr. Morkill and seconded by Revd. J.W. Bullard was not carried, some Skipton people were still hoping that the bishop might be able to live near Skipton. The Vicar of Bradford pledged that every offer of a house would be carefully considered.

Eventually it became clear that the matter of the house was not likely to be settled before the appointment of a bishop and this was so imminent that it seemed sensible to wait until the new bishop and his wife could be involved in the choice.

CHAPTER 3

CHOSEN TO SERVE

In January 1919, the Yorkshire Observer published its thoughts on the necessary attributes of Bradford's new bishop, who should be: "a youngish man, as the hills and dales would kill a septuagenarian, even if he did not first of all kill the diocese; a man who understands the north, particularly the West Riding; the blood in his veins must be warm – the climate is cold enough here without ecclesiastical freezing machines. He must talk like a man, not a gramophone – if he frequently forgets to don his gaiters and his fully- rigged top hat and discards a superfluity of buttons, Bradford will not be angry with him. It may indeed applaud. If he can enjoy a well seasoned briar pipe over a rubber of whist he will be persona grata in countless homes."

Speculation on the choice was naturally rife during the year and, until his appointment to Truro, many believed, and indeed hoped, that Dr. Warman might be appointed. Dr. Owen's name too was mentioned. It is doubtful whether any of Bradford's bishops have been accurately predicted, save possibly very quietly and discreetly by senior members of the diocesan team.

After the Order in Council brought the bishopric into actual and legal existence on 25 November 1919, Bradford did not have long to wait. The appointment of the Venerable Arthur William Thomson Perowne, Archdeacon of Plymouth, was announced on December 8th. Archdeacon Perowne did not fill quite all of the Yorkshire Observer's criteria, but certainly enough to satisfy that newspaper, which headlined the news:

Bishop of Bradford Appointed

Happy Choice

Apostle of Unity Among All Christians.

The Yorkshire Post found itself a Plymouth Correspondent, who described the 52 year old Arthur Perowne as "short of stature, having a very thoughtful face relieved by laughing eyes. He overflows with good nature and a quiet urbanity, and while always speaking most directly he has a happy way of putting strangers quickly at ease."

Urbanity might possibly not have been one of the qualities Bradford was specifically seeking in its bishop, though the quality of speaking directly would certainly be appreciated. The bishop's son Leslie remembered being with his father when one of the Sunday School workers, Miss Elliot Smith, introduced him to her landlady: "Mrs. O., this is our new bishop." The bishop beamed and said, "How do you do? I don't think I've had the pleasure of meeting you before." "Ee, well you 'ave now, 'aven't you?" came the typically local response.

Leslie Perowne described the contrast between Plymouth and Bradford. Despite the cosmopolitan bustle of its dockyard, Plymouth was still a sleepy Devon town at heart and the nearby Dartmoor, where the family took their holidays, a paradise of quiet relaxation, fishing for father and hours of unspoilt walking for the three boys; then suddenly, Bradford, with a very different atmosphere and a quickness about the people which Leslie, who has lived much of his adult life in London, likened almost to the Cockney style.

The Perownes are a family of French Huguenot descent, with a tradition of service to the Church. Arthur Perowne's grandfather was a missionary in Bengal, his father, Dr. J.J.S. Perowne, had been Bishop of Worcester, one uncle was Archdeacon of Norwich, another Master of Corpus Christi College, Cambridge. Later, a young cousin, C.R.T.C. Perowne, started his ministry as curate at St.Luke's, Manningham. Arthur himself began as a curate at Hartlebury in Worcestershire, and domestic chaplain to his father at the bishop's residence, Hartlebury Castle, then became vicar of the neighbouring village of Hallow, moving in 1904 to Birmingham, where he followed Dr. Owen as vicar of the big urban parish of St. George's, Edgbaston.

A year after his arrival in Edgbaston, the ancient Diocese of Worcester was divided and the new Diocese of Birmingham formed. Arthur became rural dean and a Canon of Birmingham Cathedral. Experience here must have been highly relevant to his appointment to Bradford, and his next move continued an almost tailor-made training when he moved to Plymouth. There, as in Edgbaston, he became known for his forceful and straightforward sermons and particularly for his efforts to improve moral standards and housing conditions in the city. He took an active part in promoting the formation of a Plymouth Bishopric although that scheme had to be postponed for lack of adequate endowment. In 1918 he became the first Archdeacon of Plymouth and Chaplain to the King.

As an organiser and administrator he was outstanding, setting diocesan finance at Plymouth on a substantial footing. One of his proposals, almost revolutionary at the time, was that churchmen should acknowledge their responsibility by a stated weekly gift which should bear some correspondence to their means. This efficient approach to diocesan finance must have found a ready echo in the hearts of members of Bradford's bishopric finance committee, and in Bradford a diocesan board of finance was set up from the start, although the legal obligation to do so did not come in until 1925. (When eventually Bishop Perowne was translated to Worcester in 1931, he found little had been done about the D.B.F. Measure there, and his administrative abilities came into play again to sort out their diocesan organisation.)

Thus Arthur William Thomson Perowne came to Bradford with experience of life in an episcopal household, diocesan administration and the birth-pangs of a new diocese. Mrs. Perowne, Helena Frances, was a cousin of the Right Revd. A.F. Winnington Ingram, Bishop of London, so the couple were no strangers to the many-faceted realities and obligations of the episcopal office.

Well aware of the demanding task ahead of the first bishop of a new diocese, his response to the call to Bradford was not a decision taken lightly. In an interview in the Church Standard in February 1920, the new bishop said, "God seemed to speak most clearly and directly the very morning I received the offer. My text for the day in my book of devotions was 'The God of our fathers hath chosen thee.' My wife's text was 'The Lord hath chosen you to stand before Him and serve Him.' I felt it was so direct a voice that I dare not disobey it."

He confessed modestly that he had neither the intellectual nor spiritual gifts so vitally important for such an office, but, "if God calls us so clearly then He will enable the particular work which He wants His servant to do. I go, confident that He has some work to do through me."

The personal style and priorities of the first bishop clearly played a part in setting the style of the new diocese. He was a staunch evangelical, though careful to avoid partisanship, but with a sympathetic and friendly understanding of widely divergent views and a readiness to appreciate good work wherever he found it. He had in particular a great respect for the work the Revd. Thomas Fullerton, vicar of St. Mary Magdalene's, was doing in one of the poorest areas of Bradford, and in 1927 appointed him as a Canon of Bradford Cathedral. The bishop's personal secretary, Miss Ruth Jeffery, was a regular worshipper at St. Mary Magdalene's and the bishop praised her to his family for her loyalty and professionalism when taking letters on matters of church policy that could not have been to her liking. Perhaps it was affection and respect for both Miss Jeffery and Canon Fullerton that took the Perowne family regularly to St. Mary Magdalene's nativity play, at the end of which the bishop gave a blessing, wearing cope and mitre, which he seldom otherwise used. Many years later, Bishop Robert Williamson explained his cope and mitre to a group of schoolchildren as being the clothes he put on for very special occasions, rather like party clothes. This led to a number of delightful letters from children, inviting him to come to their party and wear his party hat.

Arthur Perowne had been brought up in an atmosphere of ecumenical optimism. His father, Bishop J.J.S. Perowne, was wholeheartedly involved in the Grindelwald Conferences in the 1890s and had indeed been in 'hot water' for inviting all members to join in a united Communion Service. Arthur, in his turn, took every opportunity of co-operating with Free Churchmen in religious and social work, and this led to the Church Times inserting the only cautionary note into the general approval with which his appointment to Bradford was met.

Politically, he was no party man although he believed that it was essential that the Church and the new Labour Party should get to know each other and that democracy should be imbued with Christian ideals. In Plymouth, during a railway strike, daily services of intercession were held at Dr. Perowne's church and attended by the strikers, and he debated with their leaders at strike meetings. Later, in Bradford, he was to use a coal cart as an improvised pulpit when addressing Labour supporters, but he did not automatically side with any one class or movement, preferring to examine the intellectual and moral foundations of policies before making up his mind. After one by-election in Plymouth, all three parties claimed to have had his vote!

Although Arthur Perowne demonstrated great gifts for ecclesiastical administration and social reform, his organising ability was never simply for the sake of efficient machinery, and deep spiritual commitment provided his guiding principles. He was a keen supporter of foreign missions, particularly the Church Missionary Society. It must have been a source of joy to him that his new bishopric, almost as soon as it had raised its necessary endowment, launched a 'C.M.S. Forward Movement' and resolved to try to double the C.M.S. income from the diocese.

On 10 December 1919, Dr. and Mrs. Perowne paid their first visit to Bradford, to be greeted by the new vicar, Revd. William Stanton Jones, and Mr. and Mrs. Mossman. Next day Dr. Perowne received the press at the Midland Hotel, while

Arrival of the first Bishop.
Left to right: Mrs. Mossman, Mrs. Perowne, Rt. Rev. A. W. T. Perowne,
Mr. Frederick Mossman and Rev. W. Stanton Jones.

Mrs. Perowne was off to look at yet another house – they had looked at several together but found them either unsuitable or unlikely to become vacant for some time. Dr. Perowne thought that Bishopsgarth at Wakefield was a model bishop's residence, but it had been built to a bishop's design and building in Bradford at that time was out of the question. He added one more specification of his own – the house must be on a tram route as he did not propose to use a car.

Arthur Perowne was consecrated at York Minster on 2 February 1920, his enthronement was arranged for February 17th, and still the family was homeless. The Yorkshire Observer reported that while house-hunting, the bishop would be the guest of Mr. G.F. Falconer at Woodhall, Calverley. Later, while Mr. Thomas Howarth was abroad, the family moved into his house, White Lodge, in Park Drive, Heaton, a stone's throw from the eventual site of Bradford's permanent see house, although that development was well into the unforeseen future.

The enthronement itself was not without its traumas. When Bishop Boyd Carpenter of Ripon died in 1918, Ripon Diocese decided that a memorial fund should be opened and the proceeds used to provide a bishop's throne for Bradford Cathedral, but this scheme was not sufficiently advanced by early 1920 and a temporary throne had to be obtained. An account for erecting a platform for the enthronement came to a total of £12 16s 10d, which included labour costs for Man-hours, Young-man-hours and Man-and-horse-hours. Then there was the vexed question of whom to invite. Only a week before the event, when it was plain that any invitations going would have already gone, Alderman Trotter asked the Lord Mayor if the Corporation was to be recognised and invited to "this ceremony at the Parish Church." The Town Clerk explained that persons were invited by the Church Authorities and it was not for the Lord Mayor to invite anybody. The Alderman declared that he would like to record his protest as a churchman and a member of the chief public body of the city.

Revd. William Stanton Jones was approached by the press, sensing a newsworthy dispute, as has been many a Vicar of Bradford since. He expressed regret that: "it had been impossible to invite the City Council as a body. The Church Authorities had tried to make the Service as representative as possible but must consider not the City, but the Diocese of Bradford. They must remember those who had loyally supported the Bishopric Scheme from the outset and invitations had been issued to all clergy and churchwardens throughout the Diocese. The Corporation would be represented by the Lord Mayor (Alderman William Wade), the Town Clerk and other officers. A large number of regular worshippers at St. Peter's would be excluded owing to limited space, and to allocate 84 out of only 1070 seats to the Corporation would unduly entrench upon the space available to the general public." There were of course, then as now, other civic dignitaries and representatives of other local authorities to be included, since political and ecclesiastical boundaries are not co-terminous.

Describing the enthronement, the Bradford Daily Argus spoke of a 'medieval'

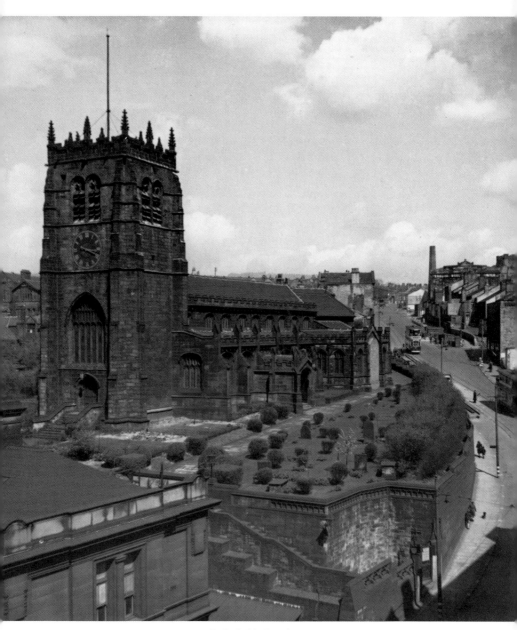

Cathedral before alterations

procession, such as had never been seen before in Bradford, although the ceremony itself was homely when contrasted with the grandeur of the consecration at York -"a simpler, sweeter character to which the homeliness of a parish church interior contributed. The Cathedral may not be a treasure house of architectural majesty towering above all other edifices, but has a thousand sanctities and traditions.... a quiet house of devotion." Bishop Perowne was enthroned by Bishop Drury of Ripon, assisted by the Vicar of Bradford, then the Chancellor of the new diocese, Sir Francis George Newbolt, took his oath of allegiance.

The new bishop's enthronement sermon made a number of points that would be equally apposite three quarters of a century later. He pointed out that the diocese was beginning its life at a critical period of our national history, when we were suffering from disillusionment, disappointment, industrial troubles, financial instability, reckless extravagance, a wave of crime, a mad rush after pleasure and a superstitious craving for contact with the unseen. All these were amongst the marks and causes of unsettlement which those of the Church of Christ were called upon to face and grapple with. Keen though he was on social reform, it was not his primary concern, but the religion of Christ must permeate the whole of life. He spoke of the task of the clergy to preach the way of love and live it. To the laity his message was to cast out jealousy, that bane of Christian workers, let friendly counsel take the place of carping criticism, let willing service and generous giving mark their churchmanship, and in business life set an example. On a topical note, he saw hope in the formation of the League of Nations and in Bradford's proposal to feed and house 1,000 children from the stricken country of our late enemies. "Thank God," he said, "for British Tommies in the Army of Occupation, who threatened mutiny because they were forbidden to help starving German women and children." A bishop's role he saw as "above all to be an example of holiness, to raise aloft the ideal of spiritual power, to show that in a world of time and sense and matter it can be a real and effective force. Who indeed is sufficient for these things? Our sufficiency is of God alone."

After the ceremony, the Lord Mayor entertained what was described as a very representative gathering to luncheon at the Town Hall. Just how representative is indicated in Mr. Mossman's letter to Dr. Perowne a couple of weeks before the event: "We pressed the Lord Mayor to allow ladies, but he won't. I'm very sorry that Mrs. Perowne cannot be there to hear your health proposed." In the event, Mrs. Perowne and the ladies of the party were entertained to lunch at the Midland Hotel by the lady members of the bishopric committee and wives of the officials.

In the afternoon and evening, receptions were held at Cartwright Hall, during which selections of music were performed by Messrs Wood and Marshall's String Band. Over 2,000 people attended to meet the new bishop, and Mrs. Perowne was not only present but made her own speech, acknowledging the kindness already shown to them both.

There followed quite a round of "meet the people" events. In March there was a reception at Skipton Town Hall, at which the bishop reminded his rural clergy that he had himself been a country parson and knew the difficulties of long distances and getting up in the pulpit to speak to three or four people. He raised here what was to be a key theme of his early episcopacy - the need to tackle the poverty of many of the country clergy.

This theme was repeated at a soirée the following month at the King's and Queen's Halls in Bradford and the bishop made an appeal for £30,000 to bring the poorest benefices up to an acceptable standard. The aim was to use donated money to augment the efforts of the poorest parishes and so bring all stipends up to a level of £400 per annum plus a house. There were many parishes providing a living of around £300, and thirteen paying less than £200, which even in 1920 was on the borderline of real poverty. In the first Diocesan Year Book, ten parishes were surprisingly listed as having no house, and only one of these, Farnley, held in plurality (with Leathley). He spoke too of the new Enabling Act - he believed the future of the Church depended on the way in which parochial church councils were used and he hoped the laity would take a far greater part than they had done in the work of the Church - they had as much right to have their say as clergy and bishops, and he hoped that awful expression "going into the church", to describe the taking of Holy Orders, would disappear.

By this time, the housing question had been settled, at least temporarily, by a decision to take up Lady Powell's offer after all, following certain modifications to the house that she had undertaken, and on the day of the soirée, the Perownes moved into Horton Hall.

In June, Pudsey's Mayor and Mayoress gave a reception at the Town Hall for Bishop and Mrs. Perowne, and again both of them addressed the gathering, both taking their new home as their theme. Mrs. Perowne spoke of being anxious to get the house in order so that they could invite people. They did not intend to give grand entertainments, but she hoped that during their time in Bradford, they would see everyone present at Horton Hall. The bishop said that he did not know whether people were going to listen to him more because he mowed his own lawn and put down his own stair-carpet, but he thought there was a deeper sympathy between clergy and laity than in the days when the bishop came down like a great lord in his carriage-and-six, like a baron of old. His father's predecessor at Worcester was remembered as having, indeed, had a carriage-and-six brought round in order to go not much more than the length of his own drive to the local church.

So Bradford's first episcopal family settled into their rented see house. Horton Hall stood at the Little Horton Lane end of Little Horton Green, opposite All Saints' Church, and was a fascinating mixture of styles. A rather grand 17th century house was built round a much earlier timber building, possibly of 14th century origin. The oldest part of the interior still featured a fine plaster ceiling and panelling dating back to Tudor or Jacobean times. A flat-topped tower had

Horton Hall

been added above the porch in 1694 to provide an observation platform for Abraham Sharp, the celebrated astronomer and mathematician. The chapel created within the house by Bradford's bishop was not the first place of worship under its roof. In 1672 the astronomer's brother, Revd. Thomas Sharp, had licensed a ground-floor room for Nonconformist preaching.

It cannot have been an easy house to run, with its stone-flagged kitchen a flight of steps down from the dining room, so that not even a trolley could be used, then more steps to the Georgian wing, another staircase to the chapel, in fact hardly anything on the same level. The Perownes did have a maid for the first three weeks, but after that, for a time, it was a case of all the family, including the bishop, taking turns to get up early to light the fires and perform other household duties. Nevertheless the bishop spoke of the house with great affection, saying he could not imagine any place which had lent itself more completely to a bishop's house. It was so comfortable and homely!

Situated as it was, well up one of the sides of the natural basin that encloses Bradford, the house offered a vista of that part of the bishop's charge. From the chapel window, the bishop's son Leslie recalled, one looked out on to about 100 black, belching, mill chimneys. He remembered too, rather foolishly deciding to sleep out of doors one hot summer night, and waking to find himself covered in soot - no Clean Air Act then, and Bradford, if not quite at the height of its manufacturing power, still presenting a picture of incredible blackness to a teenager newly arrived from Devon's moors.

As requested, the house was close to a tram route, and for his first five years the bishop got about his diocese by means of public transport and presumably the occasional lift. Eventually, in 1925, a group of Bradford's wealthy businessmen who were also staunch churchmen, bought him a Humber. Leslie, who had been taught to drive an old snub-nosed Morris by his employer's son, drove his father , in the Humber, all over the diocese and soon formed the opinion that it must be one of the most beautiful in the country. The bishop did learn to drive himself, though his son's verdict was "not very well." In many of his parishes, Arthur Perowne was the first bishop they had ever seen and by the end of his ministry his motoring around the diocese was averaging 12,000 miles a year and he had preached on some occasion in every church save one, to which he was never invited.

CHAPTER 4

AMONG THOSE DARK
SATANIC MILLS

There was more to the 880 square miles which became the new diocese than its "dark satanic mills". Within its bounds it encompassed all of the geographical features of Blake's verse - the mountains green, pleasant pastures and clouded hills; and of course its acres had their own long and varied Christian and ecclesiastical histories. It is unnecessary to describe every church in the diocese, with its date and fate (see Appendix I for a list of those now closed or demolished), but some explanation is perhaps due to account for the number of city churches of similar period and nearly all apparently too big or in the wrong place.

In Bradford itself, the mainly 15th century parish church of St. Peter's is believed to be the third on that site. Tradition links it with the earliest Christian teaching in the area in the 7th century, and two carved stones, probably part of a Saxon preaching cross, were found on the site and incorporated in the walls of the present building. Paulinus preached in Dewsbury in 627 as part of his mission to Northumbria, and whether he came in person to Bradford or not, there was certainly evangelism following his preaching, and Bradford is thought to have become part of the Saxon parish of Dewsbury, gaining its own parish status around 1150.

For centuries, the parish church, sometimes referred to in wills dating from about 1500 as "Saints Peter and Paul", was Bradford's only church, although there are others of ancient foundation nearby, notably at Calverley and Tong, and chapelries dependent on Bradford were established in Haworth in 1317, Wibsey in 1606 and Thornton in 1612. One ecclesiastical curiosity is the chapel of St. Sitha , mentioned in the York Archiepiscopal Registers as existing in 1466 and again referred to by John Leland in the reign of Henry VIII, thought to have been a wayside shrine or small chapel at the end of Ivebridge at the bottom of Ivegate. Mr. Edward Hailstone, a 19th century occupant of Horton Hall, believed the street name to derive from Ave-gate. St. Sitha's name is perpetuated as one of the Canonries of Bradford Cathedral.

The old Bradford vicarage house was in Goodmansend. The earliest reference to a vicarage house in Bradford is 1374 and it is known to have been in a ruinous state in 1695. Its site was that of the present Traffic Interchange and Vicar Lane may have been the original track from the house to the church. Prior to 1825 it was also known as Dead Lane. This house was replaced by one in Barkerend, but two of Bradford's vicars, Revd. Dr. William Scoresby F.R.S. (1839 - 1847) and Revd. Dr. John Burnet (1847 - 1870), lived at Field House, Daisy Hill. The later vicarage in Great Horton Road was still in use in 1944 when John Tiarks was appointed Vicar of Bradford. It was a big house - six main bedrooms, kitchens and a butler's pantry, built in the days when many clergy, of prime parishes at least , had private incomes with which to maintain a large house and appropriate domestic staff. Provost and Mrs Tiarks lived there uncomplaining but in some discomfort, among the many buckets strategically placed to cope with the leaking roof. Eventually a house in Heaton, Myrtle Bank, was purchased and became Provost's House until the Cathedral Close was created in the 1970s with houses for the provost and two residentiary canons.

With one exception, it was not until the 19th century that any additional Anglican church buildings were erected to provide for the growing population of Bradford. The first of these was the old Bell Chapel at Great Horton, consecrated in 1809 as a chapel of ease to the parish church. When it became necessary to enlarge this chapel, the ground was found to be undermined, so that a safe foundation for a steeple could not be made, hence the big new church of St. John the Evangelist was erected on the opposite side of Great Horton Road on land given by Mr. Francis Sharp Powell, together with a generous contribution to the building cost. Churches at this time were provided either by the personal generosity of one or more of the city's leading figures, or by public subscription.

This same Mr. Powell contributed to other churches in Bradford and was entirely responsible for the building of All Saints, opposite his home, Horton Old Hall. He received a baronetcy on the Queen's birthday in 1892. St. Columba's, Horton, was built by Sir Francis and Lady Powell in 1902. It was to have been St. Margaret's and the streets surrounding it were already named, but they visited Iona, and Lady Powell was so impressed by St. Columba that she asked to have the church so dedicated. A square of Iona marble carved with a Celtic cross is set into the altar.

The new St. John's was consecrated in 1874 and described as being of large proportions. Even so, an extension was added and opened by Bishop Ross Hook in 1980.

Assorted St. Johns' seem to have come and gone at this side of town - the short-lived St. John's at the bottom of Manchester Road, built 1838 and replaced in 1871 by St. John the Evangelist in Horton Lane, itself closed in 1965; St. John's Tong Street, which was an offshoot of the old parish of St. James' Tong, closed 1970 and replaced as daughter church to Tong by St. Christopher's Holme Wood which was consecrated in 1968, ten years after a church presence was established in a wooden hut on the new Holme Wood housing estate.

The only Anglican church to be built in the Bradford area between medieval times and the 19th century is another St. John the Evangelist, that at Bierley, built by Richard Richardson virtually for family use in 1766. The Richardsons of Bierley Hall and the Rooke family of Royds Hall worshipped at Wibsey

Chapel, which the two families had built in 1606. When Richard Richardson was refused permission by the Lord of the Manor, William Rooke, to make a new road to make the journey from Bierley Hall to Wibsey easier, the families quarrelled and Dr. Richardson decided to build a chapel at Bierley. He engaged as architect, John Carr, who also designed Harewood House, Denton Hall and St. Helen's Church, Denton. Later the building was extended to include more "free sittings" and became a centre of ministry to a very large area. This was reduced by the erection of St. Matthew's Bankfoot, St. John's Bowling and St. Mary's Laisterdyke. Bierley St. John itself became an ecclesiastical parish in 1864. Although extended and altered from time to time, it remains an elegant and attractive example of late 18th century architecture. A mission from Bierley in the Woodlands district led to the building of Woodlands mission chapel, followed by the creation of the parish of Oakenshaw-cum-Woodlands in 1877 and the building of a new church, St. Andrew's Oakenshaw, consecrated 1889.

The old Wibsey Chapel went through a troubled time in the late 18th century. Disorder prevailed to the extent that a woman was allowed to preach there! and the curate was removed by the Vicar of Bradford. In 1836 it was partially demolished and rebuilt to enlarge it and is now known as Holy Trinity Low Moor. From being one of Bradford's oldest church buildings, it has become one of the most up to date, certainly the only one with a lift to its splendid upstairs meeting room.

Thornton's old chapel was 'beautified' in 1818 during the incumbency of Revd. Patrick Brontë, though William Cudworth describes it, notwithstanding the beautifying, as "a sanctuary little calculated to inspire devotional feeling, being low, dark and damp." Its 1872 replacement, on the opposite side of Thornton Road, he hailed as "amply illustrating the better taste of the present generation of Thornton churchmen." It is clear that the Church in former times had no reservations about the Masonic craft and the foundation stone was laid with Masonic honours by the Marquis of Ripon, Grand Master of the Order. In 1921, Bishop Perowne was initiated into the Pentalpha Lodge, which brought forth the newspaper comment: "One cannot but feel what a good thing it would be for all concerned if more clergy followed the Bishop's example. It would bring them into closer touch with the laity and widen the layman's view of the parson."

By the mid 19th century the population of the urban areas was still growing. In the first half of the century a few new churches had arisen, including St. John's Bowling which was built for the benefit of families employed at Low Moor Ironworks and is architecturally unusual, if not unique, in having its interior pillars and arches in cast iron instead of stone. In 1992 this thriving church was imaginatively re-ordered, modernising its interior while emphasising the best of its architectural heritage.

Bradford and district gained several "Waterloo Churches", including one at Idle to replace its ancient chapel of ease of Calverley, and the identical buildings consecrated on the same day in 1826 at Wilsden and Shipley (St. Paul's). But

St Paul's, Shipley

to get really to grips with the needs of the growing town, the Bradford Church Building Society was formed in 1860, with the aim of providing ten new Anglican places of worship. This they achieved within twelve years (see Appendix I). Of course the Nonconformists and Roman Catholics were also expanding and building to meet growing needs during this period.

The situation in Manningham is interesting as an example of the helpful attitude of a local industrialist. St. Paul's opened in 1847. Filled to overflowing, it had led to the provision of St. Mark's on the south side of the parish and then to the clear need for another church on the north side. A period of industrial depression meant a new building would have to wait, and Samuel Cunliffe Lister offered the dining room in Manningham Mills for Sunday afternoon services conducted by the clergy of St. Paul's. This continued for five years until the opening of St.Luke's in Victor Road. The cluster of new churches and mission rooms radiating out from St. Paul's took their cue from neighbouring St. Barnabas' in choosing patron saints from among Paul's companions - Mark, Luke and Silas.

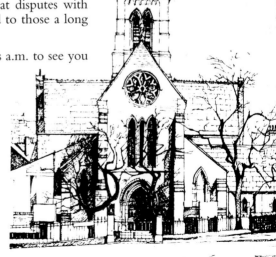

The rate of growth of Bradford is demonstrated by the saga of Christ Church, built as recently as 1815 in rural surroundings close to the Manor Hall's gardens across the top of Darley Street. By 1879 it had been demolished to open up one of the busiest roads in the town, and re-situated in Eldon Place, Manningham Lane, where it continued until 1940. A letter from one of Christ Church's churchwardens to Mr. Mossman, dated Dec. 1920, survives as confirmation, if any were needed, that there never was a golden age when all ran smoothly, and also that disputes with diocesan hierarchy are not confined to those a long way from the centre:

Sir, When I called at your office this a.m. to see you about a matter relating to Christ Church, I heard you address your clerk, a young lady, when my name was announced, thus: 'Blast him, tell him to call again.' You ought to be thoroughly ashamed of yourself, in the first place, to use such language in the presence of a young lady. Your diocesan clerk also heard your vile ebullition. A nice sort of individual to be Secretary to the Bishop of the Diocese! I shall report the incident to him today.

Yours Truly.....''

St Paul's, Manningham

By the middle of the 20th century, the population pattern had again changed considerably and far fewer people lived close to the city centre. Small in number, but significant in terms of financial support, many mill owners and other employers had moved out, to outer suburbs or surrounding villages and small towns such as Eldwick, Baildon, Ilkley. Good public transport and the dramatic increase in private motoring after the Second World War contributed to the outward movement.

High density urban housing had in many cases become unacceptably run-down, and slum clearances led to large scale re-housing, again further out on large estates. In some areas, much of the remaining housing was occupied by Asian families who had come to Bradford primarily to work in the textile industry. The upshot for the Church was that the diocese found itself with a number of large, often fine, Victorian buildings in situations where it was hard to imagine they had ever been filled to overflowing. As the life of the diocese during the different episcopates is described, the various approaches to this problem will be seen.

The situation in Keighley, the only other predominantly industrial town in the diocese, followed a similar pattern. The parish church, St. Andrew's, dates back to the 12th century, was rebuilt, badly, in 1805, and again in 1848.

Overseas aid and help for hostages got off to an early start in Keighley. The St. Andrew's Centenary book by Harry Bancroft, 1948, lists:

"1680 collected in ye parish of Kighley towards ye redemption of captives by ye Turks 19s 1d.

1681 collected in ye parish of Kighley towards ye assistance of ye Protestant Churches in lesser Poland 5s 8d. 1682 collected in ye parish of Kighley for relief of ye French distressed Protestants 8s 6d."

As in Bradford, a number of new parishes were carved out of the original during the 19th century, and as in Bradford, a proportion of them disappeared again in the 20th century:

St. John's Ingrow 1843.

Christ Church Oakworth 1846.

St. Mary's Eastwood (from Keighley and Bingley parishes) 1855, closed 1954.

St. Peter's Holycroft 1882 closed 1954.

Holy Trinity Lawkholme 1882 closed 1972.

In addition, seven mission churches were opened between 1844 and 1900, of which four have become parishes, one is still a mission church and two have closed. The complex alterations in the Keighley area in the times of the fourth and fifth bishops will be touched on in due course.

GREEN AND PLEASANT LAND

If Paulinus, directly or at one remove, was the bringer of the Gospel to Bradford, the dales have their own ancient traditions. In 690, Wilfrid, Bishop of York, baptised new Christians in the river Wharfe near Burnsall, and the church there that bears his name claims to be the oldest site of Christian worship in the dales.

There is an air of timelessness about many of the dales churches and certainly there has been far less change, in terms of church buildings, than in the urban part of the diocese. Not all country churches though are ancient and unaltered. Many have been added to over the centuries, rebuilt, restored and re-restored.

The beautiful and apparently Norman church at Conistone contains only a small portion of truly ancient work – an arcade, an arch, a window, the font. By 1846 the church had become a nondescript little building with plain windows and a wooden bell turret. It was then carefully restored in Norman style and further restored in 1957. By 1991 it had become a very model of a well loved and well

St. Mary's, Conistone

kept country church with attractive notice boards and well displayed historical information inside, sufficient to inform the visitor without intrusively creating a museum. Its prime purpose, for worship and the growth of Christian knowledge is immediately discernible, not least from its interestingly stocked bookstall.

Because of a general impression of peaceful, long-established communities, it is quite surprising to realise that over forty of the churches in the present Archdeaconry of Craven were built in the nineteenth century. This of course includes several in and around Keighley, and a few, like Embsay and Garsdale, replace much earlier buildings. Incidentally, until the late 1950s, regular services were also held in the waiting room on the "down" platform of Garsdale Station.

Yet it is true that, while new churches have appeared in the dales, few have gone. The only major re-location has been the little church at Dale Head, rebuilt in 1938 using the stones of the 1852 church after the village it served was covered by the waters of Stocks Reservoir.

The Vale of Lune Chapel in Sedbergh became redundant in 1984. It was provided by Miss Frances Upton of Ingmire Hall, originally as a place of worship for navvies engaged in building the Ingleton branch of the London and North Western Railway. The scripture reader sent to minister to these men proved so popular among local people that he was asked to stay. In 1917 the chapel was transferred to the Ecclesiastical Commissioners for the use of Sedbergh Parish, at which time it became known as the Church of St. Gregory the Great. The building has interesting stained glass depicting countryside scenes, birds and animals, and contains high quality furnishing by Waring and Gillow. Both the exterior and the furnishing have 'Listed' status and no alternative use could be found which was compatible with this, so that in 1992 the building became the only one in the diocese to be taken over by the Redundant Churches Fund, to be maintained by the State.

Another reminder of the pioneering days of the railways is to be found at St. Leonard's, Chapel-le-Dale, where many who died during the construction of the Ribblehead viaduct are buried. A plaque inside the church reads:

"To the memory of those who through accidents lost their lives in constructing the railway works between Settle and Dent Head. This tablet was erected at the joint expense of their fellow workers and the Midland Railway Company. 1869 - 1876."

Yet another memorial, this time to workers on the Leeds and Thirsk Railway, is the elaborate monument in Otley churchyard in the form of a replica of the castellated portal of the Bramhope tunnel.

It is hard to imagine that the remote hamlet of Halton Gill was once a parish in its own right, with Litton and Foxup within its bounds. Halton Gill is a natural basin and a point at which several old drovers' trails converged. In the 17th and 18th centuries quite a community existed here to supply the needs of the drovers. When movement of cattle was transferred to the railways the hamlet declined.

Halton Gill

In 1911 the benefice was united with Littondale's other parish of Arncliffe with Hawkswick, and Halton Gill church was eventually converted into a house.

It would be a mistake to regard the rural part of Bradford Diocese as an homogenous area. The individual dales were quite self-contained and distinctive in character until the huge increase in car ownership that began in the 1950s. Even two decades later than that, schoolchildren from Dent were taken for a short trip on the newly opened M6 motorway, and for some it was the first time they had been out of Dentdale except to go to school in Sedbergh. Although the children of, for example, Littondale, Langstrothdale and Upper Wharfedale now go down to Threshfield, Grassington and Skipton for secondary education and a variety of social activities, differences are still clearly discernible even between those congregations that have of necessity become part of a united benefice.

In some villages long established local families are still a majority, others have a high proportion of 'offcumdens' who have retired to the country, still others are dominated by weekend cottages and holiday lets with all their attendant problems for the day to day life of the community.

Strangely enough, one of the best known and most picturesque of the dales churches owes its very existence to catering for visitors to the dale in pursuit of their leisure activity. Soon after the Norman Conquest, a hunting chase was established, with its administrative headquarters at Buckden, stretching away up Langstrothdale. The noblemen who indulged in this sport were expected to attend Mass before the hunt, and the nearest churches were at Linton and

Bolton Priory

Burnsall. By the time they got back to the chase, the day was half gone, and so they built a small and simple chapel to which a priest could be sent from Coverham Priory. One imagines that the servants would stand outside holding the horses and as soon as Mass was over the lords would be up and away. To some extent, Hubberholme Church, the originator of the dales churches' 'ministry to tourists', still fulfils that role. Many of its worshippers are still visitors pursuing their leisure activities. The Revd. Ernest Blanchard, Vicar of the United Benefice of Kettlewell with Conistone, Hubberholme and Arncliffe with Halton Gill from 1983 to 1991, has introduced American tourists to each other who were practically neighbours back in the USA, but actually met for the first time at Hubberholme Church.

Another unusual feature of Hubberholme is that until about 1960 the public house, The George, belonged to the church and was part of the living. It originated as a house provided for the priest, not a vicarage but somewhere for him to rest before the long walk back to Coverham. After the Dissolution of the Monasteries it became a farm, then had a room set aside for serving ale. In some ways it is a pity that the church's connection with this old tradition has been severed, but there came a time when the Licensing Justices said that the licence would not be renewed without major improvements. The church authorities did not feel able to pay for the necessary work and the house was sold, not without local regret.

A little beyond Hubberholme one meets the north eastern boundary of the diocese. Backtracking down Wharfedale, through Kettlewell, the ancient sheep centre of the dale, below Burnsall is to be found one of the great historic treasures of the north. Bolton Priory is the only one of Yorkshire's major monastic ruins in Bradford Diocese. Others beyond our bounds may be bigger, more spectacular or attract more visitors, but few can rival the lovely riverside setting and only Bolton can claim an unbroken tradition of living worship from its foundation in 1155.

The Augustinian Canons who built it settled first at Embsay in 1120 and the foundations of their cloisters there were uncovered in about 1800. Their church existed up to the Dissolution, but the present Embsay church dates from 1853. During the centuries from its foundation to the Dissolution, Bolton Priory owned by appropriation the churches or chapels of Holy Trinity Skipton, Carleton, Kildwick, Harewood, Broughton and Long Preston. The canons also held the advowsons of Marton, Keighley and Kettlewell. At the Dissolution, the appropriated churches were given to the Dean and Chapter of Christ Church, Oxford, who remain their Patrons.

Since there was no other church nearby, the nave of the Priory Church itself was preserved and incorporated into the parochial system, at first as a chapelry of Skipton, only in 1864 becoming a parish. Confusion over the name of this monastic building, village and, later, parish, has existed for centuries. The Augustinian house was undoubtedly a priory, but on old deeds the terms abbey and priory intermingle. The village and parish are known as Bolton Abbey.

The Clifford family's Patronage began in 1310 was consolidated in 1542 when Henry Clifford, first Earl of Cumberland, bought the former priory and most of its estate, and has continued through the Dukes of Devonshire to the present day. The family have been concerned and generous patrons through the generations and it was only at the end of the 19th century that the congregation began to make significant contributions to the upkeep and improvement of the church. The major restoration work in the 1980s was financed by a public appeal for £300,000, of which the small congregation (1985 population 500, electoral roll 163) themselves contributed £30,000. The congregation have also committed themselves to supporting work in one of Bradford's Urban Priority Areas.

Nevertheless, not all has run smoothly at Bolton Priory since the Dissolution, or even during the short lifespan of Bradford Diocese . At a time when many country churches were facing the problems of dwindling numbers and the concomitant shortages of resources, both in terms of manpower and finance, Bolton reached a particularly low ebb. In the 1970s, with a building in sad need of repair and a congregation of less than half a dozen, the possibility of making the church redundant was seriously considered and the living was suspended. It was at this time too that monthly services stopped being held at Bolton's chapelry at Barden Tower.

The Church in this diocese has been well and faithfully served by priests too numerous to name, but Canon Maurice Slaughter must rank high among them for what he achieved between 1978 and 1986. Canon Slaughter volunteered to resign his living at Christ Church Skipton and come as priest-in-charge to Bolton Abbey where, by his own hard work and the efforts he inspired in others, the present has been enabled to keep faith with the past. Like many country churches, the congregation of the Priory Church uses the Book of Common Prayer for most of its services, feeling no doubt that time-hallowed words accord well with time-hallowed stones, and indeed the atmosphere in this ancient seat of worship has something very special to offer. It should not be forgotten however, that very different-sounding services would have been said or sung in the earliest days of that church and even for the first hundred years or so after its monastic role had ended.

There have been other monastic presences within the diocese, though little remains of the small convent at Esholt, better known in the late 20th century as the location for part of a television "soap", Emmerdale Farm, a distinction the village shares with Arncliffe in Littondale.

At Barnoldswick a group of monks from Fountains Abbey went to build a monastery, but gave up after a few years of being cold, wet, hungry and frequently attacked by robbers. The brothers looked for another site and eventually built Kirkstall Abbey near Leeds, but monks of Kirkstall were sent, possibly by Papal decree, to build a church at Barnoldswick to replace the monastery they had not completed. This they did in 1157 in the shape of St. Mary-le-Gill, a mile and a half from their original site.

The other significant monastic ruin, on the edge of the diocese, is the Cistercian Abbey at Sawley, close to Grindleton. It is possible that the Abbey Church might have survived like Bolton Priory, but for the fact that the immediate neighbourhood was already adequately provided with places of worship. There is only slender evidence for the existence of a pre-Dissolution church at Grindleton itself where the present

St. Ambrose, Grindleton

church of St. Ambrose, patron saint of bee-keepers, dates from 1805, but the parish of Mitton originated in the 12th century. The present church of All Hallows, Mitton, was begun in 1270 and its chancel screen is believed to have come from Sawley Abbey. St. Helen's at Waddington began as a chapel-of-ease for Mitton in 1338 but has been rebuilt several times since. St. Catherine's at West Bradford, built in 1896, completes this little group of churches in Bowland Deanery that have enjoyed independence or been united in a variety of combinations over the years.

All Hallows, Mitton

Changing patterns of work and leisure, and the growing availability of transport, have greatly increased the level of tourism, of which the Yorkshire countryside has received its full share. Bolton Priory was described, in a television programme in 1992, as the most visited parish church in England, and village churches are often a focal point for visitors.

Haworth, too, with its Brontë connection, is a place of literary pilgrimage for many, and a venue for thousands more with only the haziest knowledge of the daughters of the parsonage. The church itself, apart from the tower, was rebuilt after Patrick Brontë's time, the older building being demolished in 1879. Even so early, the vicar faced strong opposition from Brontë admirers, but the unpleasant reality was that the deteriorating state of the graves under the floor made his decision unavoidable. The family vault remains and there are many Brontë mementoes in the church, while the parsonage has become a museum totally devoted to the family, but perhaps the atmosphere of their day can best be experienced in the sombre churchyard and on the still-wild Pennine moors.

Devotees of the Arts and Crafts Movement will find a visit to St. Clement's, Bradford, most rewarding. The raised and painted plaster work of the chancel ceiling and the spandrels of the nave was designed by Sir Edward Burne-Jones

Haworth

and executed by the firm of William Morris and Co. Recent restoration by the Council for the Care of Churches has revealed its dramatic colouring.

The diocese has responded to the needs of visitors by the publication of leaflets and books describing some of the most historically and architecturally interesting churches, particularly "Outstanding Churches in the Yorkshire Dales", by Val Leigh, and its companion volume "Outstanding Churches in Craven", by Val Leigh and Brian Podmore. Individual churches have been encouraged to produce up-to-date guide books and leaflets. Many provide refreshments for visitors, from a cup of tea at a flower festival to the extensive service offered in the refectory at Holy Trinity, Skipton. Prayer cards in the pews and evidence of the present life of the church, in the form of well-kept notice boards and displays, contribute to a ministry to visitors. Sadly, vandalism has made it impractical for some churches to be left open during the week, but arrangements to visit can usually be made. Bradford Cathedral has its own programme of voluntary welcomers on duty, guided tours if required, and project packs for school use.

When the diocese was formed, its deaneries were: Bradford, Otley, the unimaginatively named South Craven, East Craven, North Craven and West Craven, and Clapham. In 1921 a second Archdeaconry was created and in March of that year William Stanton Jones, Vicar of Bradford, was installed as also Archdeacon of Bradford. Each Archdeaconry then had five deaneries:
Craven: Ewe Cross, Settle, Bolland (later known as Bowland), Skipton, South Craven.
Bradford: Otley, Calverley, Bradford, Bowling, Horton.

St. Oswald's, Leathley

The boundaries and even the number of the deaneries have been altered over the years but the archdeaconries remain almost as set up, with just a little adjustment moving Addingham and Bingley into Bradford and Wilsden and Denholme into Craven. It is tempting to assume that the division into Craven and Bradford Archdeaconries closely echoes the division between country and town, but the picture is more complex than that, and probably the better for it.

South Craven Deanery takes in Keighley, with urban problems and challenges closely akin to those in Bradford, as well as villages that are part of Bradford's commuter belt. In Bradford Archdeaconry's Otley Deanery, the countryside around the middle reaches of Wharfe and Washburn is softer and lusher than the limestone uplands, but no less true countryside, and villages like Fewston and Blubberhouses are quite remote from city ways. This deanery too has its share of antiquities, including the ancient parish churches of Otley and Ilkley and the Early Norman St. Oswald's at Leathley. All Saints at Weston is mentioned in the Domesday Book and there is evidence of a much earlier building, including the Viking carving known as the 'Weston Man'. The church contains an impressive squire's pew, still in use in 1993 by a squire whose own ancestors can be traced back to the Domesday Book. In the former spa town of Ilkley and the villages immediately around it, though all embrace a wide social spectrum, one finds probably the most consistently affluent concentration of housing in the diocese.

Without attempting to produce a detailed guide to all the parishes of Bradford Diocese, this and the preceding chapter have aimed to give some indication of the range of geographical and social settings that went to form the new diocese, a diocese whose size made it possible for a bishop to know and be known, and whose variety offered such a Pandora's Box of possibilities, problems and potential for Dr. Perowne and his successors down the years to come.

CHAPTER 6

A Sure Foundation

On the day of his Consecration, Bishop Perowne granted Letters Patent to Frederick Adolph Trennel Mossman, establishing him in the office of Principal Registrar and Public Scribe of the Bishop of Bradford and Successor Bishops and in the office of Registrar or Scribe of the Consistory Court of the said Bishop. This appointment was for life, as was the practice at the time, putting the office on the same terms as an incumbent's freehold. Mr. Mossman did indeed serve Bradford's first three bishops faithfully and most conscientiously from 1920 until his death in 1962, although in 1960, at the age of 82, he retired to the role of Consultant and Assistant Registrar.

Among the details of setting up a new diocese was the design of an episcopal seal. There was a suggestion that the Arms of Bradford and Craven be combined, but Mr. Mossman, in a letter to the librarian of Bradford Free Library (in Darley Street in those days), declared that, "with the Fatted Calf of Craven and the Bradford Boar's Head, the seal will be more appropriate for a butcher than a bishop!" In the event, Bluemantle Pursuivant of Arms produced a simple and suitable design incorporating St. Peter's keys and a woolsack on a blue shield, surmounted by an episcopal mitre.

Bishop Perowne's episcopal ring, carved with the bishop's coat of arms, which combined, or impaled, his personal arms with those of the diocese, was returned to Bradford after his death and is set in the stem of one of the cathedral's chalices, though it came close to disappearing from the episcopal scene when Dr. Perowne, while Bishop of Worcester, left it on the wash-basin in a Great Western Railway train. An honest and enterprising finder traced its owner by means of the coat of arms, via Bradford to Worcester.

Later in the year, a pastoral staff was commissioned by the Girls' Friendly Society as a gift from their members throughout the diocese. It was designed and made by Mr. Alex Smith, a former master at Keighley School of Art and is a magnificent piece, in Gothic style, with jewels set in silver, including twelve amethysts representing the twelve Apostles.

The Girls' Friendly Society is an organisation founded in 1875 by Mrs. Elizabeth Townsend to care for girls and women who were often working away from home. It is believed that a branch formed in Bradford within the first year. The first meeting of its Bradford Diocesan council took place on 27 February 1920 at the G.F.S. Lodge in Eldon Place, with Bishop and Mrs. Perowne present.

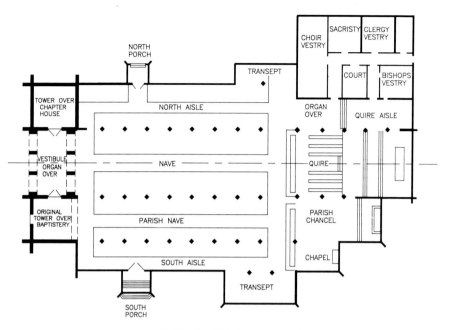

Sir Charles Nicholson's proposed extension
(simplified drawing)

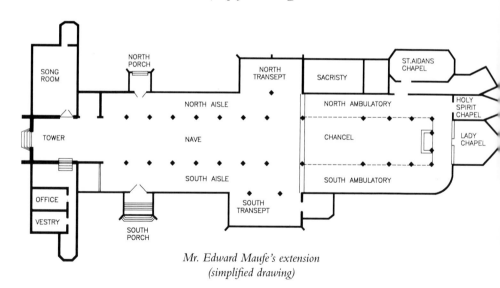

Mr. Edward Maufe's extension
(simplified drawing)

The formation of the diocese was marked with a festival held in York in June of that year, attended by about a thousand members. Branches were started in almost every parish, offering a wide range of activities including keep-fit, drama and good housekeeping. In later years, the growth of youth clubs and the availability of many other activities for young people led to rapid decline in membership. By the 1990s, most Bradford branches had ceased to exist, apart from one or two Townsend Fellowship groups for older members, although nationally the organisation continues to run hostels for young women away from home, and its overseas work is flourishing. When the house in Eldon Place was sold, interest from the proceeds was used to help with the expenses of one of Bradford's women deacons.

Towards the end of 1920, plans were commissioned from Sir Charles Nicholson for the enlargement and enhancement of the parish church into something more appropriate to its cathedral status. One of his proposals would have more than doubled its size, the existing building becoming in effect a double south aisle, with a huge new cathedral nave and north aisle with a second tower to match the present one. The immediate post war period was not a good time for building, but the main reason for not going ahead was the bishop's decision to drop an appeal for funds for the cathedral and devote his efforts to raising money for the augmentation of poor benefices. During his eleven years in Bradford, £120,000 was raised, which produced an income of £5,000 per annum to be used to supplement stipends. In addition, Dr. Perowne was known to make personal gifts to needy clergy. Sometimes, a day or two after an induction, the new vicar would receive an unexpected cheque, with a note urging him to take his family for a few days holiday, or in other cases, help with removal expenses might appear.

It was not until 1935 that the throne, or cathedra, designed by Sir Charles Nicholson as a memorial to Bishop Boyd Carpenter was dedicated, and later still that the building was enlarged, although on nothing like the scale originally considered.

In May 1920, Bradford Diocesan Conference met for the first time, opening appositely with the hymn 'Come Holy Ghost, our souls inspire.' Its agenda included the constitution of the conference, formation of a diocesan board of finance and presentation of a budget. The ending of the meeting with the equally appropriate 'O God our help in ages past, Our hope for years to come', must have been an awesome moment, bringing home to even the most confident of those present, realisation of the full weight of responsibility they now carried for the well-being of this newest unit in the "one Catholic and Apostolic Church."

In the light of 1990s discussions about how best to enable truly representative lay participation, it is interesting that weekday meetings were the norm, with morning, afternoon and sometimes evening sessions. Conference was noticeably male-dominated and membership of the board of finance actually specified adult male communicants of the Church of England. The minutes do not make it clear how this was reconciled with a motion on the Ministry of Women carried in October 1920, largely concerned with the Order of Deaconesses, but including the proposal that women should be admitted to those councils of the Church to which laymen are admitted, on equal terms. The composition of the standing committee of that first diocesan conference gives a glimpse of the social scene. The seven deanery representatives comprised four clergymen, of whom three were canons, and three laymen whose residences were Harden Hall, Newfield Hall and Skipton Castle.

However the diocese was never dominated by the aristocracy, nor burdened with medieval laws and customs designed for quite different times. Some, who have lived through the Second World War and its aftermath of social and political change, recall Bishop Perowne as an autocratic figure and he might appear so if compared directly with some of his successors. This would, however, hardly be a fair comparison and the evidence, for example in some of his conference addresses and bishop's letters, suggests that Bradford's bishop was more closely in touch with his clergy, their flocks, and the realities of their lives than many of his contemporaries. The diocese itself was set up and administered in a way that has fostered a continuing progress along democratic lines, although delayed by a later unhappy period of stagnation.

A certain early lightness of approach shows up in another conference motion in that first year, proposing that "the provision of suitable amusement for parishioners is a legitimate part of the work of the incumbent." One assumes the proposer was referring to the voluntary provision of such amusement!

BRETHREN, A FUNNY THING HAPPENED ON THE WAY FROM THE VESTRY

Before the formation of the see, activities and their funding had been in the hands of all sorts of independent societies and committees. Bishop Perowne's policy was to make the diocesan board of finance, with ten committees appointed from its membership, the key to the material working of the diocese. This secured for diocesan conference, which elected the board, supreme control of all church work in the diocese and had two beneficial results:

1. lay members of the board became keenly interested in the policies and spiritual activities of the diocese,

2. no separate appeals for money were allowed since the ten committees covered the whole range of diocesan activity.

The committees were:

1. Board of Mission	4. Training of the Ministry
2. Evangelistic Work	5. Maintenance of the Ministry
3. Social Work:	6. Pensions
Group 1. Rescue	7. Widows and Orphans
Group 2. Purity	8. Church Buildings
Group 3. Temperance	9. Religious Education
Group 4. Labour	10. Administration

The first chairman of the board of finance was Mr. F.D. Moore, who had of course chaired the bishopric finance committee, with vice-chairmen Mr. G. Ackroyd, the original chairman of the finance committee, and Mr. J.W. Morkill who so fervently championed the cause of the Craven area. Secretary to the board was Revd. C.H.K. Boughton, Vicar of Calverley, and assistant secretary one of the very few women whose names appear in the first Diocesan Year Book, Miss Kate Pickard.

Miss Pickard must have been a truly remarkable woman to hold her own in the 1920s in such a gathering of clergy and leading business men, and not as a mere taker of notes. She later became secretary to the board and in effect diocesan secretary long before such a post existed by name. She was a highly educated woman, a writer of poetry and fluent in Greek and she taught secretarial skills in her own Commercial School. It is hard to imagine now that anyone was able to cope with the secretarial needs of the diocese on a part-time basis of two days a week. Miss Pickard not only coped, but soon was reputed to know everything there was to know about the diocese. Perhaps her secret was that, short of time though she might be, she could always find time for prayer. Visitors to the office in Church House on North Parade were occasionally surprised to find the secretary on her knees. Diocesan legend, passed on by a later secretary, has it that Miss Pickard, if not otherwise able to carry the day, did now and then resort to tears – there are said to be minute books with the marks on their pages. Given the weight of the opposition she must sometimes have faced, one can hardly grudge her the use of any advantage she could find.

Bishop Perowne spent his first years getting to know and be known in his diocese. As well as setting up the necessary administrative structures, he travelled all over, preaching, confirming and particularly dedicating War Memorials. For the latter, he recommended that lists of names be kept in the form of a Memorial Book rather than tablets or plaques on the walls of parish churches. The cathedral's bells were re-cast as a lasting memorial to men of the city who had given their lives, the Colours of the Bradford Pals were dedicated and hung in the cathedral and a stained glass window installed as a memorial to the 6th Battalion, West Yorkshire Regiment .

The bishop arranged retreats and quiet days for his clergy in the relaxing and refreshing atmosphere of the dales, initiated missions of various kinds and brought in a team of Cambridge University undergraduates organised by his son Stewart to encourage the support of overseas missionary work. Early "Bishop's Letters" carefully explain and commend the various projects and contain a blend of the spiritual and an extremely practical, dare one say 'archdeaconly', insistence on correct attention to Church laws.

The first bishop set a style for the new diocese, making the most of the advantages of its relatively small size and compactness. Archdeacons are sometimes described as "the eyes of the bishop", and using these "eyes", as well as observations during his own travels, Bishop Perowne was able to keep in touch with situations in parishes in a way that has been continued and built upon throughout most of the life of the diocese. His care and sympathy, particularly for the poorer clergy, began Bradford's ongoing reputation as a caring diocese. Of course there are always complaints in any structured organisation, about the sometimes unfathomable behaviour of the undefined "them", in this case often partially defined as "them in Bradford". Sometimes decisions seem harsh to those not in a position to know the whole picture; sometimes senior staff, even bishops, get it wrong. Nevertheless, clergy and officials who have moved into or out of Bradford Diocese have commented very favourably on its standard of pastoral care in comparison with some other units of the Church of England. Senior staff in any organisation come in for criticism, not always justified. Part of the caring role of such people in the ecclesiastical situation is to absorb both fair and unfair comments without resorting to a defence that might breach a confidence or hurt a fellow-worker.

Mrs. Perowne too threw herself wholeheartedly into diocesan activities, particularly those involving women and girls. She was president of the Diocesan Mothers' Union and Girls' Friendly Society and represented the diocese on the National Council of Women Workers as well as the National Assembly of the Church. She aimed to make Horton Hall a welcoming centre of diocesan activity and, like so many of the wives of Bradford's senior clergy, had a special care for clergy wives. She was also much concerned with the 'White Crusade', a campaign launched by the bishop in 1921 to consider the state of morals in the population and the church's place in dealing with the situation. In keeping with the ecumenical approach Dr. Perowne had adopted in his earlier ministry, he elicited the agreement that the Roman Catholics and Nonconformists would work for the same cause at the same time, in an effort to bring home the message that neglect of God's law can only lead to chaos and corruption.

In 1922 personal tragedy struck the Perowne household when, after a long period of ill health, Mrs. Perowne died, aged only 53. Mrs. Stanton Jones, writing on behalf of the women of the diocese began with the words, "The Diocese of Bradford will always be the richer for the fragrant memory of its first Bishop's wife - one of such vivid and striking personality. When she came to the Diocese, she quickly won for herself in a remarkable way a very warm place in the hearts of all who met her." Mrs. Perowne was buried in the churchyard at Calverley, the first parish to which she had come when she left her Plymouth home. In 1923, the G.F.S. held its birthday celebrations in Bradford, only the second time the event had been held out of London since its founding in 1875. Bradford was chosen in honour of the splendid work done for the organisation by the late Mrs. Perowne. In 1924 a stained glass window was placed in the south transept of the cathedral, given in her memory by "many women and girls who knew and loved her."

In October 1922, the Ven. Henry Cook had retired as Rector of Skipton, by no means the almost automatic procedure it would be today. It was necessary then to invoke the Incumbents Resignation Acts of 1871 and 1887 and enquire into "the expediency and alleged ground of the resignation." The enquiry obviously proved satisfactory and the archdeacon vacated his benefice with a

Bishop Perowne and Senior Clergy at Horton Hall 1928.
Left to right: 7th Archdeacon Howson, 10th Rev. S. E. Lowe, 11th Archdeacon Wilson and
16th Canon Ackerley

pension of £100. He remained Archdeacon of Craven until his death in 1928, when he was succeeded by Canon James Francis Howson, Rector of Guiseley, giving rise to a distinguished family double – his brother, the Ven. G.S. Howson being Archdeacon of Liverpool. Although the new archdeacon remained based at Guiseley in the Bradford Archdeaconry, he was well acquainted with the Craven district, his family having long lived in the Settle/Giggleswick area.

Among many other events and activities over the next few years, was a series of public lectures at Church House, speakers including Dean Inge, Lady Astor and a certain Canon E.W. Barnes who spoke on "The Bible and Modern Thought." (As Bishop of Birmingham he was to cross swords with Dr. Perowne's successors.) There was a Mission of Grace in 1924, conducted by Canon Cecil Wilson of Swansea, and plans were set in motion to build a new hall behind the cathedral for diocesan and parochial use. A certain amount of controversy was unleashed when the bishop licensed the Revd. James Hickson to exercise a Ministry of Spiritual Healing in the diocese and concern of a different kind followed the discovery that a temporary curate at Pudsey was not in fact in Holy Orders, had not been a missionary in the Congo as claimed, nor did he hold the degree he professed. Furthermore, he had performed two weddings at Queensbury!

At one of the parish events, the bishop had a lucky escape. He was preaching in Wilsden at a service to mark the centenary of St. Matthew's Church when, about half way through the sermon, there was a sensationally loud crash, which, to his credit, he did not allow to interrupt his words. Those who went to investigate found to their horror that the vestry roof had fallen in, on and around the chair on which their bishop had so recently been sitting! St. Matthew's was demolished in 1962 and rebuilt on a different site in 1975.

So far as social activities in the diocese were concerned, sales of work and bazaars abounded, often lasting all day and evening and sometimes for as long as four days. Some had elaborate themes such as the Orange Grove Bazaar at St. Chad's, Bradford, or the cathedral's Grand Bazaar of 1925 when the rooms of the King's Hall were decorated to represent Haddon Hall. Each day had its own distinguished chairman, opener and host and hostess, and each stall had its own committee and list of helpers. There were concerts in the evenings and a 'Café Chantant' offered afternoon teas with entertainment. The Men's Class ran an extremely profitable stall selling tobacco and smokers' accessories, while the Business Women and Girls rather daringly offered 'Everybody's Fancies'. A huge amount of time and effort went into these events, which ensured that everyone, of whatever means, could contribute to the cause being supported, by buying, selling, making, serving meals or otherwise lending a helping hand.

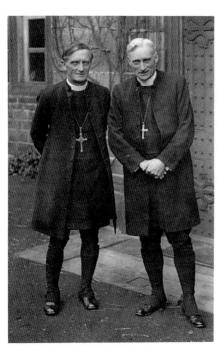

Bishops Stanton Jones and Perowne, 1930

In 1926 Bishop Perowne re-married. Miss Mabel Bailey was an old friend of the Perowne family, having been a Sunday School teacher at St. George's, Edgbaston, while Arthur Perowne was vicar. She went to India with the Church Missionary Society in 1912 and became Principal of a school for boys and girls at Nasik until her return in 1925. After her marriage, Mrs. Perowne continued to take a great interest in the church overseas and doubtless her influence contributed to the support Bradford Diocese gave to this work. The C.M.S. and the Zenana Missionary Society were among the organisations supported by the diocese from the start.

In 1928 came another change of archdeacon when William Stanton Jones was consecrated Bishop of Sodor and Man. In nine years of untiring work for the Diocese and City of Bradford he set the pattern for the balance between the needs of a cathedral for the diocese and a parish church for the city and it is thanks to him that from February 1920 all seats have been free. In the church's relationship with Bradford's businessmen, his cheerful, extrovert nature was a perfect complement to the bishop's rather more restrained style. He was succeeded by his old friend Cecil Wilson, who knew Bradford from the Mission of Grace. He had been a Chaplain to the Forces and was described in 'The Sentinel' as a liberal evangelical of wide outlook and attractive personality.

It seems at first sight strange that no church building dates from the period of Bishop Perowne's episcopate, until one takes into account the great spate of such activity in the latter half of the 19th century plus the eleven churches built between 1900 and 1914. Some parochial changes did take place, notably the re-grouping of some of the dales parishes and the transference of a number of patronages to the bishop. St. John's, Idle, in Cavendish Road, the forerunner of the church at Thorpe Edge, built as a mission church in 1874, gained parish status in 1924. In that same year St Saviour's Fairweather Green became a parish, based on the Jesse Street church until a new building was opened in 1966.

In January 1931, Arthur Perowne was invited to become Bishop of Worcester. Although he left with regret the diocese and home he had grown to love, he unhesitatingly took up the new task set before him, becoming as he did so, the first son to follow his father as bishop of the same see. The move to Hartlebury Castle was literally a going home. Inevitably there was speculation as to his successor in Bradford, but the circumstances of this move were quite unusual, and Bradford did not have long to wait!

Archdeacon Wilson and Bishop Perowne

CHAPTER 7

A LIGHTED CANDLE

St. Werburgh's is a fine, big building in 19th century Gothic style. No one in its large and active congregation in the 1920s could have dreamt that by 1990 it would have closed as a place of worship and become a rather exclusive shopping and art and craft precinct, with a café under the great mosaic in what had been the sanctuary.

Here, in the centre of Derby, Alfred Walter Frank Blunt ministered from 1917 to 1931, with a staff of two curates and Deaconess Perry, at whose door can be laid his lasting appreciation of the value of properly trained women church workers. Here he developed the social Gospel he had first propounded in his earlier ministry at Carrington, near Nottingham, convinced more than ever that to convert the individual and to work for a just society were inseparable aspects of Christian ministry. Here nine of his books were written; here his preaching and teaching, his thriving church and high standing in the town, all combined to inspire a number of bishops to put forward his name for consideration for a bishopric. The Labour Member of Parliament for Derby, Jimmie Thomas, had also brought the canon's name to the attention of Prime Minister Ramsay MacDonald. The M.P. and the churchman had formed a friendship and a working relationship as together they visited the factories and railway works of Derby.

In 1930, Bishop Ernest Pearce of Worcester died, and the Prime Minister, convinced that Alfred Blunt would be a refreshing asset to the Bench of Bishops, offered him the see on December 3rd. After conferring with his wife and with Bishop Edmund Pearce, Bishop of Derby and brother of the late Bishop of Worcester, Canon Blunt gladly accepted the offer – then dropped his bombshell in a second letter to the Prime Minister: "I ought to tell you that, if I go to Worcester, I shall not live at Hartlebury Castle and will try to dispose of it."

He later enlarged on this, explaining that he did not intend actually to settle the fate of the castle himself, but would invite the Diocesan Board of Finance to consider the problem: "Sooner or later the diocese will have to face the question of selling the house or adapting it for other diocesan purposes besides episcopal residence. I should invite them to grasp the nettle at once. In doing this, I should feel I was conferring a real service on the diocese."

But Worcester, with the backing of the Archbishop of Canterbury, was not quite ready for such a change. Canon Blunt was persuaded to reconsider and reluctantly agreed to move in on an experimental basis, and with that agreement the appointment was announced. By the end of December, without making the move, he had finally and irrevocably withdrawn.

The reason given publicly was that Canon Blunt felt unable to take on the burden of the see house, and this was indeed true, since the Blunts had no private income and the castle was deemed to require eight indoor and four outdoor servants. In John Peart-Binns' biography of Bishop Blunt, he discloses that a question of Mrs. Blunt's health arose, but her husband asked for this not to be made public at the time.

Apart from the expense, Hartlebury Castle epitomised those grandiose aspects of the Church of England that Alfred Blunt thought least appropriate to its ministry, and the national press generally agreed with him. The Manchester Guardian, for example, warned that unless the Church of England faced up to the questions raised, it could lead to the appointment, not of the best men available, but of those "whose financial resources enable them to live in houses for which their official income is inadequate. This is hardly a policy that can result in the strengthening of church life."

Canon Blunt must have suspected that he had given up his only chance of exercising a wider than parochial ministry, but Ramsay MacDonald was still keen to have him among the bishops, and of course still needed to fill the Worcester vacancy with someone prepared to take on the castle. There was an admirably qualified man who had lived at Hartlebury before, and might be prepared to do so again. Like Alfred Blunt, Arthur Perowne was not convinced that that scale of housing was appropriate to the 20th century episcopate, but on being offered the nomination, he did accept the see, and with it the expectation that he would live in the see house. In an interview in the Yorkshire Observer he said, "There is a great deal to be said against a big house like this being a burden on the income of the see, but so long as it is felt that it is indispensable that the bishop should live there, I shall feel it my duty to do so until such a time as some other plan for using the house for church purposes has been evolved."

In fact this appointment only postponed the "Hartlebury decision", Bishop Perowne being the last bishop to occupy the whole house. Handed down in the Perowne family was another variation on the reason for Canon Blunt's withdrawal - that Mrs. Blunt had said no on the grounds that the children might fall into the moat!

Thus the appointment of Alfred Blunt as second Bishop of Bradford was announced in February 1931.

Illness, most likely brought on by overwork in Derby and the stress of the Worcester decision, delayed his consecration until July. His enthronement was planned for September and the bishop took a month's break and set off on a long dreamed of visit to Greece. Early on the trip he became very ill with tonsillitis and was taken into hospital in Athens. The infection, serious in pre-

Enthronement procession: Bishop Blunt and Mr. F. Mossman

antibiotic days, the heat of Athens, frustration and anxiety about the future, brought a hitherto fit and active man to a very low ebb. When the enthronement eventually took place on St. Andrew's day, Nov. 30th, the sufferings of the preceding months were reflected in the new bishop's request to the people of his diocese for prayer that "God's strength might be revealed in human weakness, and that a very earthen vessel might yet by God's mercy be used as an instrument of His grace."

On the afternoon of the enthronement, Bishop and Mrs. Blunt followed the pattern set by their predecessors and held a reception at Cartwright Hall. Bradford's declared policy of no palatial residence for its bishop must have accorded well with his beliefs and the city that gave birth to the Independent Labour Party would also strike a chord with him, but so far as the Blunts' four children were concerned, the style, churchmanship and politics of Bradford Diocese were of no great importance. What really counted, specially for the boys aged nine and fifteen, were the exciting prospects of a motor car and a house with electric light!

During the months between the departure of one bishop and the enthronement of another, much of the administrative work of the diocese fell on the shoulders of Cecil Wilson, Archdeacon and Vicar of Bradford, who had been appointed as the Archbishop of York's commissary during the vacancy in see. The "Bishop's Messenger" of Nov. 1931 carried the announcement that: "The Archbishop of York has decided that the provision in the Cathedrals Measure which provided that the Incumbent of the Cathedral Church shall be styled Provost shall take effect immediately. The Archdeacon of Bradford therefore, in relation to the Cathedral may now be styled 'The Very Revd. the Provost of Bradford.'" Thus Cecil Wilson became the first Provost of Bradford. Although he was never actually installed as such, the 'Vicar's Letter' was headed 'Provost's Letter' from this date and Archdeacon Wilson signed himself 'Provost' in matters concerning the Cathedral.

Like Bishop Perowne, he was of evangelical persuasion and it is easy to envisage a number of matters on which he and his new bishop did not see eye to eye. While in Derby, Canon Blunt had practised a central churchmanship but it is likely that it was here that unease with the Simeon Trust and the strand of Protestantism it represented first took root. When the Diocese of Derby was created in 1927, the Bishop of Southwell was patron of St. Werburgh's and the Simeon Trustees of All Saints'. All Saints' was chosen as cathedral and an arrangement made to exchange the two patronages. The first the vicar and congregation knew of this was when it was publicly announced, a situation which caused a great deal of hurt and resentment.

Interestingly, the Church Assembly Cathedrals Commission had recommended that the patronage of Bradford Cathedral should not remain in the hands of private trustees. They suggested that the patronage be transferred to the Crown, although for cathedrals such as Bradford, which were also parish churches, they made an alternative recommendation that the incumbent might be appointed by the bishop . The Bishop's Commission on the Needs of the Diocese of Bradford, in 1928, favoured a transfer to the Crown, "because the Crown necessarily has a wider field of selection and an incumbent comes to his office with higher prestige if appointed by the Crown." Archdeacon Stanton Jones, who was a member of the Bishop's Commission and also one of the Simeon Trustees, was asked to ascertain whether the patrons would be willing to make an exchange for a Crown Living. Such an arrangement would certainly have been more acceptable to Bishop Blunt, but nothing came of it, possibly because Archdeacon Stanton Jones left the diocese that same year, to become Bishop of Sodor and Man.

In his early years in Bradford, Bishop Blunt aligned himself with the anglo-catholic minority in the diocese, partly from his own leaning to the catholic view of the Church and a liking for a certain amount of ceremonial, but partly also in keeping with his life-long inclination to side with those who felt themselves to be oppressed or marginalized.

However, in spite of the bishop's dislike of the starkness of the cathedral worship and the provost's unwillingness to compromise, when Cecil Wilson was appointed as Suffragan Bishop of Middleton in Oct. 1932, Bishop Blunt was generous in his tribute, speaking of one who, as provost, has made the cathedral tell in the life of both city and diocese; as archdeacon has been a friend and counsellor whose judgement and sympathy could always be depended on. "To myself personally, the loss is a very heavy one. I cannot even begin to say how

Bradford Pageant 1931: Archdeacon Wilson as Paulinus

much I owe to him for his kindness, advice and support during this difficult first year. Mrs. Wilson made the vicarage a place to which we were all glad to go." There was only a slight sting in the tail when he asked for prayers for wisdom for the Simeon Trustees to whom would fall the appointment of the new vicar and provost, and concluded: "The appointment of the archdeaconry however, does not come to them but to me."

Although cast in the role of stern and pious Protestant in his relationship with the bishop, it would be unfair to leave that as the complete picture of Cecil Wilson. Another aspect shows up in the way he wholeheartedly threw himself and his church into that spectacular event, the great Historical Pageant of Bradford held in Peel Park in 1931. The name of the archdeacon appears on the Executive Committee and as chairman of Episode II, which became, appropriately, the responsibility of the church. The episode depicted the arrival of Paulinus and his monks in Bradford Dale and the conversion of the Saxons. The archdeacon himself portrayed Paulinus and thirteen more reverend gentlemen took part or assisted with the production. The photograph of Cecil Wilson in the souvenir programme shows a shrewd and humorous face.

He was succeeded as vicar and provost by Edward Worsfold Mowll, a big man both in nature and stature, at six feet three inches in constant danger from the low beams of Horton Hall. He and Bishop Blunt got on well. Out of respect for the bishop's preferences he so far defied Simeon tradition as to keep two candles on the High Altar of the cathedral, which were lit whenever the bishop was present. His son, the Revd. John Mowll, recalls that he had quite an eye for dignified ceremonial. Such details may seem trivial in retrospect, but one should not underestimate their importance to those concerned at the time. Just as aspects of liturgical worship have symbolic values way beyond the actual physical acts or objects used, so small visible concessions had a symbolic value in the corporate life of the diocese.

Provost Edward W. Mowll

For those who explore the cathedral, the dates on the provost's stall may be puzzling. There is no mention of Provost Wilson and Provost Mowll is given the date of 1936, although his appointment dates from January 1933. The explanation seems to be that the stall itself was dedicated in 1939 and the Constitution and Statutes of the Cathedral Church were made official by order of the King in Council in July 1936.

Bishop Blunt's choice as Archdeacon of Bradford had the extraordinary effect of giving the diocese an Archdeacon of Craven whose parish was in Bradford Archdeaconry and an Archdeacon of Bradford who was Rector of Carleton-in-

Craven. Frederick George Ackerley was the son of the Revd. G.B. Ackerley, Vicar of Mitton, and followed his father into the living of Mitton twice, once from 1925-29 and again from 1936-45. After curacies in Keighley, Eccles and Washington, he had gone to Libau in Russia as S.P.G. chaplain, and there met his wife, the daughter of the Vice-Consul. Like her husband, Mrs. Ackerley was a linguist, but is remembered in the parish of Mitton for the unusual distinction of singing tenor in the choir. Archdeacon Ackerley was fluent not only in Russian, German and French, but also in Romany. He was a member of the Gipsy Lore Society and published works on dialects of gipsy speech. He was a man of rather fearsome appearance, bearded, with a stiff triangular moustache, and even Bishop Perowne's son remembers the then Canon Ackerley as a forbidding figure.

Although Bishop Blunt had been known as a first rate administrator in his earlier ministry, as bishop he was content to leave much of this aspect of the work to his archdeacons and other officials. He appreciated too that Bishop Perowne had laid such excellent foundations of administrative structure that his best contribution in his first years was to leave well alone and concentrate on other aspects of diocesan life, including of course becoming acquainted with its great variety of parishes.

The industrial life of the diocese was of great importance to Bishop Blunt, but when he discovered the dales, he quickly grew to love them and said he couldn't imagine a more lovely diocese of which to be bishop. An ally in exploring this part of his domain was the diocesan registrar, Frederick Mossman. The bishop's son David recalls that the two of them developed an unemotional but good and lasting friendship, to the extent that after Bishop Blunt's retirement, Mr. Mossman always spoke of: "Bishop Perowne, *the* Bishop, (Blunt), and the present chap."

They must have made a striking pair, two pipe-smoking gentlemen, the cleric short and decidedly broad, the lawyer, in Lord Coggan's words, " a big man with a voice like a thunderclap." A story told often enough to have some foundation is of a visitor to Mr. Mossman's office who, hearing a great noise within, was asked by the clerk to wait a few minutes because, "he is speaking to Birmingham," to which the visitor replied, "Why doesn't he use the telephone?" This outwardly fierce personality was, for those who got to know him, a front for a kind heart and a sense of humour. A picture in the anteroom to his office showed two farmers engaged in a tug of war, one at each end of a cow, while in the middle sat a lawyer milking it! A less anticipated talent was that of being an expert on the hostelries of the Yorkshire Dales, and the quality of their food and beer, which expertise he was happy to put at the bishop's disposal.

It is generally held that Mrs. Blunt played little part in public life, and it is true that being in the public eye and making speeches was not at all congenial to her. On a number of occasions their elder daughter Amy would accompany her father, or take up the mantle of bazaar opener. To her the bishop explained, "I didn't marry your mother for her ability to make a good clergy wife or bishop's wife. I married her because I loved her." That this love was deep and mutual, no one who knew them well could doubt. A difference in background, particularly educational background, (Margaret's was that meagre share that so often had to suffice for daughters in the 19th century), meant that their expectations of an understanding companion were not always capable of being realised. If visitors to Horton Hall sometimes detected a measure of unhappiness, what they would never detect was any lessening of loving commitment one to the other.

Congenial or not, newspaper reports of the time show that Mrs Blunt did more than is often thought, at least in the early years. She hosted a tea-party for lay readers at Horton Hall and is reported as showing them round the house, pointing out everything of interest and bubbling over with information. She came to love the hall, despite its practical difficulties, and it became very much her enclave. Her son David describes her as wrapping the house around her and it becoming almost her whole world in the last years of their living there.

But certainly in the 1930s we see Mrs. Blunt at a sale of work in Kettlewell in aid of Anglican and Methodist missionary societies, at Horton Mothers' Union Festival, with the bishop at the dedication of a memorial window in Denton, at the Regimental Ball of the 6th Battalion West Yorkshire Regiment, and many other events. Ordination retreats were conducted by the bishop in his home, and his wife played her part by catering, often unaided, for the twenty or so

Mrs. Blunt and the Bishop at Missions to Seamen Exhibition

young men and being on hand with a beaker of hot milk and words of comfort for the nervous. Horton Hall was also the scene of a sale of dolls in aid of the Waifs and Strays Society (later the Children's Society), and of regular Church Missionary Society bazaars. CMS, the Zenana Mission and Missions to Seamen were causes embraced by Mrs. Blunt, for which she worked with enthusiasm, and in this she was supported by the bishop, who believed that bazaars and the like should, whenever possible, be for special causes, and the giving of church people should keep the church going.

What clear lessons in stewardship Bradford's bishops have given, and how slowly, slowly their flocks have responded.

CHAPTER 8

BURNING BRIGHT

Bishop Blunt's early years in Bradford were a time of boundless energy. He continued to publish, no single great work but a whole series of small books, many of lasting value. In his writing, as in his preaching and teaching, he demonstrated a clarity of mind and expression that made his deep theological insights available to a wide range of readers and listeners. David Blunt believed his father's greatest gift to the diocese was his teaching. Academically brilliant, with an Oxford double first, he could nevertheless, "put scholarship into the language of the people; theology seemed to matter when you heard him; he could expound the Trinity so you could understand it!"

Although some responses to issues of the day are inevitably dated, much of his writing is as clear and applicable many decades later as it was at the time. A Primary Visitation Charge to the clergy of Bradford Diocese in 1933, published as "The Church of England - What Does it Stand For?" could have a wonderfully concentrating effect on some of the woollier minds around in the 1990s.

Some of his earlier academic works, and notably his fine commentaries in the Clarendon Bible series, were written at least partly from the need to supplement his stipend as a young clergyman with a growing family. Others simply had to be written, the theology poured out almost spontaneously, as in "Our Need for God", written in a deck-chair on Folkestone beach, of which a review said, "One of the things which justly entitles the Bishop of Bradford to assume a position of leadership in the religious thought of today is his capacity to combine sound scholarship and deep personal knowledge with a remarkably accurate knowledge of what the ordinary man is thinking."

Within the diocese, Bishop Blunt followed and built on Bishop Perowne's concern for, and pastoral care of, his clergy. Like Dr. Perowne, he too rejected a grandiose scheme for the cathedral, this one involving a new building, with bishop's house, guest house, car park and aeroplane landing strip! He was not even prepared to ask the diocese to raise funds to implement Sir Charles Nicholson's earlier plans while funds for current work were scarce and possibilities for spiritual effectiveness were hampered by lack of money. He did not, he said, undervalue the inspiration of a fine cathedral, but he maintained that it was not right, in such circumstances, to spend money lavishly in order to provide a magnificent edifice. That would be to prefer stones to bread.

Thereafter, national and international events closed the door on any thought of non-essential building work, not just for the Church of England, but throughout all aspects of United Kingdom life. In noting the general lack of church building during Bishop Blunt's long episcopate, one needs to remember the war years and the post war period of restrictions and controls.

Though this bishop did not provide the diocese with new bricks and mortar, what he did bring it, very much by his personal endeavours, was a considerable influx of young clergy of high calibre and ideals. The sad thing was that he was not able to keep many of them for more than a few years. There are advantages to a small diocese, but a serious drawback is the lack of parishes to which the most able men can be 'promoted'. With only a handful of 'important' parishes, scope for movement into or within the diocese is limited.

The dales parishes offered small populations but physically demanding geography, particularly when two or more villages were combined into one benefice, making them neither what the keen young men were seeking nor yet ideal for those coming towards the end of their ministry.

This is a problem successive bishops and committees have faced, and is to some extent a problem of the rural church all over the country, not yet satisfactorily resolved, and it was not a new problem in Bishop Blunt's time. In the early years of Ripon Diocese in the nineteenth century, it is recorded in parish returns for that part which later became Bradford, that at least thirteen incumbents were non-resident. Among them, the Vicar of Kirkby Malham was also Vicar of Burnsall and headmaster of the grammar school there, while the Vicar of Long Preston was headmaster of the school at Brewood, Wolverhampton. The Rector of Guiseley was a professor at Cambridge, and the Vicar of Carleton-in-Craven lived in Berkshire where he was the Vicar of Bray!

What many village congregations would most like, of course, is their own church and their own vicar (possibly in that order), but with populations in the hundreds rather than thousands, and churchgoers of any denomination but a small fraction of that, this is no longer possible. At the same time, the miles, often up hill and down dale, between the villages, make city and suburban solutions of closures and mergers inappropriate.

While recognising the different practical needs and problems of its various parts, Bishop Blunt was a great believer in the value of the fellowship of the diocese and in 1932 addressed a gathering of rural clergy at Gargrave on the importance of playing their full part in chapters, conferences and committees. He set up residential courses at which clergy from all over the diocese could share in several days of real study, with the bishop himself and other high-powered lecturers.

Later, that institution with such a potential for mischief, the anonymous Crockford's Preface, claimed that "dioceses so small that an episcopal superior is always at hand, reduce the independence of character, outlook and status of the clergy." Bishop Blunt firmly believed that he was at hand to be a source of help and support when needed, rather than to be constantly looking over a man's shoulder, and he replied in his diocesan letter, "I suppose there are servile clergy, though I should have to look a long while to find one; and if I suffered from the temptation to be an autocratic bishop, I rejoice to think I should not make much of a success of an attempt in this diocese. The accessibility of a bishop to his clergy need not impair their independence. After all it cuts both ways; if he sees them frequently and at close quarters, they see him "unbuttoned". It is hard for a Bishop of Bradford to be a grandee. It may need a special grace to save the bishop of a large diocese from becoming one."

The bishop was a great enthusiast for work with children and young people and spoke forcibly on the rights of the child, for example at a Greengates Sunday School Festival, where he declared that a child was not simply the property of its parents, still less of the state, but had rights of its own which were sacred in the eyes of God. Finding the level of Sunday School provision in the diocese varied and largely unsatisfactory, he appointed Deaconess F.M.(Prudence) Bullock as full time Diocesan Sunday School Adviser in 1932. This was not, at first, a popular appointment. Many of the clergy were content with, and even proud of, the way their Sunday Schools were run, with large classes often of very mixed ages. There was suspicion, and not a little resentment, at the prospect of diocesan interference, but Deaconess Bullock was prepared to work patiently and prayerfully, and made no move to implement changes until she had first made friends with the clergy of the diocese.

She and the bishop were keen to introduce principles of educational psychology that were in use in secular schools, and to encourage the use of good books, such as those by Phyllis Dent, which combined sound doctrine with well-planned lessons. They wanted the children to be well informed about the life and teaching of Jesus, just as Bishop Blunt wanted adult Christians to become knowledgeable about their faith and about the doctrines of the Church. This emphasis on knowledge and understanding underlies much of the bishop's writing, preaching and public addresses.

Together, Bishop Blunt and Deaconess Bullock started diocesan evening classes for Sunday School teachers, and Summer Schools in partnership with Manchester and Chester Dioceses. The clergy were also strongly encouraged to attend annual periods of instruction in

Deaconess F. M. (Prudence) Bullock in 1992

this aspect of their work. As well as running clergy schools, the deaconess lectured on the religious education of children to Mothers' Unions, men's groups and anyone else whose activities might touch on this work. Within two years, she had been welcomed into every parish but one, and so valued was her work that the diocesan conference readily agreed to the appointment of Joan Harcombe as the first of a number of assistants.

The bishop was also concerned about religious instruction in general education and held a three-day refresher course for schoolmasters from Sedbergh and Giggleswick Schools, which proved so useful he later repeated it for Secondary Modern School teachers. He was also a great believer in and supporter of Church Schools.

Although a fair and conscientious father-in-God to all his clergy, the bishop did enjoy the careful and dignified ceremonial of much of anglo-catholic worship and this alignment led to an event which would not have taken place in Bishop Perowne's Bradford. In 1933, clergy of all persuasions had requested and supported a celebration of the centenary of the Oxford Movement. The evangelicals stated that they were ready, while admitting disagreement with some of the forms of activity and tendencies in anglo-catholic teaching, to thank God wholeheartedly for the general result of the Movement in the life of the Church. Encouraged by the success of the centenary, the anglo-catholics held a big congress in Bradford the following year, with the bishop as president and many distinguished speakers. High Mass was sung in different churches each day and the congress ended with a dramatic and colourful procession from All Saints' Church, Little Horton, to a final service in the courtyard of Horton Hall.

Later, Bishop Blunt stepped back from his involvement with the anglo-catholics, the relationship marred by a few extremists he felt were trying to manipulate him for their own ends, to the detriment of his relationship with the evangelical clergy in the diocese. It would be presumptuous to describe a man of his spiritual and intellectual gifts and achievements as naïve, but, himself a man of straightforward integrity, he did display a simple trust in his fellows that occasionally led to hurt and disappointment.

As well as issues that were traditionally and conventionally seen as within the province of the Church, Bishop Blunt was outspoken on social issues. In 1935 he wrote, "Some years ago, I was offered a parish in the London slums. After much heart searching I refused. I could better serve the underprivileged by tackling the rich and comfortable." In Bradford he organised clergy conferences on unemployment, economics and other political matters, and pressed his social gospel to the point of causing consternation among employers and leading citizens. He visited slums and appealed to the City Council for better housing. When slum clearances began, he challenged the policy of offering compensation based only on site value, and personally inspected houses declared unfit for human habitation, challenging reports on condition, and hence valuation.

The General Strike and the unemployment situation had led him to membership of the Labour Party and to association with some more extreme left-wing groups, but he later withdrew from any party membership. He still believed that socialism was the solution to social problems, but was unhappy with the way it was being worked out. He regretted that socialist parties had become very much 'anti' some people, instead of being 'pro' everyone. He rejected communism, saying, "The change in shape from capitalism to communism is taking shape only as an exchange in position between bottom and top dogs. This produces no radical amendment in the situation if both remain dogs. The only fundamental improvement would be one which would teach both sets of dogs to become men and live together as men. But that would be a spiritual revolution and not merely a functional alteration. Christianity and communism move on different levels. Christianity is concerned with the inner inspiration of human life; communism is concerned with the political and economic structure of society, and to turn it into a gospel is to offer men stones for bread and machinery for life."

In addition to his work within Bradford Diocese, Bishop Blunt was much in demand at home and abroad, to lecture, preach and lead courses. In 1936 he gave a series of lectures in the Guildhall at Bath, for which extra seats had to be brought in, suggesting a speaker of the same force and attraction as Bradford's sixth bishop, Geoffrey Paul, who similarly filled Hull City Hall. There was a pilgrimage to the Holy Land and preaching engagements from Westminster Abbey to New York.

In spite of the ever increasing work load, Bradford was too small to be allocated a suffragan bishop although Bishop Blunt tried to have one appointed, to be situated at Skipton. Fortunately, in 1935, the Rt. Revd. Rupert Mounsey, formerly Bishop of Labuan and Sarawak, consented to act in an honorary capacity as an assistant bishop. Bishop Mounsey was a member of the Community of the Resurrection and lived with the Community at Mirfield, only a few miles from Bradford, though not within the diocese. He was of invaluable help during the bishop's travels, and later during his illness. A Bradford clergyman said of him, "During prayers he looked up, and you felt he was looking right into the heart of Heaven."

The 1930s brought more changes in senior staff. In 1934 Archdeacon Howson died. He was a generous man, of great artistic taste, and a knowledgeable antiquarian who did much to beautify Guiseley church. In his memory, a sum of money was raised sufficient to produce £15 per annum to assist with the training of candidates for ordination. He was a man who combined piety and reverence with a zest for life and an infinite interest in people, which Bishop Blunt summed up as "a genius for lovableness, the secret of which lay in his own lovingness."

To succeed him as Archdeacon of Craven, the bishop chose Archdeacon Ackerley who was already based in the Craven Archdeaconry. From 1925 to 1929 he had been Vicar of Mitton, as had his father before him, and in 1936 he returned there. To be twice vicar of the same parish and also archdeacon of both archdeaconries, is an unusual pattern of ministry, as befitted an unusual man. In addition to his other linguistic abilities, Archdeacon Ackerley made his Service book entries in Latin, and as a very old man he was visited in hospital by a young curate, who found him sitting up in bed learning Chinese!

Sidney Edward Lowe, Vicar of Otley and Rural Dean of Otley Deanery, was appointed as Rector of Guiseley and Archdeacon of Bradford. He was an outspoken preacher and lecturer, and also became widely known as 'Yorkshire's sporting parson'. While at Guiseley he organised a series of Sportsmen's Services, and as well as being a keen follower of Yorkshire Cricket Club and Bradford Northern Rugby League team, he was a regular member of the Yorkshire Gentlemen's Cricket XI and even rode pillion on a speedway bike on the Odsal track.

Much of the administrative work of the diocese fell to the archdeacons, including chairing committees of the diocesan board of finance, and their bishop's policy was very much to leave them to get on with it, giving them a considerable work-load, considering that each had a parish to care for. Guiseley in particular was and is a substantial parish with a mission church at Carlton and a large community to serve.

Bishop Blunt was president of the Actors' Church Union and in this capacity visited theatres around the country, including of course Bradford's Alhambra,

Alhambra Theatre Pantomime

where his children were always taken backstage at the pantomime. On one occasion in 1935 he confirmed three girl dancers in the chapel at Horton Hall. They had been prepared partly by correspondence and partly by the theatre chaplain at their previous venue. The show in which they were appearing was "Gay Divorce", an ironic forerunner to the next major event in the life of bishop and nation.

In January 1936 King George V died. Edward VIII was King and his Coronation was planned for 1937. For his diocesan conference address on 1st December 1936, Bishop Blunt chose the subject of the Coronation, planning the discourse to answer two specific points. The first was a proposal by Bishop E.W. Barnes of Birmingham that the Coronation should be separated from a service of Holy Communion so that Free Church ministers could take part. Bishop Blunt had never been opposed to ecumenical involvement where it was appropriate, but this, he felt emphatically, was not a situation where that applied, for reasons which he clearly explained and which were appreciated by at least one Bradford Congregational minister who wrote, "We Nonconformists pride ourselves on being free from state control in matters of worship. Repudiating the whole concept of state religion, asking for a share in the ceremonies is illogical and unreasonable. The bishop is to be congratulated on his clear and sound reasoning." The relationships between denominations, it must be remembered, were not at the stage they had reached even by the 1953 Coronation.

The second point concerned the religious nature of the whole ceremony. A business man had commented to Provost Mowll, "You parsons are trying to make us take a religious view of the Coronation. What's the use when the principal actor in it has no use for that sort of thing himself?" Without the Abdication issue, the whole address was a clear and masterly exposition of the nature of the ceremony and the roles of king, priest and people. With the situation that pertained, one paragraph only sprang into prominence and was used to unlock floodgates that could not in any event have held for much longer. Reading it, what stands out is how little encouragement the press needed to break their self-imposed silence:

"The benefit of the King's Coronation depends, under God, upon two elements: Firstly on the faith, prayer, and self-dedication of the King himself; and on that it would be improper for me to say anything except to commend him and ask you to commend him to God's grace, which he will so abundantly need, as we all need it - for the King is a man like ourselves - if he is to do his duty faithfully. We hope that he is aware of his need. Some of us wish that he gave more positive signs of such awareness."

Newspaper men assumed the words to be a reference to the King's relationship with Mrs. Simpson, and further assumed that the bishop would not have made the reference unless authorised, presumably by the archbishops. It was not too distorted a chain of reasoning to further assume that this indicated some sort of Establishment intention that the British public should now hear what was being openly discussed in Europe and America.

Bishop Blunt himself claimed, and there is no reason to doubt him, that the whole address was composed and typed in October, at which time the bishop had never heard of Mrs. Simpson. His words referred to the King's lack of public religious observance, the very attitude that had given rise to the comment by the provost's acquaintance. The bishop was not, he admitted, in a position to know whether the King was aware of his need for God's grace, but he was quite entitled to express the wish that he gave more positive signs of such awareness. The bishop explained that at the Church Assembly meeting in November he was shown some American newspaper cuttings by Bishop Michael Furse of St. Albans, and in the light of these he did wonder whether to alter his words, but decided not to "for the simple reason that as the words had no reference to the King's love-affair, they could not be twisted to contain such a reference. So I delivered the words as originally written. Sancta Simplicitas!" Unusually for him, he read his speech, an indication of his determination not to deviate in the slightest from his original text.

The Duke of Windsor in his memoirs wrote, "The immediate effect of the Bradford bombshell was to shatter all my hopes of settling my problem one way or another by private negotiation with my Ministers." Much has been written elsewhere about the Abdication and events surrounding it and it is not part of the Bradford story to re-examine it here, only to say that it seems improbable that the final outcome could have been other than it was, no matter whether silence had been maintained for days or weeks longer. It is hard to imagine that a matter of such constitutional importance and such dramatic media potential could ever again be kept 'under wraps' for so long in a non-totalitarian society.

For a short time the bishop became almost as newsworthy as the King. The day after the diocesan conference, he was in Sedbergh for Confirmation Services, in Sedbergh School in the morning and in the parish church in the afternoon. The nation's press descended on the little market town and police protection had to be provided for the bishop. In the days that followed, his postbag was bursting, some for, some against, and the usual sprinkling of cranks. Among the bishop's supporters were a number from the U.S.A., some commenting on the harm the King was doing to the esteem and affection in which the British Royal Family had been held. Many expressed thanks for his moral courage, and a Greek journalist and member of the Orthodox Church likened him to St. John Chrysostom reminding Empress Endoxia of her duties.

His unwitting part in an unprecedented national crisis was to haunt Alfred Blunt for the rest of his life. Without it, it is unlikely that in 1955 the national press would have sought the views of the ageing bishop of a small north-country diocese on the question of Princess Margaret's possible marriage to the divorced Peter Townsend. Bishop Blunt's low key, factual statement of the Church's attitude to such a marriage gave rise to such headlines as "Prelate who Rocked Throne warns Meg," and "Call it off, Bishop tells Meg. Cleric the One who put Whammy on Windsors." Indeed the issue followed him to the grave, featuring in obituaries, to the exclusion of some of the achievements of the early Bradford years, for which he surely deserved to be remembered.

CHAPTER 9

PERILS AND DANGERS

Towards the end of the decade, international events overshadowed the whole country. In the Church of England such niceties as cathedral extensions, candles on altars, even whether one's parish was in the most appropriate diocese, moved, quite properly, so far down the order of priorities as virtually to disappear off the end. Expressed views of English Church leaders, as Europe moved uneasily towards disaster, ran the gamut from unwavering pacifism to Bishop Headlam of Gloucester's misguided sympathy for Nazism. Leaders of the city of Bradford, and through the person of its bishop, the diocese, published a forceful and honourable protest at the persecution of Jews as far back as 1933.

Initially Bishop Blunt supported the Munich agreement as being preferable to war, but by early 1939 was supporting the Government's re-armament programme as a Christian duty. To diocesan conference he said the point had been reached when, "it is my firm conviction that for us not to fight would have been a worse sin than for us to fight. We have sinned, I have agreed, by political blindness and folly; we should then have added to this sin the sin of treason to the ideals of Christian civilisation. This is the point at which I join issue with the Pacifists. To them no sin is greater than war. I cannot agree with them. War is an awful evil, and modern war diabolical in its destructiveness. But to betray Right is a worse sin than to fight Might. To submit to Hitlerism – still more to leave others a helpless prey to it - would be to betray every principle of international right, which civilisation has slowly come to acknowledge, and to let the world sink back into the barbarism from which it had so painfully emerged."

He saw this war as a war of religion, the issue between Christ and antichrist. In an address to Bradford Rotary Club in 1940 he told them that this war was different from previous wars for hundreds of years. In the 1914-18 war the German nation and the Kaiser were in the same cycle of civilisation as ourselves. In this one it would not be so much Germany conquering Britain as a particular philosophy of life conquering another philosophy of life. He summed up: "The struggle is going on to settle the question whether man shall live in the future under a system in which man will be regarded merely as a creature of the State, owing no duty except a duty to his nation or his class, or whether man shall live in a system in which he shall be allowed to think of himself as a child of God who owes a duty not only to his nation, not only to his class, but to the development of mankind."

Canon T. J. Williams and the Bishop

In respect of the Church's role in time of war, the bishop urged that churches should be kept open during daylight hours, to provide a place for prayer, that regular and frequent celebrations of Holy Communion and services of intercession should be held, that preaching should not constantly be about war but about fundamental Christian values, and that visiting and ministry to hospitals should be the chief occupation of the clergy. The bishop himself visited factories and canteens, and walked about the city talking to those he met, sometimes going out very early to encounter people on their way to work.

He ordained all the diocese's deacons as priests, so that they could fully serve wherever needed, and authorised parochial lay readers to act as diocesan lay readers. The role of the parochial reader was much narrower than that of his equivalent several decades later. He (there was no question of 'she' until 1969) could assist the vicar, for example by reading lessons, and diocesan readers were allowed, in an emergency, to take Sunday Morning or Evening Prayer at other churches within the diocese. For this they needed to have the permission of the vicar and churchwardens, but were not allowed to preach if a clergyman was present.

The newly priested young men were likely to find themselves looking after parishes, as parish clergy volunteered for war service as chaplains. Queensbury is one example of a parish cared for by a curate 'lent' from Shipley when their vicar, the Revd. Kenneth Kay, volunteered for sea at the outbreak of war. He had already served as a naval chaplain before coming to Queensbury, and in 1939 was posted to a warship which escorted convoys on the dangerous northern route to Russia. There were many narrow escapes, and on his final convoy, this time to Malta, the ship was badly damaged by torpedo and took four hazardous days to limp back to Gibraltar. The Centenary Souvenir of Holy Trinity., Queensbury, records, "with pride and pleasure the fine service rendered to Queensbury Parish and his country by the Revd. Kenneth Kay." Although the Service chaplains were volunteers, they had to be selected by their bishop and also had to have at least five years parochial experience. It is interesting that chaplains were commissioned to the relative rank of Captain in the Army and Squadron Leader in the R.A.F. In the Royal Navy, the chaplain was not given a rank, but assumed the rank of any officer he was dealing with at the time, be it Midshipman or Admiral!

One who went as a senior chaplain was Canon T.J. Williams, who was to be the next Archdeacon of Craven. He had already served as a chaplain from 1916 – 1918 and been awarded the Military Cross. The Revd. Geoffrey Young, curate of Guiseley, with responsibility for Carlton, was stationed with the Gunners in Malta and a letter from him, describing the heavy bombing the island was enduring, was read out to his parishioners. In 1943 he was reported missing but in 1944 he was again writing home, from a prisoner of war camp in Germany. This letter spoke of their inspiring Easter Services in the camp and a Theological School for ordination candidates he was helping to run. Geoffrey was welcomed back in 1945 and later became Vicar of Thornbury.

The only son of Archdeacon Lowe, serving with the R.A.F. in Singapore, was also reported missing in 1942. Throughout the war the Archdeacon published in the Guiseley Messenger vigorous letters of encouragement to his flock, emphasising the need to prosecute this war to a successful conclusion. It was not until November 1945, when the war was over, that Archdeacon and Mrs. Lowe learnt that their son was dead. The bereaved father wrote: "We are very proud of dear Peter and thankful that he has taken his part, along with so many, in defeating a great evil, and we pray that we who remain may go forward worthy of those who opened up the way." He paid tribute to all those other families who had been so wonderful and so brave throughout the war.

The diocese as a whole was relatively unscathed by the war, in comparison with other parts of the United Kingdom, and casualties in the Services were lighter than in the previous conflict, as can be seen from any War Memorial, but it was still a cause of deep distress to many homes. Mr. and Mrs. Mossman lost their only son, and Bishop and Mrs. Blunt's younger son Geoffrey, a pilot officer in the R.A.F., died in 1941 at the age of 19. Only days after his death, the bishop wrote a very beautiful and moving article which was published in the Sunday Chronicle, and which gave hope and comfort to many.

Churches throughout the diocese adapted in various ways to the war situation. The cathedral's large east window and some of the smaller ones were bricked up as an air-raid precaution, though Bradford actually escaped lightly from this aspect of war. Evensong was switched to 3 p.m., and instructions were issued that, in the event of an air-raid, those present should shelter close to the walls below window level and occupy themselves with prayer or singing hymns. Many parishes likewise changed their Evensong to afternoon to comply with blackout regulations. Though Bradford was not seriously bombed, it was not unresponsive to the needs of others, and congregations contributed to air-raid distress funds. One parish sent its Sunday collection to All Saints' Church, Grimsby, on hearing that this had been hit.

At St.Luke's, Manningham, the school building became a NAAFI canteen for troops stationed in the district. Sunday School was held in church and parochial organisations met in the vicarage. Youth work, which had been thriving, was so severely curtailed that it never really recovered, although there were other social factors involved in the gradual decline of the parish from having been one of the most important in the Ripon Diocese. Their mission church, St. Silas, in Fairfield Road was closed and taken over by the ARP for the duration of the war. The church hall at All Saints' Keighley was requisitioned as a first aid post and decontamination centre, and a section of the churchyard was turned over to vegetable growing as part of the 'Dig for Victory' campaign.

Individuals and congregations, were involved in sending gift parcels to men serving in the forces. The people of St. Jude's for instance, applied themselves to knitting for the benefit of the skipper and crew of HM Trawler 'The Girl Winifred'. A certificate displayed in St. Andrew's, Blubberhouses reads:

"Presented by the Lords Commissioners of the Admiralty to the Civil Parish of Blubberhouses to commemorate the adoption of H.M.S. Speedwell during Warship Week, March 1942."

Many churches lost their iron railings and gates to the war effort, which proved to be more of a symbolic than real help, as much of the metal collected was unsuitable for melting and re-using. Bazaars and sales of work diminished, partly because strict food rationing was not compatible with cake stalls and afternoon teas, but mainly because of the lack of people with time to organise them. As well as the men and women in the armed services and those engaged in essential war work, more women than ever before were going out to work to fill the many civilian vacancies. Where fund-raising activities were taking place, the money might well be for some cause not usually associated with church life, such as War Ship Week, or Wings for Victory.

A typical little incident from the magazine of St. Jude's and St. Aidan's in 1941 illustrates a very English, understated reaction to the trials of war, and determination to make the best of things. Father Whitehead was moving out of the diocese and he wrote that rationing made it impossible to invite friends to drop in and take pot luck, but, "there is a fine garden which is very suitable for picnic teas. Even in these days we can provide hot water." He then gave instructions for reaching his new parish, some 25 miles away, by bicycle.

It is hard to imagine now how slender the chances of defeating, or even halting, Nazism looked in the early years of the war. Later, when Russian and American involvement made Allied victory only a matter of time, the Bishop of Bradford turned to another moral aspect of the war. The 'hate Germany' propaganda from the War Office worried him. He declared that Nazism was the worst enemy of Germany's soul and that to defeat Germany thoroughly was the most loving thing to do to her, but, he warned, to hate Germany now is to spoil our victory before we win it. These sentiments were not in tune with the general feeling of the times, although Churchill's "in victory, magnanimity", grasps a similar vision. To the diocesan conference in 1944 the bishop said, "It seems to come to this. So long as men have no real 'enemies', we may preach 'love your enemies' as much as we like. Nobody will mind; also nobody will heed. But as soon as men have real enemies, the words of Christ are called 'vapid sentiment' and 'sob stuff', especially by people who do not know what Christ means by Love. In other words, Christianity is all right so long as you do not let Christ mean what He says. But treat Him once as if He does, and you become a nuisance."

CHAPTER 10

IMPROVE EACH SHINING HOUR

In 1944 Bishop Blunt suffered another breakdown in health, but made a good recovery, and with the end of the war was ready and able to apply himself again to the needs of the diocese. The report of the diocesan board of finance for the year ending Dec. 31st 1944 began: "The war with Germany is now in God's Providence ended. The Diocese is free of debt, there are accumulated funds for some purposes, but there must be a great Forward Movement if God's work is not to suffer. The long awaited diocesan appeal can now be launched."

F.D. Moore had been succeeded as chairman of the board by W.B. Gordon, then E.C. Woodman, and in 1937 another of the 'great names' of Bradford's laity had taken over. Mr. John Foster Beaver had been a member of the original bishopric committee and a member of the board of finance since 1922, becoming its joint treasurer in 1924. He remained chairman until he decided it was time to retire in 1973 at the age of 82. The diocese owes him a lasting debt of gratitude, both for his personal generosity of time and money and for his skilful management of its affairs over half a century. The money now known as diocesan reserve came into being as the chairman's fund, into which Mr. Foster Beaver gathered up any surpluses or profits that occurred, and which he controlled with a fair but extremely firm hand.

At a meeting of diocesan conference in April 1945, Bishop Blunt launched the Forward Movement Appeal, setting a target of £200,000. Mr. Foster Beaver explained that the need was for new church buildings, clergy stipends, new vicarages, improvements to schools, training for teachers and clergy, moral welfare and youth work. The Vicar of St. Clement's, Bradford, the Revd. Charles Forder, later Archdeacon of York, agreed to be secretary of the appeal, although the extra curate he was promised never materialised. Appeal work took him out into the dales, where the country clergy seemed to him to be lonely and very pleased to see someone from Bradford. Five years of the wartime slogan 'Is Your Journey Really Necessary?' had seriously reduced contact between different parts of the diocese. Short staffed in the parish, Mr. and Mrs. Forder used their day off for this work. Sadly, there was poor response to the appeal from the business world, with very few firms contributing, partly due to straitened circumstances, but also, Archdeacon Forder suggests, partly due to the bishop's unpopular left-wing views.

Mention was also made at the April conference of a separate appeal to be launched for the needs of the cathedral, and when this came, later in the year, there is no doubt that it detracted from the bishop's appeal - not the last occasion for such a clash of interests. By the end of the following year, the bishop was referring to the number of appeals in existence for large sums of money. He pointed out that people had become accustomed to having their church privileges on very cheap terms and had not valued them properly. Any gift beyond a modest coin in the offertory was looked on as a work of supererogation and they had a sense of acquiring superfluous merit. And they expected to be begged for it! So many of the clergy were forced into feeling their affinity with the daughter of the horse leech! The bishop proposed that at least one month before a public appeal for money was made by any parochial authority, the promoters should inform the archdeacon and undertake to observe such regulations governing the appeal as he may make.

Canon W.J. Perrett, Rector of Shipley, chaired the finance committee of the diocesan board of finance, and took responsibility for the Forward Movement Appeal. He was a small man, forever busy, likened by one of his parishioners to a robin bobbing about. Men who were curates or young vicars in his time recall with gratitude his efforts on behalf of the clergy, raising the Forward Movement fund and disbursing much of it for the augmentation of stipends. Canon Perrett retired at the end of 1953, and in June 1954 Mr. Foster Beaver gave the final report on the appeal. It had raised £123,757, about 60% of target, and this mainly from the parishes. Almost all of it had been paid out, mostly for stipends, which were by this time as high as the standard in any diocese, and for help with the training of ordinands. Church Day Schools were also to benefit from the fund. Later chairmen of the board of finance may find it hard to believe that it had been possible to work to the same diocesan budget, of £8,250, from 1930 to 1953. At that point it became necessary to raise it to £12,500, which was presented in 1953 as the budget for 1954, 55 and 56.

This however, is to run ahead of the events of the immediate post-war period. 1943 had seen Provost Mowll consecrated as Bishop of Middleton, following in Cecil Wilson's footsteps. The preacher at his consecration was one of his former curates from his time as incumbent in Southport. This young man, John Gerhard Tiarks, had gone on to make his mark as a dynamic and effective leader of a number of Lancashire parishes, and in January 1944 he arrived in Bradford as its new vicar and provost.

John Tiarks quickly made his presence felt in Bradford, becoming as recognisable a figure as the bishop. He was a tall, imposing man, with a Shakespearean forehead and piercing eyes. Though he made headlines by arriving in Bradford wearing what was in 1944 an informal outfit - lounge suit, soft collar and tie - he adopted the traditional garb of his rank for public occasions. This gave rise to a suggestion at Sports Day at his daughter's school that gaiters, being more streamlined than the wide-legged trousers of the day, gave him an unfair advantage in the Fathers' Race. The local paper records that he did not win, but acquitted himself well, with a rare turn of speed. At services, in the cathedral and elsewhere, his long fur tippet soon assumed almost the role of a trademark.

Mrs. Tiarks, even with the addition of hat and high heeled shoes, scarcely came up to her husband's shoulder, but was just as full of energy and enthusiasm, throwing herself wholeheartedly into Mothers' Union and other cathedral activities, as well as looking after husband and children and running an almost impossible house. Provost's House, Bradford Vicarage, was in Great Horton Road, next door to what was then the Technical College. The provost's daughter, Mrs. Ann Remfry, recalls not only leaking roofs and a huge expanse of black and white tiled hall to be scrubbed, but also baths so high she almost needed a ladder to get in and out. The house was a long way from the cathedral and another clear memory is of setting off with mother and brother to walk to church, father having gone earlier, and of "haring down Great Horton Road, usually late."

The "haring" would be absolutely essential, as punctuality was something of an obsession with the provost. Later, when the family had moved to Heaton, there was an occasion when he walked the three miles to the cathedral in thick snow and still arrived in time for the service, for which the Lord Mayor, who only had to cross town from City Hall, was late. "I wait for no man," said the provost, and began. Well known friends, who once arrived late for dinner, were surprised to be greeted by the reproachful ticking of a clock on the doorstep! One of his curates once remarked that he didn't know what the provost would do when there was all eternity!

The voice of John Tiarks was soon being heard in Bradford, speaking out about declining moral standards. His first big public speech came soon after his installation, at the 37th annual meeting of St. Monica's Homes, a church-led organisation for the care of unmarried mothers and their babies. He spoke of the twin roles of the Church in moral issues: of picking up casualties at the bottom of a precipice, but also providing a fence at the edge to prevent people falling over. He praised St. Monica's for not only picking up casualties, but putting them back on the right side of the fence.

Propaganda for un-chastity singled out for criticism included films, novels, a certain type of cheap magazine, and even some of the "alleged comedy of the BBC." Of sex education in schools, he said, "It can never be anything but an evil. It may be the lesser of two or three evils, but it remains an evil and can never produce a full understanding of the subject. Sex education, of which biological facts are a part, but not the chief part, can never be learnt outside personal relationships." He stressed that sexual morality was not the whole of morality, and would not attribute general decline wholly to the war, but pointed out that a revolt against Christian ethics was due to repudiation of the doctrines on which it was founded.

He opposed the Sunday opening of cinemas, which was originally at the request of the Military Authorities so that troops might have somewhere to go, his opposition summed up in a statement equally applicable to the Sunday trading issues of the 1990s: "I am not anxious for the cinemas to close in order to help the churches. I simply suggest that this willingness to treat Sunday as any other day of the week is a tragic symptom of the disease of irreverence which has smitten modern man. Unless he be a Christian and a churchgoer, he has nothing before which he must stand and bow his head. The whole matter of keeping Sunday as a national (not personal) day of change from normal weekday activities, runs down to this question of whether we are to keep alive in England 'the little flower of reverence', as Emerson called it."

Later, in 1947, the provost joined with other religious leaders in Bradford in a short experiment in taking the Gospel directly to the people who had opted for the cinema. On four Sunday evenings, the programme at the Odeon was interrupted for a three or four minute talk, the first one being given on December 21st. by the provost, who delivered a Christmas message which was greeted with resounding applause.

A different approach to moral issues came with the formation in 1948 of the Bradford Diocesan Moral Welfare Council. Bradford was a late starter in this work, which had arisen out of an Archbishop's Advisory Council on Moral Welfare set up before the First World War. There was opposition to the idea from many in the diocese, partly because there was little money to spare for the work and partly because people were uneasy about the Church appearing to equate morals with sex.

The council might well never have been formed but for the efforts of the Vicar of Idle, the Revd.(later Canon) Guy Waddington. He was already working among the poorest and most disadvantaged members of society, and most keen for the Church to be seen in action as well as heard talking. His strategy was, according to one of the leading professional workers for Moral Welfare, Miss Elsie Cunliffe , "to go and annoy everyone until they gave in." He was, she says "the most militant pacifist I have ever met."

The object of the council was 'the co-ordination of thought and action in relation to the place of sex, marriage and the family, in Christian life.' The name was later changed to Family Welfare, as more accurately describing its range of activity. In practice, initial referrals to the council always came as a result of an unwanted pregnancy, but the workers soon found themselves involved in a wide range of family problems and attitudes within an equally wide range of social classes. Like many Bradford Diocesan projects, the council ran on a shoestring, with a small office in Church House and at first only one paid official. Later, some secretarial help was added and more social workers, including Mrs. Slaughter, wife of the Vicar of Christ Church, Skipton, to look after the Craven area. Two additional part-time workers were appointed after the council added the task of being its own adoption agency.

Many parishes supported the work by organising yearly house to house collections, but there was always some opposition. At a meeting of diocesan conference in 1956, Canon Waddington said he hoped those who were critical of the work would remember that every human life belongs to God and that He does not renounce His claim to it, no matter how degraded it might be. The council put less direct emphasis on religion than did St. Monica's Home;

its workers simply tried to live out their Christianity. An old clergyman in the dales used to complain to Miss Cunliffe that they were given all these reports on the work the council had done, but no mention of how many souls they had saved. At last Miss Cunliffe was driven to reply, "Do *you* know how many souls you have saved?"

The council continued to work until 1975. Ironically, the beginning of the end was brought about by Bishop Michael Parker, 4th Bishop of Bradford, who was himself deeply interested in the work. He visited the office every week and regularly invited the workers to 8 a.m. Holy Communion at Bishopscroft. He declared that welfare workers should not have to go round asking for their salaries, and so put an end to the annual house to house collections and included the cost in the quota required from the parishes. This was a source of frequent complaint and made the council vulnerable when diocesan finance reached one of its recurring low ebbs. However, it must also be admitted that by the time it was disbanded, much of its work was being undertaken by Local Authorities. In fact three of the diocesan welfare workers were able to transfer to the Social Services' Adoption Unit. It could be argued that the Church had fulfilled its task by making sure the work was started and carrying it forward until it was taken up by others. There are parallels with the Church's role in health care and education over the centuries.

To return to the work of Provost Tiarks, he built on the relationship with the business community established by his predecessors and, in addition to the usual Civic Services, introduced occasional business men's services of intercession. At his first Harvest Festival he emphasised Bradford's particular harvest with a display in the cathedral of wool in various stages of manufacture. Co-operating happily with the Free Churches, he spoke at various anniversaries and special services, including the 40th anniversary of the Bradford Methodist Mission at Eastbrook Hall.

In 1945 of course, the war in Europe ended. On the 8th and 9th of May, 12,000 people attended cathedral services which went on until after midnight. On V.E. Day, Thursday 10th May, six 15 minute services were held at intervals in the cathedral, with a one hour service at 7 p.m. Next day began with Holy Communion, followed by a Civic Thanksgiving Service at which Bishop Blunt preached, and Choral Evensong with the provost as preacher. On Sunday the 13th, the British Legion service at the cenotaph at the bottom of Morley Street was conducted by the Revd. Kenneth Kay, Vicar of Heaton. There was a ceremonial parade and a Civic Service in a packed cathedral in the afternoon, when Bishop Blunt again preached. This service was relayed to hundreds of people in the cathedral grounds and in Forster Square.

At 12.30. p.m. the provost addressed not only a full cathedral and people of the diocese, but countless members of the armed forces, when the service was broadcast on the B.B.C. General Forces' Programme. One of the letters in response to this came from a Royal Air Force sergeant in Burma: "It was a hot, sweltering afternoon. We were resting, not particularly interested in much, when someone turned on a portable radio. Your service had just started and 30 of us listened. We had heard many programmes during the week of celebrations of V.E. Day, but I do not think any of the programmes were received with more enthusiasm and interest than your sermon and the beautiful singing of the choir. Dare I ask you to pass on to them my thanks and appreciation? It was really grand. The service brought to us a bit of dear old England and the message of the sermon a hope for the future."

So successful was the broadcast that the BBC asked John Tiarks for a series of five short services which they called "For Isolated Units", intended for members of the armed forces in out-of-the-way places, who had no padre with them. Thereafter, the Provost of Bradford was a frequent broadcaster, in the "People's Service" on the Light Programme, Community Hymn Singing from Bradford Cathedral, an evening service from the Bradford Royal Infirmary nurses' chapel, at which the address was given by the Matron, Easter services in 1947 when the sound of Bradford Cathedral's bells rang round the world on the BBC's short wave service, and "Lift Up Your Hearts". Pictures of cathedral and provost appeared regularly in Radio Times, and Christmas 1947 was dominated by the city, with the cathedral bells, People's Service, and Wilfred Pickles' Children's Party from Bradford Children's Hospital.

An innovation in religious broadcasting was the 'listener's seat', an idea suggested by the provost to enable the listener to hear the service as if from a seat half way down the aisle, rather than from the choir, where the microphones were normally installed. The broadcast started with an invitation: "We have kept a seat for you, halfway up the middle aisle; just slip into it...." In 1949 Bradford Cathedral was the venue for the BBC's first broadcast of the whole of a Holy Communion Service. An article in Radio Times explained that broadcasts of the Communion Service were experimental and would be restricted to the major festivals of the Christian year. John Tiarks conducted the service and Bishop Blunt preached. In these days of television, it is hard to imagine what a controversial decision this was. In 1951, the opening of the Holme Moss TV transmitter was marked by a televised Evensong from Leeds Parish Church. The preacher was John Tiarks, described in a press report as "one of the most successful of religious broadcasters in the north, who is going to be equally fitted for television broadcasting."

High among the provost's achievements, and forming a lasting memorial to him in Bradford, must rank the long-awaited metamorphosis of the parish church building into the present cathedral. In his farewell message to Bradford, Provost Mowll had said that he would like to see in Bradford a cathedral building worthy of the city. During the war years it was realised that some structural repairs to the east end were needed, as well as extensions more than ever being desirable, but the Cathedral Council were opposed to a public appeal at such a time. Echoing the situation in the First World War, when the bishopric endowment was needed, Provost Mowll and People's Warden Mr. A.E. Simpson quietly began to raise money and invest it in Savings Bonds.

In 1944 an exhibition entitled "Rebuilding Britain" was mounted in Brown, Muff's store in Bradford. One of the exhibits was a picture provided by the

Telegraph and Argus, showing Forster Square as it might look if the General Post Office building in front of the cathedral were to be demolished. Complementary to this was a drawing by the Ilkley-born architect Mr. (later Sir) Edward Maufe, of proposed extensions to the cathedral.

The plans submitted by Mr. Maufe, who also designed Guildford Cathedral, were approved by the Cathedral Council. The estimated cost was £175,000, and in November 1945, an appeal was launched at a luncheon in City Hall, when prominent citizens were the guests of the Lord Mayor, Alderman Cecil Barnett. Three phases of building were planned, starting with wings at the west end to flank the tower, followed later by enlargement of the south aisle, and finally an extensive renovation and remodelling of the east end. In 1953, phase one began to take shape when the foundation stone of the north wing was laid by H.R.H. the Princess Royal, sister of King George VI and the former King Edward VIII.

Architect's visualisation of completed Cathedral, 1944

CHAPTER 11

OPENING AND CLOSING DOORS

With such a dynamic personality as John Tiarks at the cathedral, and an exciting building programme beginning, it is inevitable that the story of the diocese in the 1940s and 50s seems to focus on the city of Bradford, rather to the exclusion of the rest of the 880 square miles. The relationship of the provost to the civic and business community is an important one in both his roles, as provost of the cathedral and Vicar of Bradford. Although the bishops have been, to varying degrees, involved in the public life of the city (and later the Metropolitan District), this is only a part of their concern and the diocesan bishop is the one man above all whose overall charge is the whole of the diocese.

In 1950, Bishop Blunt was 71 years old. The custom of moving meetings of diocesan conference around the diocese had lapsed, and most of the meetings of the 50s were held in Bradford. Yet along the valleys of Aire and Wharfe and among the smaller dales and hills of the rural part of the diocese, the Church's work went on, in less headline-making ways, but of no lesser value for that. One key appointment in 1948 was of enormous value here and arose directly out of the Lambeth Conference of that year.

The bishop took the opportunity the conference gave of re-inforcing diocesan interest in overseas work by inviting to Bradford the Bishops of Damaraland (in South Africa); Kingston, Jamaica; Newcastle, New South Wales; and Northern Rhodesia, who were among those attending. He was thrilled by the response when thousands of churchgoers processed through the city with the bishops. The crowd was so great it had to be divided between the cathedral and Eastbrook Hall, and all four bishops spoke to both congregations.

Bishop Blunt found the conference itself an inspiring occasion and among the new friends he made there was the Rt. Revd. Alexander Ogilvie Hardy, Bishop of Nagpur. Bishop Hardy and his wife, Dr. Ruth Hardy, had meant to stay in India for the rest of their lives, but changes in that country had led to such a reduction in income that they could no longer manage to educate their five children. So the bishop was resigning at the Lambeth Conference, and when he had completed some deputation work in Scotland, he was hoping to find a position in the Church of England. He had never worked in England, having served a curacy in Londonderry before going to India with the Dublin University Mission, but he knew Yorkshire from having spent a portion of each home-leave with the Mirfield Fathers.

Bishop Alex and Dr. Ruth Hardy

Bishop Blunt invited Alex Hardy to become Vicar of Gargrave and Assistant Bishop of Bradford, primarily for the Craven Archdeaconry, with special regard to the pastoral care of Craven's clergy. The only finance available was the Gargrave stipend, but Bishop Blunt rather typically added £100 a year out of his own pocket for the assistant bishop's expenses. Although the Blunts and the Hardys had never met before 1948, they discovered an earlier connection when it turned out that a little book called "Worship and Intercession", for which Bishop Blunt had written the foreword in 1934, had been written by Ruth Hardy before her marriage.

The family moved into the old 14-roomed vicarage in December, and loved it, though Ruth had to do the decorating and it was furnished with a van load of bits and pieces from her mother's home and items picked up at auctions. They kept open house, making the vicarage the centre of parish life in the same warm and friendly way that they had used Bishop's Lodge in Nagpur. Hearing that the people of Gargrave always washed the floor of the church before Christmas, Ruth put on an apron and got down on her hands and knees with the rest, which was not quite what the parish had been used to, the vicarage in times past having been very much regarded as one of the "big houses" of the village, even having a footman.

The Hardys had no car and though they would sometimes be taken into other parts of the dales by friends, most of their visiting was done by train and on foot. They would set off and walk from parish to parish, having morning coffee at one vicarage and lunch at another, getting to know many of the clergy of the archdeaconry. Being themselves based in a parish, they had a great understanding of parochial problems.

Bishop Blunt kept up his involvement with the Public Schools at Sedbergh, Giggleswick and Bentham to the end of his episcopate, but from 1948 on, Alex Hardy was the ever-present and active father-in-God to the dales clergy, the more so when Ven. T.J. Williams, already in his 60s, became Archdeacon of Craven in 1950, while remaining Vicar of Otley. Bishop Hardy was also available to ordain and confirm when Bishop Blunt was away or ill, as was increasingly the case (and in fact confirmed the author at St.Luke's, Manningham in 1951). Although Bishop Hardy was so much help in the diocese, the parish of Gargrave was in no way neglected. His PCC secretary, Derrick Watson, recalled him systematically visiting every house in the parish - "a shepherd who knew all his sheep by name." An informal arrangement with the local doctor made him a prompt visitor of the sick. Meticulous in his duties and an imposing figure when robed in the Indian vestments he brought with him, Bishop Hardy also presented to Gargrave a most human face. He was a smoker, who grew his own tobacco as an economy measure, and dried it in the vicarage attic, and when he had worked up a thirst by cutting the churchyard grass, he would stroll across to the Masons' Arms with a big enamel jug to be filled with beer.

Ruth Hardy was also much involved in parish life, organising sales to support missionary work and annual Nativity and Passion plays. These events did much to bring the Anglicans, Methodists and Roman Catholics of Gargrave together. For one of her early productions , Dr. Hardy asked the Roman Catholic priest for the loan of a thurifer for one of the Three Kings, and it was at first refused because the play was not to be in a Roman Catholic church. Eventually he did get permission from his superiors to lend it and co-operation between the churches progressed over the years until the plays became totally ecumenical events. As an indication of how far we have moved in interdenominational relationships, in the Hardys' first year in the diocese, Dr. Hardy preached in Settle Baptist Church for Women's World Day of Prayer, and caused, she said, "uproar in the diocese - the assistant bishop's wife at the Baptists!" The Hardys' life and witness in Bradford and the dales made its own contribution to the much improved co-operation between Christian people at all levels.

Dr. Hardy also involved herself in the Moral Welfare Committee for Craven and was a speaker at Mothers' Union meetings, although she declined to be Enrolling Member except for a very short time when the member in office in Gargrave died. She felt strongly that it was better for the vicar's wife not to hold that position since it could cut her off from women who, for any reason, were not eligible to be members. A Boys' Club was run in part of the vicarage and the family generally revelled in the joys a big house full of people could bring, rather than dwelling on the drawbacks. They became good personal friends to the Blunts and Ruth would visit, to give Margaret some company when, in their later years, she hardly stirred out of Horton Hall.

The youth work Bishop Blunt had been so keen to build up throughout the diocese was under the care of a Diocesan Youth Committee from 1944, but its secretary, treasurer and organiser (and vicar of a parish) Revd. Robert Allan, resigned, and the structure was found to be unworkable. In 1949, the Revd. (later Canon) Charles Goodchild was appointed to the small parish of Tosside, specifically so that he could take up the duties of Youth Chaplain to the diocese.

After a couple of years at Tosside he moved to Settle, and having the Youth Chaplain based almost in the geographical centre of the diocese must have been an encouragement to the country parishes.

As well as encouraging more local clergy to start youth groups, Charles Goodchild organised day conferences with visiting speakers e.g. on marriage preparation and on vocational training such as nursing, when some of the meetings were held at St.Luke's Hospital in Bradford. Diocesan or other group events were a great help to those parishes with too few young people to support strictly local activities. One of the highlights of the year was the big rally at Bolton Priory on Easter Monday. Groups of young people from all over the diocese would plan a day's walk, ending by coming together at the Priory for cups of tea provided by Mrs. Goodchild in the parish room, then an outdoor service in the ruins. Canon Goodchild continued as Youth Chaplain for eleven years, at Settle until 1958 and later at Tong and Holme Wood.

Bishop Blunt was a great believer in the episcopal role of enabling, rather than keeping a close and possibly interfering eye on those he appointed. Another man whose specialised ministry was furthered by the bishop's attitude was the Revd. Norman Goodacre. He came into Bradford Diocese as a young curate in 1936, attracted by having read Dr. Blunt's publication, "The Church of England, What Does It Stand For?" In 1938 he became Vicar of Thornbury, and writes of some of his colleagues of those days: "During the war a few of us, all incumbents in the city, met at intervals to talk about our work. One was my neighbour Charlie Forder, then Vicar of St. Clement's in Bradford, who went on to become Archdeacon of York and wrote a famous pastoralia classic, 'The Parish Priest at Work' (1947). Another, Chat Hammond, was Vicar of St. Luke's Manningham : later he had a very successful ministry in the south as Vicar of St. George's Beckenham in Kent. Max Johnstone, who was at that time Vicar of St. Margaret's Frizinghall, and very musically gifted, went on to a residentiary canonry in Bristol Cathedral. I was Vicar of St. Margaret's Thornbury, two miles from the city centre. After the war I accepted the smallest living in the Bradford Diocese, St. Peter's Coniston Cold (now joined with Kirkby Malham) where I was able to continue the peripatetic ministry of the late Revd. Dr. R. Somerset Ward (1881-1962) who made himself available for spiritual direction in twenty centres throughout the country." (After 1958, Mr. Goodacre continued this ministry, working from a house given for this purpose, in Harrogate.)

Leaving Bradford for the quiet depth of the countryside, Mr. Goodacre discovered, did not mean leaving the company of spiritually and academically distinguished men. With such priests as Archdeacon Ackerley, George Midgley, Vicar of Long Preston and author of a book of meditations, and the internationally renowned classical scholar and author, Dr. Ernest Evans as Vicar of Hellifield, clergy chapter meetings were more like an Oxford or Cambridge High Table, and presented wonderful learning opportunities for younger clergy. Through the ministries of such men, Bradford Diocese exercised an influence throughout the Anglican church.

Sector ministry, combined with a parish, has its drawbacks, not least that each of the half jobs usually ends up needing two thirds of the officer's time, but those parishes enjoying, or suffering from, a part-time vicar and part-time something else might be interested to realise how traditional the situation is. Indeed, even the archdeacons had parishes, and theirs were often among the biggest and busiest, albeit with the help of one or more curates. Advantages of this system are that an officer keeps closely in touch with the realities of parish life and also has the support a parish provides from any assistant clergy, churchwardens and PCC. Financially it means a lot to a diocese with few historical resources, not to have to raise money for salaries in addition to stipends. It also means that some small parishes are still able to have their own vicar living among them when otherwise a merger or even a close-down might have been the option.

In the last years of Bishop Blunt's episcopacy, some aspects of diocesan administration and overall strategy were falling down. The ideals and ideas were still there, but follow-through was patchy. There were many vacant parishes and some of the later appointments had been of not very active men. Archdeacon Ackerley's successor, the Ven. T.J. Williams, was himself of an age when many men retire, and the younger Archdeacon of Bradford, the Ven. Kenneth Kay, Vicar of Heaton, had suffered a severe illness from which he never fully recovered. Bishop Hardy supplied pastoral care, but his role was not an administrative one. Of the senior staff, only John Tiarks was forceful and effective, but his sphere of authority ran only to the cathedral and Bradford parish.

On June 9th 1955, Bishop Blunt was too ill to attend the diocesan conference, but his prepared address was read out by Archdeacon Kay and in it he gave warning of the need for a new appeal for money, linking it with the Evangelistic Committee's call to prayer and service. The money was to be for new church buildings, most obviously needed in Bradford and to a lesser extent in Keighley, where the new housing estates were growing. His successor is often, and rightly, credited with the provision of these much needed new churches, but it is also right to make it clear that this was exactly the work Bishop Blunt foresaw as the immediate need, and had he been younger and stronger, this is the programme on which he would have embarked.

On the 18th of June, the bishop went to Bentham School for their Confirmation Service and preached a typically fine sermon. His son David remembers him coming home, seeing the car coming up the drive and through the archway of Horton Hall, his father looking perfectly all right, but having to be helped out by the chauffeur because his legs wouldn't obey him. As he entered the house, he had a severe stroke and his family very soon realised that his working days were over, and his retirement was announced to take effect from October of that year. If he had retired earlier, the memory of his episcopacy would not have been marred by the general run-down of the last few years. His son believed he could not face the prospect of retirement and nothing to do, for although the outer man was old and ill, his inner self still blazed with zeal and eagerness for his Master's service.

When Alfred Blunt came to Bradford, it was generally expected that in due course he would be moved to higher office. Some have suggested that Worcester, which he refused, might have proved a better 'jumping off' point, but nothing about Bradford has held back some of its subsequent bishops. Certainly his bouts of ill-health may have influenced the issue, as may his politics, given the changes of Prime Minister during his career. The Abdication events too may have played their part - the 'Establishment' is not kind to those who rock the boat, no matter how urgently it needed rocking.

Bishop Blunt died on the 2nd of June 1957, Margaret in 1962. They are buried in Calverley churchyard beside their son Geoffrey. At the dedication of a memorial in Bradford Cathedral (the two archdeacons' chairs in the chancel), the preacher was Canon Hugh Hunter, who had served the whole of his ministry in the diocese. He said, "In his early years at Bradford he had hopes of high preferment. It is most probable that if his health and strength had been maintained, this would have come his way. But it was not to be. What he had to give was given here, and from here. And only God knows how much he gave."

CHAPTER 12

THIS IS THE DAY

Less than two weeks before Bishop Blunt's episcopate officially ended, the Principal of the London College of Divinity received a letter from Prime Minister Anthony Eden, asking him to allow his name to be put forward for the Bishopric of Bradford.

Frederick Donald Coggan had an impressive scholastic record, with a First Class Cambridge degree and a whole string of prizes and scholarships to his credit. He had lectured in Hebrew at Manchester University before ordination, served a curacy in Islington, then in 1937 went to Canada as Professor of New Testament at Wycliffe College, Toronto, and while there received his Bachelor of Divinity degree, First Class. In 1944 he returned to England and a desperately run-down London College of Divinity. His call to Toronto had been as part of the Wycliffe Principal's plan to build up the standing and academic standard of that college, and in London he carried much more responsibility for an even more formidable task, and one he was rather loath to leave just as the worst of the struggles seemed to be over. Margaret Pawley's official biography of Donald Coggan graphically describes the L.C.D. years and the stresses imposed on the Coggan family.

Before accepting Bradford, Dr. Coggan consulted with Archbishop Fisher, whom he remembers giving him undivided attention and carefully considered advice, even though the arrival of H.M. the Queen was so imminent that he was asked to walk up the edge of the stairs as the red carpet had been prepared. The Archbishops of Canterbury and York were both keen for him to accept. A man was needed who could relate to Bradford business-men, who would attract a high standard of ordinand to the diocese, and who above all could release the Church in that part of the North from the stagnation of the last few years. Donald Coggan's evangelical churchmanship accorded well with most of Bradford's clergy and he also had a reputation for working well with people of different views. Although his experience of parish ministry had been so very limited, his capabilities as a teacher, administrator, organiser, and above all a builder-up of institutions which had fallen sadly below their full potential, were well known in Anglican circles.

Donald Coggan had preached a couple of times in Bradford, but knew nothing of the area outside the city centre. Jean Coggan could only think of an educational card game she played as a child, in which the Bradford card depicted wool and smoky buildings, but when they arrived for a proper look, like the two previous episcopal families, they found the reality a pleasant surprise. In one of his books, "Convictions", Dr. Coggan wrote, "What better diocese could a new bishop go to than Bradford? It was - and is - unbelievably beautiful (most of it!)......The response and the warm-heartedness of the people would have heartened any man, and there was much to encourage."

By coincidence, Bradford and Worcester were again vacant at the same time, but this time it was the Bradford see house that almost proved a stumbling block. On visiting Horton Hall, the bishop-elect announced that either a new house or a new bishop would have to be found. As far back as 1943 Bishop Blunt had said Horton Hall was too big, too costly and altogether too grandiose for his requirements. Had it not been for the war, he would have moved, and he forecast that after the war clergy would be expected to live a simpler life. By the time house-hunting was again feasible, the Blunts, Mrs. Blunt in particular, could not face the upheaval.

Jean Coggan was shown round by Gwyneth Tiarks, and was getting more and more despondent at the stone corridors and blackleaded grates, when they reached the top floor where the ordinands had slept the night before ordination. "If I had been one," said the provost's wife in a loud whisper, "I would have recanted on that last night." Jean's mounting feeling of sickness was dispelled in laughter and the two ladies, who eventually were near neighbours, became firm friends. Meanwhile, Donald had met Bishop Blunt, expecting to be given some guidance on the task ahead, perhaps along the lines of the book of "Notes for my successor" Bishop Perowne had sent to Bishop Blunt, but all he got was, "It's very easy to run, very easy to run", and a few dusty envelopes that were the filing system. Had the meeting taken place even twelve months earlier, there would doubtless have been a very useful exchange, but as it was, following Bishop Blunt's severe stroke, it was 'in at the deep end' for the newcomer.

Donald Coggan's Consecration in York Minster on 25 January 1956, was attended by 2,000 people from Bradford Diocese, and another large congregation filled Bradford Cathedral for his Enthronement on the Feast of St. Blaise, patron saint of woolcombers, 3 February 1956. The Yorkshire Post and Leeds Mercury described the arrival of the third Bishop of Bradford: "Present to greet him at the West Door were Provost Tiarks, the Chancellor Mr. Raymond Hinchcliffe Q.C., Assistant Bishop Hardy, Diocesan Registrar Mr. Mossman, members of the Cathedral Chapter, Mr. J. Foster Beaver (Chairman of the Diocesan Board of Finance), Mr. J.H. Shaw (Chairman of the Cathedral Appeal Committee), the Cathedral Wardens Mr. J.J. Cullingworth and Mr. A.E. Simpson, and the Vergers. Bareheaded and dressed in his Convocation robes - white rochet and scarlet chimere - the Bishop walked towards the Sanctuary with its High Altar, his step measured, his youthful face serene."

Words from his sermon set the tone for his whole ministry, in Bradford and later on a wider stage: "I cannot align myself with those who, wistfully looking back to the Victorian era or some other by-gone age, dismally hanker for the good old days. **This** is the day which the Lord hath made; we will rejoice and be glad in it. Behold now is the accepted time; behold now is the day of salvation."

Enthronement of Dr. Donald Coggan by Provost John Tiarks

Like the Perownes, the Coggans were in need of a temporary home. They were not prepared to move into Horton Hall and the Church Commissioners' architect agreed that it could not be altered to form a suitable permanent see house. Mr. Mossman took the opportunity of reminding the Commissioners that when money had been subscribed to endow the bishopric 35 years ago, that portion of it designated for the see house had not been spent and the Commissioners, therefore, should have the means to buy a house now.

Dr. Coggan looked at the geography of the diocese and was determined that it should not be treated as "Bradford with bits added on." He seriously thought of living at Skipton, and a house at Burley-in-Wharfedale was nearly bought (but was instead taken over as an Old People's Home). For five and a half months the Coggans lived in an hotel in Ilkley and the diocese was run partly from there and partly from an office the provost made available in the cathedral. The Coggans' two daughters loved spending their school holidays in the hotel and choosing meals from the menu, but it was a great joy for the whole family when a house was eventually bought. They had not had a satisfactory home together since Donald left Canada in 1944. Jean and the girls were unable to get a passage until after the war, and housing for the Principal of L.C.D. had been far from suitable for family life.

The house chosen was 'Fieldhead' in Heaton, renamed 'Bishopscroft'. The bishop promised he would not forget the dales as he moved closer to Bradford and immediately re-instated Skipton as the venue for June diocesan conferences and for alternate meetings of the Dilapidations Board. As an encouragement, bus and train times were printed on the conference agenda papers.

Bishopscroft is conveniently situated north west of Bradford, and more than one occupant has commented on the symbolism of its windows, some of which look on to the chimneys of the city and some out to the moors. The house needed only slight modification, although it has been altered more radically since in order to separate the official and family areas. It has six bedrooms, three bathrooms and a further two lavatories with wash basins, sitting room, dining room, family room, kitchen and pantries, chapel, study, office and chaplain's office. It is interesting to compare it with the specifications in chapter two, as set out by the Bishopric Committee, and also to note how close it is to the area in which they first concentrated their search. The girls were allowed a free choice of decoration for their bedrooms, and Mrs. (later Lady) Coggan recalled that one of her daughters chose a very worldly looking wallpaper with bottles all over it. The son of a later bishop decorated one of the bathrooms with explicit murals of bathers, which proved quite a talking point for guests, but was not the bathroom allocated to Princess Anne when she stayed there.

Rumours that one third of the livings in the diocese were vacant were an exaggeration, but the situation was quite bad enough, with nineteen actual vacancies and a further five on the point of occurring. The new bishop lost no time in filling as many as possible, some with his former students. One of these was R.W. Neil, appointed to Cowling after an eleven month interregnum.

The mill villages of the West Riding presented their own problems and Cowling is in some ways typical. The parish was carved out of the huge, ancient parish of Kildwick in 1844 and its church was one of the second wave of 'Waterloo' churches, built when more money unexpectedly became available. Unfortunately, one of the conditions laid down by the Church Building Society was that the new churches should be of a size to accommodate a quarter of the population, irrespective of how many other denominations were active in the parish. Cowling was a Nonconformist stronghold and the Anglican church seldom had a congregation of more than a tenth of the 533 it could seat. Under Mr. Neil the church prospered sufficiently to put in new choir stalls made by the celebrated Thompson of Kilburn, whose trademark is a little carved mouse, and these were duly dedicated by Bishop Coggan.

A more controversial appointment was of the Revd. Patrick Ashe to Otley, where he certainly enlivened the church scene. His insistence that the parish gave away as much money as they spent on their own church needs was sometimes carried to impractical lengths when repairs were left undone until twice the cost could be raised, but Otley did gain a reputation it has kept, for its high level of giving to mission and charitable work. He also caused something of a stir by putting up a large notice bearing the accurate, but not wholly popular announcement: "This Church is for Sinners Only."

By December of his first year, Donald Coggan had instituted or licensed twenty six incumbents. The number of vacancies, coupled with a shortage of curates, had placed a heavy burden on those who were in post, and Dr. Coggan appreciated that many parish clergy had to settle for holding the status quo, even if they were aware of areas where advances should be made. To relieve the situation, he quickly brought in two Church Army captains and declared his intention of appointing more captains, Church Army sisters and lady workers.

He also arranged a residential conference at St. John's College, Durham, for the spiritual and intellectual refreshment of his clergy, to be a coming together for prayer, study and conference, in that order. He urged parishes to consider making a goodwill gift to their clergy, to help with the cost, and many were happy to do so. Reporting on the success of the event, the bishop said that during their days together, they had come to realise that they were not isolated individuals, each with the most difficult parish in England, but members of a great diocesan family, itself part of the infinitely greater Anglican Communion, which was in turn only a part of the ecumenical Church of God.

1956 saw the sudden death of Archdeacon Williams and the following year Archdeacon Kay resigned, although he remained as Vicar of Heaton until his death in 1958. As a Naval Chaplain and as Vicar of Queensbury and then St. Barnabas, Heaton, Kenneth Kay had been a fine preacher and a loved and respected priest, and had, up to his illness, been an effective archdeacon. He was by nature a quiet man , in marked contrast to the genial and voluble 'Taffy' Williams. Bishop Blunt used to comment that he had two archdeacons, one who never said a word and one who never stopped talking. Although Canon

Kay remained Vicar of Heaton, the diocese gave him sick leave for the last twelve months and brought in a retired priest, the Revd. Neville Pedley, to run the parish.

Bishop Coggan appointed the Rector of Skipton, Arthur Sephton, as Archdeacon of Craven, much to the benefit of that archdeaconry, for which he worked tirelessly, gaining a reputation for knowing everyone and everything in Craven. For Bradford, the bishop sent for Hubert Higgs, who had been Publications Manager for the Church Missionary Society when Donald Coggan wrote "The Glory of God" under C.M.S. auspices in 1950.

Archdeacon Arthur Sephton

The bishop was concerned to ensure a succession of high calibre ordinands and, in addition to the normal range of archdeaconly duties, Archdeacon Higgs was to be responsible for the care of those preparing for ordination or exploring the possibility. He was to formulate an educational policy for clergy and lay people and be responsible for the post-ordination training of young clergy. He was also to be chairman of the Diocesan Missionary Council. Small wonder then that Hubert Higgs became the first archdeacon in the diocese not to occupy a parish. Instead, to give him the equivalent of a parish base and a worshipping community to

Left to right: Mr. A.E. Simpson, Bishop Coggan, Archdeacon Higgs, Canon Guy Waddington and Provost Tiarks

which the family could belong, he became the first Residentiary Canon of Bradford Cathedral, and took some services there, which was a help to Provost Tiarks.

Archdeacon Higgs admitted that he was not particularly good at some of the more prosaic aspects of his office - diocesan politics, financial affairs and the ubiquitous drains and church roofs - but he was acknowledged to be quite charming even when his handling of parish problems was causing some frustration. He was at his best in the pastoral and educational work for which he was primarily appointed. There was no Cathedral Close at this time and Archdeacon and Mrs. Higgs lived in Shipley in Rowan House, unofficially and affectionately known as "The Higgery". Here, every month, junior clergy would come to spend a whole day in discussion and Bible study. Elizabeth Higgs (Betty) was a great help, although she had come reluctantly to Bradford, simply because she was so happy being a vicar's wife that she didn't in the least want to become "Mrs. Archdeacon". However, she soon made this into an equally fulfilling role and joined Mrs. Coggan in work with clergy wives. She said she hoped they felt she was a friend who had two ears and no mouth!

Jean Coggan resolved to take her time settling into the role of bishop's wife and certainly not to become automatic president of anything. Just one organisation defeated her. Although Mrs. Coggan told Miss Walker, who had run the Girls' Friendly Society for many years, that she was not going to be president of anything for the first year, but take her time to discover what God wanted her to do, the reply was, "I'm afraid you have to be our president. It's in the constitution."

Other than that, Jean drew on her training as a social worker in becoming involved with voluntary mental health work and work with handicapped children; but above all she felt her calling was to help and support wives of the clergy. She believed that lack of parish experience beyond that first curacy was not a drawback, but even an advantage in that she had no stereotype role to colour her approach.

As for her husband, he was not a man to acknowledge drawbacks, but in any case felt so called to the Bradford task that he was willing to trust that they would both be led along, step by step. Both the Coggans drove and did not make use of a chauffeur, but went together into the parishes whenever possible. At Confirmations and other parish events, Jean made a point of chatting with the clergy wives and eventually set up an organisation whereby they met in different vicarages, sometimes just for a social get together, but often to talk through issues that really mattered to them.

Their greatest problem was a combination of loneliness and being taken for granted. Jean told them that they had a very special gift to give, but also that the traditional role of vicar's wife was not one everyone had to accept. She reassured them that if they had been trained for some other job, this too could be what God wanted of them. She particularly praised those unsung women who fostered needy or 'problem' children. The 1950s were early days for married women to have jobs of their own and for clergy wives this was rather frowned on by some diocesan bishops. Bishop Coggan did not share this view and never expected Jean to become an example of a model clergy wife. In fact by working along slightly different lines, they found they enriched each others' lives.

The Church, which works so hard to care for others, has been slow at times to realise the needs of the carers, and although Bradford has a better record than some, arrangements for bereaved clergy families were not always good and help was not well organised. One of the achievements of the Clergy Wives' Fellowship, under Mrs. Higgs and with Mrs. Coggan's help, was to set up a little fund, raised by selling nearly-new clothes, out of which a clergy widow could immediately receive a small sum as of right, to tide her over. This was started in response to an actual case, where the couple had been missionaries with no savings, and the wife was suddenly left literally penniless.

Jean found that some of the least happy times of her own life, the separation of the war years, the difficulties of domestic life at L.C.D., had provided her with experiences she could helpfully share with the other wives. She found too that Bradford was a wonderful preparation for life at York and Canterbury in later years.

CHAPTER 13

A TIME TO BUILD

With an office in the cathedral, Dr. Coggan naturally saw more of the provost than he would otherwise have done and the two men found they had much in common. Both were hard and efficient workers, whose practicality and drive impressed the local business community.

The cathedral was positively humming with life. If there was a fault, it was, perhaps, a lack of emphasis on its role as Mother Church of the diocese, but as a church with something to say to the city of Bradford, it was extremely active, offering comfort, instruction and opportunities for worship to those who lived within its parish and also to the civic and business communities.

Inevitably, given its cathedral status and the charisma of its vicar, the main Sunday services drew a large eclectic congregation and anyone not there half an hour before Evensong was unlikely to find a seat, but the cathedral's outreach day by day was among its own parishioners. It functioned as a caring parish church, particularly to those in the humble streets that then clustered around Church Bank, including the one known as Hand-in-Pocket Street because if you didn't keep your hand on your money, it vanished! The provost was assisted by curates and parish workers of various kinds - Church Army sisters, deaconesses, lady workers - giving rise to some confusion among those visited, and a reported puzzled comment when Miss Beatrice Kennedy began her ministrations: "We don't understand. Deaconess A. came round in a navy blue uniform, Sister B. in a grey one, but Miss Kennedy comes round in nowt!"

A whole host of organisations thrived, including Mothers' Union, Sewing Circles, a Housewives' Group for women not eligible for membership of the M.U., and many uniformed youth groups. Many such have flourished at various times, not only at the cathedral, but in parishes the length and breadth of the diocese, designed to meet the needs of different groups in congregation or community, men women and children. Of them all, the best known, most enduring and most widespread at every level - parish, deanery and diocese - must surely be the Mothers' Union. A summary of key dates in the M.U.'s story forms Appendix II.

There were Bible classes and very thorough Confirmation classes. Clinical Theology seminars were run by Dr. Frank Lake, first in a bedroom of the Clergy House, where the curates lived, and later at St. Clement's in Barkerend Road. Dr. Lake was a lay reader at Ben Rhydding whilst undertaking psychiatric training at Scalebor Park Hospital. The Bradford branch of the Samaritans also started in the Clergy House, organised by Miss Kennedy, who stayed with the Revd. and Mrs. Chad Varah and their social worker to learn about the organisation. Chad Varah insisted that it should be actually led by a clergyman, and the Revd. Malcolm France, Vicar of Esholt, was chosen. Later this organisation became independent of the Church although many church people continue to be involved.

There were Lent breakfasts – Wednesday morning services followed by breakfast in the Cathedral Hall, and the first Sunday in the month was a Youth breakfast. Once a year there was a very popular Family Pew Service, for which parishioners were encouraged to reserve a pew for their whole family. During this service the Girls' Bible Class presented religious tableaux on the chancel steps in front of the blue curtain that screened the Sanctuary when the rebuilding of the east end began.

John Tiarks, with only the help of his part-time secretary Mrs. Kitty Hartley, raised a huge sum of money for the cathedral appeal, much of it from Bradford firms who responded to his personality and style, and subscribed generously. Cathedral Warden John Cullingworth launched the fund with a gift of £10,000 from his company and others soon followed. Fortunately money came in quickly as well as generously, and the provost was in a position to halt his appeal and support his new bishop in setting up a campaign to bring in money for building new churches. Furthermore, he lent Dr. Coggan the invaluable Mrs. Hartley, who eventually became full time secretary to this bishop and the next two.

Explaining his plans to diocesan conference, Dr. Coggan reminded them that as far back as 1902 a report had said that a mission church was needed for Horton Bank Top and Clayton Heights, Bradford, with a view to forming a new parish. A tiny church, St. Thomas of Canterbury, had been made out of two derelict cottages in Beacon Road, but had proved to be in the wrong place and was now redundant, meanwhile buildings were rising like mushrooms, full of young families all neglected by the Church of England.

One serious problem was that Bradford, unlike most other Corporations, refused to sell land for church building – some Local Authorities even made sites available free of charge. Other urgent needs were at Wrose and Woodhall, Pudsey, where congregations met in small halls. The site for St. James' Woodhall was already owned by the church and the bishop expressed the hope that England's former cricket captain, Sir Len Hutton, would very soon have something more entertaining to look at than a cabbage patch.

To examine the whole situation, Dr. Coggan set up two committees. The Survey Committee was not only to survey new areas of need, but also to report on the difficult matter of redundant churches. The bishop said he was well aware that this could be a painful duty. When a person had worshipped in a place for fifty years, been baptised, confirmed and married there and struggled to keep it going, it was hard to look dispassionately at the prospect of closing it down. Manningham was one example that had changed almost beyond recognition and it was wrong to try to maintain all the churches in that area.

The second committee, Ways and Means, was to determine the best way of raising the money. "In asking for money," the bishop said, "we have nothing to apologise about. This is the work of God. Money is a sacred thing, a trust from Him to us. 'The silver is Mine and the gold is Mine, saith the Lord of Hosts.' So said the prophet Haggai, who, had he been prophesying in Bradford rather than Jerusalem, would no doubt have added 'and the brass'. Yes, there must be an appeal and we will face it joyfully. But not unthinkingly."

One of Dr. Coggan's early ideas could have made a general appeal hardly necessary. He suggested that every Christian on an electoral role should give one day's pay. A number of keen and devoted people did so, but there was no great general enthusiasm for the scheme. Many, no doubt, felt they were already giving, Sunday by Sunday and in other ways. So the appeal was officially launched in June 1957, calling for a quarter of a million pounds. Dr. Coggan sent out 25,000 personal letters to individuals and industrial concerns and gave lunches for leaders of the communities and representatives of industry in Bradford, Yeadon, Keighley, Skipton and Settle. He pledged to conference that money would not be found by increasing the quota, and paid tribute to John Tiarks: "Behind it all has been the provost, thinking, prodding, chivvying, inspiring – no word that I can speak can express the debt that this operation owes to him."

In the first six months, £100,000 came in and work was able to start on some of the more urgent needs. Bradford Corporation had a change of heart and the diocese was able to buy land on new housing estates. During this episcopate, five new churches were completed : St. Aidan's Buttershaw, more appropriate to the new areas of population than earlier ideas about Horton Bank Top and Clayton Heights; St. James the Great, Woodhall; St. Cuthbert's, Wrose; St. Martin's, in Haworth Road, Heaton; and Holy Trinity, the long awaited

St. Aidan's, Buttershaw

new church for Barnoldswick. In addition, St. John's, Great Horton, was rebuilt after a serious fire in 1955 had closed it, and work was started on others. A programme to replace run-down and over-large vicarages began with those at Thornbury, Ingleton and Gargrave.

The bishop's concern to get a visible church presence into the new housing areas was given a sudden impetus when in 1958 an exciting opportunity presented within the parish of Tong with Tong Street. Bradford Corporation offered for sale a site on the new Holme Wood estate which would enable the Church to get in on the 'ground floor' of a housing development which was planned to be completed by 1961, with a population of about 10,000. Dr. Coggan moved the Youth Chaplain, Charles Goodchild, to Tong, and entrusted him with building up a congregation on the new estate and building a church.

To provide a visible presence as early as possible, a builders' mess hut was obtained. The Medical Officer of Health promptly asked the vicar if the building could also be used as a child welfare and ante-natal clinic, so the first building was, to quote a tenth anniversary booklet, "to provide succour for both the soul and the body." The first Eucharist was celebrated in the wooden hut on 21 December 1958. Plans to build a permanent church began almost at once but ran into all sorts of delays. At last it was possible to lay the foundation stone in February 1961, the last such ceremony performed by Dr. Coggan as Bishop of Bradford. The new building was a dual purpose hall used for worship until in 1968 St. Christopher's Church proper was consecrated.

More important than the physical building of the church was the building up of a congregation, and the level of pastoral achievement is a tribute to Mr. Goodchild, who still had the care of both the village church at Tong and St. John's Tong Street, which only closed in 1970 after housing clearances made it no longer viable. A curate was appointed in 1961. Before this there had been help from a Church Army captain, but the vicar wanted Eucharistic services whenever possible, with vestments, to bring colour into people's lives, and the cathedral staff enjoyed helping with these. Up to 1966, the vicarage was still on Tong Street and Mrs. Goodchild would go out on Sundays to open the church. If she saw the cathedral curate's motorbike, she would walk down the hill, but if it was the provost's car, like most people who had dealings with John Tiarks, she would run!

The bishop's concern for pastoral needs was not confined to the urban scene, but solutions were harder to find in the countryside. It was not a matter of wholesale movement of population, as with the new housing estates, nor a case of a dwindling population being served by four or five churches within a few minutes' walk of each other. The village churches, though some were barely viable, each served a distinctive community.

Various groupings were tried out, such as the plurality of Marton-in-Craven with Thornton-in-Craven, to which Broughton was later added. Barnoldswick and Bracewell became a united benefice, and the living of Wilsden was suspended and placed under the supervision of Harden, with a Church Army captain

Howgill Holy Trinity Church

appointed. It was at this time that the parishes in the Sedbergh area were re-grouped to give one plurality of Sedbergh, Cautley and Garsdale and another of Killington, Howgill and Firbank. Dr. Coggan was a practical bishop, who would see that such necessary steps were taken, but never at the expense of the main thrust of the Church's mission. He set up and provided lectures for a series of monthly schools of evangelism and 1957 saw three major evangelistic efforts in the diocese. In the Keighley Campaign in March, seventy Church Army evangelists worked with the local churches. Early May brought the Bradford Churches Campaign, with the young David Sheppard among the visiting missioners, and in late May the Village Evangelists organisation visited some of the villages north of Skipton.

In June, Dr. Coggan commented to conference on the outcome of these campaigns. They had been successful in bringing into the central life of the churches some of those who were favourably disposed to them, but had been content to support from the outside. In other words, some buttresses had been converted into pillars. They had not had much impact on those outside that second layer, and this he believed was a typical result of such campaigns. This reinforced his determination to get the Church into the places where people now were and to make sensitive but unsentimental decisions about those buildings that were no longer in the right place.

It also gave strength to his concern for more lay involvement in church services, for meaningful responses and for understanding. He called for revision of the Psalter and was in fact appointed chairman of the Commission to undertake this. He urged that the new translation of the Bible should be used when it became available, strongly believing that worshippers should understand the words they said or sang, and in the case of hymns, those which were intended to be joyful should sound so! He was known to have stopped a congregation in mid-song and called for it to be started again with appropriate speed and vigour.

In 1957, illness forced Bishop Hardy to retire. He was advised to live somewhere less hilly than the Yorkshire Dales and chose Cambridge. Good wishes and gratitude went with him and Dr. Ruth, from many Yorkshire men and women, and particularly from the people of Gargrave. When the bishop died in 1970, his ashes were buried in Gargrave churchyard, marked by a simple cross, a copy of those in the graveyard of the Community of the Resurrection at Mirfield, made by his former PCC secretary, Derrick Watson.

Many dioceses acquire episcopal assistance when retired bishops come to live within their bounds. There are rumoured to be pleasant towns in the south where one is in danger of tripping over such retired prelates, but Bradford Diocese rarely seems to have attracted them. With his chosen archdeacons in office and himself young and full of energy, Donald Coggan saw no need to look for another assistant bishop. Diocesan conference met only twice a year and while the finance committee had its many subcommittees, there were fewer bodies requiring the bishop's direct participation than became the case under the later synodical system of church government.

All the same, Lord Coggan's own comment about there being less demand on diocesan bishops in those days, modestly omits the extra-diocesan engagements added to his work-load. In 1957 his duties as President of the United Bible Societies took him to Rio de Janeiro, Santiago, Valparaiso, Lima, Colombia, Panama, Jamaica and New York. 1958 brought a conference in Ghana and a visit to Nigeria.

Even with an increasing volume of high-level work on the national and international Church scene, Bishop Coggan kept his pastoral concern for the clergy and lay people of Bradford. He was approachable and sympathetic, only impatient with those who offered careless or sloppy service to the Lord. He had a great gift for remembering those he met, demonstrated when, many years after leaving the diocese, he returned as Archbishop of Canterbury to a school speech day, met the churchwardens of the parish, and remembered their names without any prompting from the vicar.

One project within Bradford Diocese, though not, as will be seen, precisely a diocesan project, became very dear to both Bishop and Mrs. Coggan. The

Scargill Community was an unexpected outcome of the Village Evangelists' Campaign in 1957. Scargill, between Conistone and Kettlewell in Wharfedale, is sometimes referred to as "in the diocese but not of it", or "not quite like Parcevall". (Parcevall Hall, the diocesan retreat house, of which more later).

So what is Scargill, and how does it fit into the diocesan story? In the post-World War II years, a number of religious communities have come into being, differing in detail from each other, and considerably from traditional monastic orders. One such is the Lee Abbey Community in Devon, begun in 1946, a large part of whose function is to provide a Christian holiday centre. A sense of need for something like it in the north of England was growing, and a number of people from the north, who had benefited from a stay at Lee Abbey, were praying about the provision of a similar establishment .

Among them was the Revd. Bernard Jacob, who had stepped in at the last minute to lead the Village Evangelists' team when, by a strange combination of circumstances, the original leader was taken ill and a different mission that Mr. Jacob was to have led, was cancelled. During the mission, he stayed with Mr. and Mrs. D.A.R. McCauley at Rylstone, and naturally talked to his hosts and other local people, wondering if perhaps this part of the country might be right for the project. One morning, Mr. McCauley opened his copy of The Times and saw advertised for sale a house and estate a few miles up Wharfedale. Set on the lower slopes of Great Whernside, the house took its name from a natural limestone scar above and behind, bounded on one side by a dry gully or ghyll.

Other supporters of the concept were sent for, to look at the property, particularly the Revd. Harold Frankham, Vicar of Middleton, and the Bishop of Bradford. The estate included not only the main house and four lodges, but also two farms, two cottages in Kettlewell, shooting rights on the moors and fishing rights on the river - far more than was needed or could be afforded - and yet the feeling grew that this was the right place.

Three local landowners were interested in the farms and shooting and fishing rights, but none of them wanted the house. They approached the bishop with the offer that they should combine to buy the estate and divide it, the Church to take the house, lodges, cottages and seventy acres of land. The little group of Christians decided to go ahead in faith, with Dr. Coggan as their spokesman and negotiator, though not in his capacity as Bishop of Bradford. Indeed, he assured Bradford Diocesan Conference in December 1957 that not one penny of the Church Building Appeal or diocesan funds would go to support the project. "Its work will be on a scale beyond the bounds of the diocese, but it is in our midst and calls for our prayer support and general sympathy."

The purchase was financed by gifts and loans, which came pouring in from the little group who had been praying for such a house, and from members of the Lee Abbey Friends Association. Once its programme began, the house was self-supporting. It is managed by a council and run by a warden and resident Christian community. Bishop Coggan was the first chairman of Scargill Council. Bishop Geoffrey Paul, who had been Warden of Lee Abbey, was a later chairman, while

Scargill in the snow

Bishop of Hull, and Bishop David Evans, a later Assistant Bishop of Bradford, was a council member. Bradford's other bishops have taken a friendly interest but been less directly involved. The purpose in setting it up was to bring renewal to the Church in the north of England and although it is used by parishes, groups and individuals from Bradford Diocese, its guests also come from much further afield. In the Yorkshire Dales, the holiday season is short and Scargill has developed a role as a conference centre for business and industry, and has hosted many diverse groups. Up to ninety guests can be accommodated in pleasant and comfortable surroundings.

The most striking architectural feature of Scargill is the chapel, with its steeply pitched, soaring roof and limestone walls, joined on to the house as a sign that worship, work and living together are all part of the whole. Its light and spacious interior forms a setting in which patterns of worship can be explored with a greater freedom than in most parish churches.

The first warden was the Revd. Arthur Barker, who moved in with his wife and children. He stayed until ill-health made retirement inescapable in 1961 and is fondly remembered as the father of the community. He was succeeded by his assistant, a former Bradford Cathedral curate, the Revd. Dick Marsh. In 1964 he and his partner, Leslie Ashburn, went to the Lake District to select a camp site and suitable rock-climb for a group on a 'Fathers and Sons' course. Dick had climbed in the Himalayas and been chief climbing instructor at an Outward Bound School. The community, and above all Dick's wife Shirley, were stunned by the news that the two men had fallen to their deaths on Dow Cragg. Dr.Coggan, by this time Archbishop of York, gave the address at Dick's funeral, and the conference lounge added to Scargill the following year was dedicated to his memory.

That then is Scargill, a community outside diocesan structures and yet located within its bounds, available to anyone who wishes to take advantage of the blessings it has to offer.

(The early story of Scargill in much greater detail can be found in a book produced for its tenth anniversary, "My Name Shall Be There - the Story of Scargill" by Miss Margaret Leach, to whom, with Miss Irene Price, I am indebted for the information I have used.)

CHAPTER 14

A SPLASH OF COLD WATER

The Second World War had brought about even more social upheaval than the First, and by the mid fifties it was clear that all that had been tossed into the air was not going to fall back into the same old pattern, so that even the most progressive of pre-war thinkers had been overtaken by events. Dr. Coggan's episcopate can be seen in retrospect as a watershed in the history of Bradford Diocese. There were still links with old days and old ways. Mr. Mossman and Mr. Foster Beaver, those two giant personalities from the very foundation of the diocese, still held office.

The registrar in particular had taken upon himself, for the best of motives, much of the administration of the diocese, requiring Bishop Blunt's signature to documents as little more than a formality. The first time he asked Dr. Coggan to sign a paper, he was much put out when the bishop insisted on first reading it through carefully. A later registrar has recounted the story of the short, sharp crossing of swords that ensued, to establish who was the actual, as opposed to titular, captain of the ship.

In 1960 Mr. Mossman retired, but not without one final victory. His son George had a best friend, a fellow solicitor, and after George's death, Mr. Mossman was known to hope this man would be his successor. When Dr. Coggan asked for a short list of possible names, he applied a little elementary psychology and put Henry Firth at the bottom of his list. The ploy was successful, but there was no loser in this little game. Mr. Mossman got his way, and Dr. Coggan, who thought he had made an independent choice, got a first-rate registrar, although they were not, in the event, to work together for long.

Henry Firth was a short, plump, jolly man. devoted to his family, his home and garden. At work he was a perfectionist and grudged no amount of time to make sure everything was just right. Later he dealt meticulously with all the changes the introduction of Synodical Government meant. He was always slightly surprised to have been chosen, but thoroughly enjoyed the committee aspects of the work and dealing with senior staff. Ceremonial held less appeal. He felt everyone but him knew what they were doing and only found out later that there were rehearsals, to which he was not invited because they assumed he was too busy. He also suspected he looked silly in his wig. "Well he did," conceded his clerk, affectionately, "because he was small." In much of English ceremonial there is a very fine line between silly and dignified, and an imposing stature certainly helps to tip the balance.

In his continuing desire to take the Gospel message to the people, Dr. Coggan encouraged experiments with open-air services in the dales, and in Bradford an ecumenical group of clergy took the Good News into six of the city's parks on Whit Sunday afternoon. The bishop himself drew a crowd of two or three thousand in Lister Park. A similar exercise was carried out in 1992 in Peel Park, under the heading "God in the Park", organised by the North Bradford Council of Churches, with the Revd. Robin Gamble, Vicar of St. Augustine's, Otley Road, very much involved. This ran for six nights and attracted average attendances of 600.

The Church played a part in awakening Bradfordians to race relations issues when Bishop Trevor Huddleston of the Community of the Resurrection, then Bishop of Masai, spoke to two thousand people in a packed St. George's Hall, but in the late fifties, the Church of England as a whole was barely starting to address questions of race relations in England. This was of particular significance in Bradford, where large numbers of Asians, mainly from Pakistan, were arriving, attracted by opportunities to work in the textile industry, and Bishop Coggan was one of the early speakers on this theme in the House of Bishops at York Convocation in January 1959. He referred to this speech in his address to diocesan conference in June, pointing out the need to extend the hand of friendship at neighbourhood level to those of different cultures and colours of skin who were beginning to appear among us.

Some of his suggestions - serious study of the problems, a ministry of reconciliation, employment of former missionaries as interpreters - were made much of by the media, but were ahead of general public opinion of the time. Gradually, as will be seen, the Church in Bradford Diocese built well on the foundations he laid. However, the main thrust of his message concerned the work of the Church overseas, where he saw the Church, not in an isolated preaching role, but bound up with the concept of social justice. Recognising the seeds of the 'greedy society' of the western world, he urged on Christians the need to support improvements in living standards for other countries before talking about doubling our own. He took up this theme again when Christian Stewardship, the last major innovation of his Bradford episcopate, got under way.

"The Christian Stewardship of Money" was published as an initiative of the Church of England's Central Board of Finance. Bishop Coggan drew the attention of conference to this with the words, "I think a new era is beginning to dawn in the Church of England in regard to the churchman's attitude to his money, or, rather, to the money which has been entrusted to him by God." Typically, he set up a small committee to advise on the application of the proposals in the diocese.

The keynote of their report was the need to establish the principle that Christian stewardship is an acknowledgement that all things come from God and that this principle involves the financing of the Church by direct giving, without the seeking of material benefits in return - a concept which Bradford's first and second bishops would have had no difficulty in recognising and which both had commended to their flocks, although without the high profile of the ensuing campaigns.

Although Dr. Coggan's committee realised that careful teaching and preparation would be needed, if parishes were to embark on stewardship campaigns, the actual scheme used was based on campaigns mounted by the American-based Wells Organisation, whose thrust was wholly financial. Of the dozen or so larger Bradford parishes to take it up, some grasped the underlying theology and experienced benefits in terms of their financial situation and also in general renewal of parish life. Others were so poorly prepared that a totally wrong emphasis was given, and the antagonism generated to the very idea of stewardship lasted for many years.

That some failures were coming to light was clear from Dr. Coggan's Presidential Address at the December 1960 conference. He warned that Christian stewardship was not mere fund-raising and the motives behind a campaign must be ruthlessly analysed - "Is it because we want a new boiler, or organ, or what-have-you, or because we want to tackle a fundamental privilege and duty?" He was, he said, not sure that anything like enough thought was given to the use of money brought in by the campaigns. At worst, it could lead to an internal parochial spending spree, ministering to selfishness and stultifying stewardship in years to come. The health of a parish was reflected in their decision about what percentage was to stay inside and what to go out. They must consider diocesan needs, since each parish was part of a family, but, said the bishop, "I think especially of the Church overseas. I would like every parish to plan that a worthy proportion goes overseas, and this is particularly urgent for those having campaigns."

The Revd. Raymond Smith, Vicar of Weston and Denton, was appointed as Diocesan Stewardship Adviser, and under his guidance, the concept of stewardship of not only money, but time and talents, was found more acceptable.

Later, in 1971, Mr. Peter Davies was appointed to be in charge of stewardship for the Dioceses of Bradford, Wakefield and Ripon. The difficulty of running programmes over such large areas became more and more apparent as the 1970s progressed, and in 1978, the Revd. Bernard Gribbin was asked to consider and advise on future policy for all three dioceses, and as a result, each decided to appoint its own adviser. Bernard Gribbin had had experience of what were now called stewardship missions in two parishes, as Vicar of Denholme and later of Bankfoot, Bradford, and he became full-time adviser for Bradford Diocese in 1979. He had a committee to support him, and for several years an assistant, Mr. Edward (Ted) Garnett, a lay member of General Synod. By the time Mr. Gribbin left in 1986, to become Precentor of Chester Cathedral (later a Canon of Chester), over half the parishes of the diocese had held a full stewardship mission.

At this stage, the Archdeacon of Craven was asked by the bishop to review the work of stewardship in the diocese, and the next Stewardship Adviser, the Revd.

Peter Burwell, had the benefit of this report when formulating his own policy. His was a much less structured approach, helping parishes to decide their own programme, often suggesting a Parish Audit as a first step. Perhaps this has been a useful approach for those who have not felt that a full-scale programme was right for them, but sometimes the presence of external advisers can be a help, and a formal framework, sensitively handled, can enable a parish to get to grips with uncomfortable realisations. In 1992, under new diocesan structures, stewardship became part of the brief of the Bishop's Officer for Parish Mission and Development, the Revd. Ron Jackson.

In spite of early mistakes and patchy response, the concept of Christian Stewardship has played an important part in teaching something of obligations and duties, and, above all, a right attitude in response to all the good gifts God gives to His people; in relatively affluent England, this must include material possessions.

The Church of England in Bradford Diocese has never had an insulating layer of historic resources and, as the proportion of diocesan budget provided by the Church Commissioners steadily diminishes, it becomes more than ever important for church people to realise that true commitment must include a realistic financial element. While there is never occasion for complacency, Bradford has been for many years in the top handful of English dioceses in terms of average giving per head. Bishop Donald Coggan's role in this was to give his people a good, hard, push in the right direction, or, as he described it," a splash of cold water on a sleepy man's face - a bit unpleasant to begin with, but utterly necessary and utterly refreshing."

Early in January 1961, the Bishop of Bradford was commanded by the Queen to preach at Sandringham. In the middle of the month, on the occasion of the Northern Convocation in York, the Coggans were staying at Bishopthorpe as guests of Archbishop and Mrs. Michael Ramsey, and it was there that the telephone call from Prime Minister Harold MacMillan was received. Geoffrey Fisher had announced his resignation as Archbishop of Canterbury, Archbishop Ramsey was to succeed him, and Donald Coggan, only five years a bishop, was to be Archbishop of York. Bradford received the news with a mixture of sadness at their loss, and enormous proprietorial pride. Fourteen years later, Archbishop Coggan was appointed to the senior position in the Anglican Communion and enthroned with great ceremony as the one hundred and first Archbishop of Canterbury.

Looking ahead to the elections to diocesan conference in 1961, Dr. Coggan had spoken of the importance of attracting younger men and women, and realistically accepted that few people with the qualities needed would be available during the working week. Therefore he had announced that, beginning in 1961, conference would meet on Saturdays for a three year trial period. Little did he expect that the first of these would also be his last, and on Saturday, 10th June, in Skipton, he would be giving his farewell Presidential Address.

He paid tribute to his wife, for the happy home background that had enabled him to put so much into his work, and to John Tiarks who had been both colleague and friend. (It was appropriate that almost his last engagement in Bradford as its bishop was at the laying of the cornerstone of the new east end of the cathedral by the former Archbishop of Canterbury, Geoffrey Fisher. This stone rests, symbolically, on two historic stones, one from Ripon Cathedral and one from York Minster.)

Giving a brief retrospective of his Bradford years, Dr. Coggan stressed that it was much more important to look forward than back. He envisaged and hoped for Bradford a deepening sense of the diocese as family, with strong parishes helping the weak, a cathedral growing in beauty and dignity as the mother church, and in every parish a strong worshipping community with the two foci of Word and Sacraments. "Happy the man, "he said, "who comes to this diocese, surely one of the fairest in this fair land, as its chief pastor."

Archbishops Michael Ramsey and Donald Coggan in York

CHAPTER 15

DECENTLY AND IN ORDER

It is hard to say whether the man who came to "this fair diocese" saw its geographical features as a particular source of happiness.

Clement George St. Michael Parker, who was enthroned in November 1961, had spent his entire ministry, from ordination as deacon in 1923, not only in the Diocese of Birmingham, but largely within the conurbation of that city, as curate, vicar, rural dean, Archdeacon of Aston and, from 1954 to 1961, as Suffragan Bishop of Aston.

In some of his writings and addresses he certainly paid tribute to the wonders of nature, but it was the orderliness of creation that he seized upon, speaking of the great pageant of the seasons and their application to spiritual life. Of flowers in church he wrote, "Use those in season. Artificial flowers are wholly unsuitable and should never be used." Again he stressed the theology underlying the direction, "Flowers are an expression of thanksgiving for our creation, preservation, redemption and sanctification."

Untamed uplands, broken only by a limestone wall straggling away out of sight to heaven-knows-where, farmsteads from which no neighbouring habitation could be seen, twilight and darkness in unlighted lanes - with such as these, Bishop Michael Parker was not at ease. Once, at the highest point of the old 'coal road' between Garsdale and Dentdale, the bishop got out of his car to survey the magnificent scenery stretching before him in the sunshine. He turned to the rural dean and said, "I think I'd better consecrate you bishop of these parts and leave them to you; I'll then concentrate on what I understand." One possible alternative for the see house, though less than twenty miles from Bradford, was turned down flat because there were no street lights outside the front gate.

Gardening was an acceptable point of contact with nature, but here too with an emphasis on bringing order. A story is told from his time as archdeacon, which also serves to demonstrate his kindness at a very personal level to young clergy under his care. An appointment had just been made to a run-down parish, with a Victorian vicarage almost submerged in undergrowth. The archdeacon decided to do an afternoon's work in the garden to make it look better before the new man moved in. Off he went, in proper archidiaconal garb, stripped off to shorts and casual shirt, and hung his trousers and clerical collar on a tree. Some hours later, the undergrowth had been cut down and consigned to a large bonfire, but alas, too close to the aforementioned tree, so that the conflagration engulfed the clothes. The archdeacon had no choice but to walk home in shorts and open necked shirt, which was considered a bit out of the ordinary in 1950s Birmingham.

Michael Parker's care for his clergy was demonstrated many times in Bradford. This would not seem remarkable in the 1980s and 90s, but at that time it was by no means automatic that a bishop would be so interested in the junior members of diocesan staff. He took great care over the placing of curates and working out suitable future moves for them, and would look in on the young clergy families to make sure they were settled into their homes, although as a bachelor he was not always sympathetic to some of the domestic requirements. One wife got short shrift when she asked if her husband could be given a parish where the vicarage was not at the top of a hill, now that there was a pram. The bishop was a shy man, not relaxed with the social side of diocesan occasions - confirmation and induction 'bun fights' and the like, and not at ease with women, although clergy families remember his fondness for their children, once past the baby stage. He peered into one pram and said, "Just like George Robey. All babies look like George Robey."

Very soon after Bishop Parker's arrival, the interesting possibility of yet another see house arose. The lovely, historic rectory at Guiseley was proving far too large for Canon Wrangham Hardy and his sister. The front portion of the house mostly dates from 1601, with walls of older houses still intact inside, and this was the portion the rector's household used. There were eleven unoccupied

Mr. John Foster Beaver and Bishop Parker at Airedale Show, Bingley, 1962

rooms in a Victorian wing added in the days of plentiful domestic staff, and the house had its own chapel. Representatives of the Church Commissioners, Bishop Parker, the Archdeacons of Bradford and Craven, Canon David Rogers and the chairman of the Diocesan Board of Finance visited Guiseley, and agreed that the house was distinctly possible as a bishop's residence, although less accessible from the north western part of the diocese. It was John Foster Beaver who delivered the final veto. The reorganisation of local authority boundaries and formation of large metropolitan districts was already in the air, and it was unthinkable, he declared, that the postal address of the Bishop of Bradford should be Leeds!

So the bishop remained at Bishopscroft, but the Coggans' cherished family home was used in a very different style by Bishop Parker. While he was appreciative of other people's comfortable homes and attractive possessions, he felt no need for such things himself and gave away almost everything that was given to him. The only room he carpeted was the chapel and, being a non-driver, he had his office transferred from the cathedral to the house. Other than that, the bishop virtually camped in a corner and commented to his secretary Mrs. Hartley that he could do with a bicycle to get around inside the house. Domestic arrangements were presided over by the formidable housekeeper, Lily, a large lady with a strong Irish accent and a fiercely protective attitude to her employer that visitors sometimes found disconcerting.

Although he lived frugally, the bishop was no recluse within his house and frequently invited clergy to join him for early morning Holy Communion and then have breakfast with him, and there would be a breakfast invitation to new incumbents and their wives on the mornings of their institutions. Ordination retreats were held at Bishopscroft, with trestle tables brought in for mealtimes, and if the house was full, a young ordinand could find he had been given the bishop's bed, while the bishop 'made do' in the study.

There was an occasion when the 'making do' was exposed to the gaze of any curious passer-by. Bishop Parker had been visiting the new church at Thwaites Brow, in which he took a keen interest. On one visit he enquired about a blue brick contraption in church and was told it was to be a pulpit/lectern. The vicar, the Revd. (now Prebendary) Robert Sharp, took him home and the following day received a telephone call from the bishop asking him to drive him to Thwaites Brow yet again. On arriving at Bishopscroft, he was told that the bishop had been unable to sleep on account of the blue brick contraption. He said, "It looks like a urinal wall and must be modified." Later he said that the church also needed a warm colour and when they got back to Bishopscroft he would take down his study curtains (which he proudly said he had bought from Donald Coggan), and Robert must drape them over the nearly completed altar for a week or two. "They are just the right colour for the hessian you are going to purchase." Robert was amused to note that the soon-to-be-ordained priests and deacons were in residence, with the usual arrangement about use of the bishop's bedroom. It never occurred to the bishop that without the study curtains he would be somewhat exposed.

It has been remarked that Bishop Parker was at heart a parish priest of the best and most conscientious kind, and that he saw the diocese very much as his bigger parish. He believed deeply in his pastoral ministry to his clergy, and as he became known, so he became much loved by many of them. Problems were quietly and efficiently handled without leaks or scandals, so that often only those immediately concerned knew just how much had been done.

Running in tandem with this quiet and very personal approach, and at first sight slightly at odds with it, was a whole series of directives, pronouncements at diocesan conference and publications, rather stern and dry in tone, not very quotable for newspapers looking for topical comments of general interest. At one conference, for example, he condemned a careless attitude to the upkeep of electoral rolls by many parishes and set out quite detailed suggestions for the proper running of an annual parochial church meeting.

The bishop had been badly injured in a motor accident while in Birmingham, and in consequence was plagued by much pain and spent time in hospital in Bradford and Birmingham. During one of these periods of enforced idleness he produced, in the form of a small booklet, "The Constitution and Regulations of the Diocese of Bradford." This gave an outline history of the diocese, lists of former bishops, provosts and archdeacons, the composition of the various boards and committees and a set of regulations covering aspects of parish life from 'Administration of Baptism', to 'Trees, removal of from vicarage gardens.' This was followed a few months later by another little book - "Let All Things Be Done DECENTLY AND IN ORDER." This covered every imaginable aspect of use, maintenance and procedure within the church building and was illustrated with photographs of good examples taken around the diocese. It is a detailed and factual manual, offered, as the introduction explains, "as an encouragement to make the best use of what we have inherited in both the setting and form of traditional Anglican worship." If there was any raising of hackles, or resentment at the implications, it can only have been a case of "if the cap fits...."

Bishop Parker was not opposed to experiments within church services, to bring fresh life and meaning into parish worship, so long as everything was done within the Church of England's legal framework. The new services leading up to the production in 1980 of the official Alternative Services Book were beginning to appear at this time, and Canon John Clayton, one of Bradford's representatives on the Church Assembly, asked to be allowed to try out one of the proposed new forms of Holy Communion. It was no good, he said, just voting in London for something they had never seen or tried out. The bishop replied that it was illegal and he forbade it. The canon persisted. A few days later there was a telephone call from the bishop: "All you Assembly people be at my house at 7.30 a.m.. My chapel is not a parish church and doesn't come under the same rules. We'll have it there."

One of Bishop Parker's early actions was to pick up the work Bishop Coggan had been unable to finish, concerning the changing pastoral needs of the urban part of the diocese. The commission he set up in January 1962 had as its terms of reference, "To consider the present position of the parishes in the Deaneries of Bradford, Bowling, Calverley and Horton in relation to the City Development Plan in respect of

1. Population,

2. Buildings – church, vicarage, hall, residence for assistant curate, and to make recommendations for the more efficient working of areas (including possible changes in parochial boundaries) in respect of pastoral, financial and material needs."

The commission included the City of Bradford's Chief Engineer Mr. S.G.Wardley, so accurate information regarding the City Plan was always to hand. Their report was published in 1963 and many, though not all, of their suggestions were acted upon.

Bishop Coggan is remembered by many for the upsurge in church building during his time, and Bishop Parker gained something of a reputation for closing and demolishing, but it was all part of the same movement and a study of the report shows how inevitable the closures were. The City Development Plan involved demolishing 11,500 dwellings in inner Bradford, affecting 30,000 persons. New homes in central Bradford were to be provided for 8,000, with an overspill of 22,000 into other parts of the city. The churches to go were those where the local population was declining rapidly and only industrial or commercial development was planned. Some, even at this stage were being kept up mainly by congregations made up of those who came from outside the parish boundaries.

Those with a high church tradition, St. John's Tong Street, Holy Trinity Leeds Road, St. Jude's Manningham, may have been hoping for a more sympathetic approach from a bishop of higher churchmanship than his predecessor. Some may even have been aware of his serious quarrel with Bishop Barnes concerning matters of churchmanship, when Michael Parker was a curate in Birmingham, so serious that, for his principles, he endured eleven years without any official appointment. But for these decisions, tradition was not among his criteria. For Bishop Parker, if a church was needed, it had to be of the best, and, whatever its style, all things done 'decently and in order'; but just as he had no personal attachment to possessions, so as Bradford's chief pastor, he had no attachment to buildings other than for their role in the spiritual life of the community. At the closing service at Holy Trinity he said, "The Church of God is neither a parish nor a building, nor indeed a single congregation, however united and expressive of Christian devotion it may be. Though your spiritual hearth is to exist no longer, your Church remains. Enter into the life of neighbouring congregations, thereby enriching them."

In keeping with these views, one of his chief dislikes in the hymn book was "We love the place, O God,". Canon Bruce Grainger was acting as bishop's chaplain at a Confirmation at which this had been chosen as the first hymn. "You'll have to change it," said the bishop, "I don't like it." The vicar protested

St. Saviour's, Fairweather Green

that the choir had practised it and they were going to sing it, to which the bishop replied, "Well I shall stay in the vestry till it is over." So bishop and chaplain stood in the vestry meditating until the hymn ended and they processed in. The musical tables were nearly turned on the bishop by the organist of another parish. In his opening address to diocesan conference, the new bishop had revealed that St. Paul had used for 'steward' a Greek word actually meaning 'oarsman', and had developed a long metaphor about being in the same boat, pulling our weight and rowing together in perfect rhythm. The organist terrified his vicar by threatening to play "Michael Row the Boat Ashore", when the bishop visited their church. Alas, decorum won the day.

Pastoral reorganisation was not all demolition, and church building continued around the edges of the city where populations were increasing. St. Christopher's Holme Wood was completed, St. John's Idle relocated to Thorpe Edge, St. Hugh's Baildon and St. Aidan's Crossflatts were established as daughter churches of St. John's Baildon and All Saints Bingley, respectively, Cottingley Church was resited to suit the growing village, and St. Saviour's Fairweather Green, whose first priest-in-charge was appointed in the first year of Bradford Diocese, finally got their church building. This is a striking design, in a decade not renowned for its secular architecture, by George Pace, who was also responsible for the chapel at Scargill. The architect planned everything in St. Saviour's, even down to the kneelers, and specified that nothing be changed during his lifetime!

Many of the findings of the Bishop's Commission on the Bradford Deaneries, and subsequent actions, had been almost self-evident. This was not the case for the Bishop's Commission set up in 1967 to examine the situation in Keighley. At this time, Keighley comprised a single united benefice embracing the parish church of St. Andrew's, All Saints' Highfield Lane, St. Mark's Uttley, St. Barnabas'

Thwaites Brow, Holy Trinity Lawkholme, St. Matthew's Braithwaite, St. Peter's Holycroft (whose church building had been closed some years previously) and St. John's Newsholme. There was one Parochial Church Council, and councils for individual churches to deal with local, day-to-day matters.

The basic problem was that of the country as a whole - decline in church-going, and population changes, exacerbated when different units did not always work in harmony, and curates did not stay long enough to make for any measure of continuity. Commission members found no easy answer and submitted a divided report, one group proposing more or less a continuance of the united benefice but with the creation of a team ministry staffed by a rector, two team vicars and a curate. The other group urged division into three separate parishes. Debate and discussion continued, sorely trying the patience of all concerned. An added factor was the similar decline in the Methodist Church, leading the minister of Temple Street Church to approach Canon E.C. Hamer at St. Andrew's in 1969 about the possibility of a sharing arrangement. Nothing immediately came of this and the whole Keighley situation dragged on, unresolved in Bishop Parker's time although he and the Diocesan Pastoral Committee put in a great deal of time and thought.

In his successor's episcopate, some changes were made. The least controversial was the transfer of the little church at Newsholme, which had been formed out of a room cut off from Church Farm, to the care of Oakworth Parish, on whose electoral roll most of its worshippers already appeared. The community at Thwaites Brow was smaller than the Church Commissioners generally thought acceptable for the creation of a new parish, but, given its geographical isolation from Keighley and the strong local feelings, it was agreed that it could be treated as a special case, and the parish came into being in 1974. The sharing arrangement between St. Andrew's and the Methodists also began in 1974 and later the Methodists built a hall in the churchyard and a grant from Bradford Diocese enabled the church to be re-ordered.

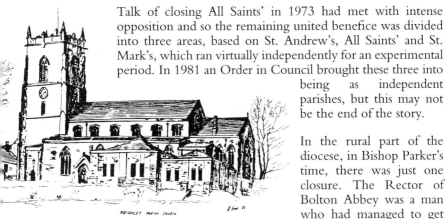

Talk of closing All Saints' in 1973 had met with intense opposition and so the remaining united benefice was divided into three areas, based on St. Andrew's, All Saints' and St. Mark's, which ran virtually independently for an experimental period. In 1981 an Order in Council brought these three into being as independent parishes, but this may not be the end of the story.

In the rural part of the diocese, in Bishop Parker's time, there was just one closure. The Rector of Bolton Abbey was a man who had managed to get very much at odds with the

St. Andrew's, Keighley with the Methodist Hall

trustees for the Devonshire estate, particularly over questions of maintenance, and he had also given up holding monthly services at the little chapel at Barden Tower, which was a part of his charge. This building, inside and out, was in a deplorable state, and while the Duke of Devonshire accepted responsibility for the fabric and had it repaired, the furnishings were not his concern. Getting no satisfaction from the incumbent, Bishop Parker set to and cleaned it out with his own hands before closing it down in 1968. Since there is no record of the building ever having been consecrated, there was no problem over its eventual change of use to a tea room.

And there was a rural opening! To celebrate his birthday in 1962, Bishop Parker invited representatives from every parish to come to see Parcevall Hall, near Appletreewick in the heart of Wharfedale. This lovely house, with its serene terraced gardens and pools and its view across the fells to Simon's Seat, was to become Bradford's Diocesan Retreat House.

When Sir William Milner bought the Parcevall estate in 1928, the house was a nearly derelict farmhouse in the traditional dales longhouse style. An architect by training, and a dedicated and knowledgeable gardener, Sir William restored and extended the house, planted trees and created gardens. In the 1950s he set up a charitable company to manage the estate, the directors being the Guardians of the Shrine at Walsingham. On his death in 1960, he left the whole estate, including the house and its antique furnishings, to Walsingham to use as they thought fit. Members of the Scargill Community were invited to look at the house with a view to running it, but being themselves so new, they did not feel it right to take on anything else. The Walsingham Trustees then most generously offered the house to the Diocese of Bradford, at literally a peppercorn rent, and with an undertaking that Walsingham would look after the gardens and help in other ways.

Archdeacon Sephton was particularly enthusiastic and much involved in the early days. He delighted in the house and would often visit to talk to the warden and staff. Bishop Parker's birthday party came just before the second anniversary of Independence Day in Nigeria. In preparation for their celebrations, Miss Pam Bradley, Principal of an Anglican teacher-training college, took some of her students into Ondo to buy supplies. Waiting for them, she opened her mail from home. Included was a magazine from her home parish, St. Laurence, Pudsey, and in the magazine a leaflet about Parcevall Hall which indicated that a warden would be needed. Miss Bradley wrote to the archdeacon and by Christmas she had accepted the post of assistant warden to Deaconess Gibson, without ever having seen the house.

Illness forced the deaconess to resign before the house opened, leaving Miss Bradley, a helper from Scargill and a large house full of workmen. In defiance of the difficulties, they opened in July 1963 and took their first party of 27 teenage members of the Girls' Friendly Society, and this without the benefit of the new wing. The warden's own bed was whisked away into a guest room, mattresses put on floors, and a great, if hectic, time was had by all.

Gradually during that first year, work was completed and groups began to use this new facility. The first Christmas was spiritually and socially warm but physically cold since holes had been knocked through to where the new wing was to be.

Staffing has often been a problem for so remote a house, but early visitors would have fond memories of Jessie from Dent, who gave sterling service as cook, and cheroot-smoking Eleanor, who came to Parcevall after retiring, intending quietly to fade away, but changed her mind about fading, became housekeeper and turned her hand to almost anything needed. Pam Bradley stayed until 1973 and has been followed by Miss Irene Price, Dr. Heather Beaumont, Miss Anne Lessiter and Miss Florence Begley. All have made their contributions and developed the life of the house. It is used for clergy and lay retreats, working meetings of various diocesan bodies, holiday breaks and various short courses, some with a programmed spiritual content such as 'Prayer and Painting' weekends. Whatever the activity, the place itself seems to impart an air of calm and tranquillity. Its benefits to the diocese can be summed up in words Miss Begley wrote in a publication to mark its silver jubilee as a Diocesan House: "A retreat is an opportunity for renewal, re-appraisal, creativity, reflection, prayer, silence, stillness and discernment. It is a chance to stop deliberately and to step out of the head-long rush of life with all its complexity and triviality, in order to be still, to listen and to discern the deepest realities of life. A retreat experience will be different for each person, but basically it is an experience of God, of self and of others. The peace and quiet that surrounds Parcevall Hall makes it an ideal place for prayer for many people. The Lord Himself found it necessary in His lifetime to escape from the crowds and the hustle and bustle of every day life, to go away to a quiet place and rest a while and pray. The people of Bradford Diocese have a real gift in Parcevall Hall for promoting the spiritual life of the diocese."

Parcevall Hall

*Provost and Mrs Tiarks with pastoral staff presented
by the Cathedral congregation*

CHAPTER 16

JUBILEE

Pressing needs in the urban areas, particularly in relationship to Bradford City Development Plan, kept the bishop well occupied with this part of his diocese. Perhaps it was this which was responsible for the lack of rapport between Michael Parker and his Archdeacon of Craven. Whatever the reason, there was little warmth between the two men and the archdeacon, on several public occasions, such as diocesan conference, took a contrary line to his bishop. If the archdeacon felt the bishop did not understand the ways and needs of country people, it is a pity that he was not able to offer help and advice rather than opposition, or that the advice offered on less public occasions was not heeded. Whether as cause or effect of this flawed relationship, this bishop spent less time in the rural areas than others before or since, and some of the painstaking efforts from 1919 onwards to build up a feeling of family within the diocese received a setback. This was particularly sad, as Michael Parker clearly saw the needs of his 'diocesan family' as the main thrust of his episcopal ministry. He had little time for London and central affairs, and never took the seat to which he was entitled in the House of Lords. These difficulties, however, were later at least partly outweighed by the family-feeling generated during the Jubilee celebrations.

Although Arthur Sephton resigned as Rector of Skipton in 1964, he continued, as was his right, as archdeacon for the whole of Michael Parker's episcopacy, making it impossible for the bishop to have a man of his choice in Craven.

Other senior staff changed during this time. In 1962, John Tiarks, who had become almost synonymous with Bradford Cathedral, received richly deserved preferment when he was appointed Bishop of Chelmsford. Canon Gordon Hewitt, in his 'History of the Diocese of Chelmsford', suggests that approaches were made to John Tiarks earlier, but there were tasks at Bradford Cathedral which he felt it was his duty to see through to completion. Although he made a fine and able bishop, and he and Mrs. Tiarks enjoyed Chelmsford, their daughter believes that Bradford was closest to their hearts and the Bradford years were the happiest of their lives.

It was entirely appropriate that when, in 1963, the Sanctuary, Lady Chapel and Chapel of the Holy Spirit of Bradford Cathedral were consecrated, the High Altar was consecrated by Donald Coggan, Archbishop of York, and the Altar of the Lady Chapel by John Tiarks, Bishop of Chelmsford. Again in 1965, at the Festival of Thanksgiving and Dedication upon the Completion of the East

End of the Cathedral, the Bishop of Chelmsford was the preacher at two of the three services. He and the architect, Sir Edward Maufe, are commemorated as two carved heads in the chancel, the architect looking westwards, surveying the fruits of his labour, and John Tiarks looking towards the Altar. In the ambulatory between the High Altar and Lady Chapel are to be found carved heads of the two long-serving cathedral wardens, Mr. J.J. Cullingworth and Mr. A.E. Simpson.

The new provost, the Very Revd. W.H. Alan Cooper, came to Bradford in July 1962, from St. Andrew's Church, Plymouth, which had already supplied Bradford's first bishop and a distinguished organist for the cathedral, Dr. Charles Hooper. John Tiarks, after nineteen years, was by any standard a 'hard act to follow', and Alan Cooper's style was entirely different, quieter and in some ways more formal. Seeing the building work through to completion occupied much of his first three years, but then there were fresh challenges to face. The first was to rethink the pattern of worship. People were beginning to prefer morning services rather than evening ones and also to require more Sacramental worship.

Secondly, the cathedral team set themselves to forge a link with the rest of the diocese. Parochial clergy were invited to take part in cathedral services, and the Cathedral Choir was made available to sing Evensong in some of the country churches. The cathedral staff also pursued a policy of trying to interest senior pupils from Bradford schools, although careful not to 'poach' those who already had links with other churches.

Provost Cooper found it a distinct handicap living out at Heaton, and during term time, he and Mrs. Cooper used one of the flats in the Clergy House. Eventually it became possible to build three houses, for a provost and two residentiary canons, on the closed graveyard on the north side of the cathedral. At that time, an Act of Parliament was needed to allow secular building on consecrated ground and 495 graves were removed and the remains re-interred in Calverley churchyard in 1971. This development, with a sweep of lawn between the houses and the cathedral, the old stone cleaned to match the honey colour of the new, has created, in the heart of Bradford, a lovely and peaceful close, worthy of any cathedral city, and a summer oasis for city centre office workers to picnic and enjoy the sun in their lunch hours.

This arrangement also made it easier for provosts, canons, and the junior clergy living just across the road in the Clergy House, to work as a team and to adopt a pattern of corporate prayer and worship. It was Provost Cooper who first introduced the idea of having volunteer guides, or welcomers, on duty in the cathedral, to welcome visitors, answer their questions, and show them round if required.

In 1965 Bradford supplied yet another bishop when Hubert Higgs became Suffragan Bishop of Hull, following the Rt. Revd. George F. Townley, himself a former Bradford clergyman. George Townley had been one of Bishop Perowne's first ordinands and had served curacies at Keighley and Bingley before becoming Vicar of Lidget Green, where one of his curates was Bernard Markham who was later consecrated Bishop of Nassau.

Hubert Higgs was succeeded as Archdeacon of Bradford by the Ven. William Johnston, who was no stranger to Yorkshire, having served in a number of parishes in neighbouring Ripon Diocese before becoming Vicar of St. Chad's, Shrewsbury. His wife Marguerite spent her childhood at Cautley, and both Bishop Perowne and Bishop Blunt stayed at her parents' home when they had business at that end of the diocese.

There was a suggestion that the archdeacon should again have a parish and the small living of Esholt was proposed. However, he was to be Diocesan Missioner as well as archdeacon, and responsible for the post-ordination training of curates, and for taking retreats. The decision to leave him free from parish ties proved a blessing for the diocese, and particularly for two parishes living through unusually long interregna.

Firstly, while house-hunting, the Johnstons lived in the empty vicarage of St. James', Bolton Road, making the Revd. Geoffrey Ashford wonder whether he was the only curate to have an archdeacon as his assistant. When St. Paul's with St. Jude's, Manningham, was vacant, Archdeacon Johnston took it on almost as his parish and brought to it great spiritual gifts, combined with humour and shrewd common sense, to help the former parishioners of those two parishes through the difficult early days of their amalgamation. His work as Diocesan Missioner took him all over the diocese, so that he was better known than most Archdeacons of Bradford in the Craven Archdeaconry and was soon much in demand to lead retreats, quiet days, and Lent courses.

Archdeacon Johnston and Bishop Parker became good friends and the archdeacon's brisk practicality made up for episcopal shortcomings in this area. Arrangements made through either the archdeacon or the bishop's secretary worked efficiently, but left to himself, Michael Parker was liable absentmindedly to double book himself, or do something quite unscheduled, on impulse. In a manner reminiscent of the T.V. series "All Gas and Gaiters", the bishop would sometimes make out that he was terrified of being caught out by the archdeacon when embarking on some impractical course of action, but in reality a deep affection developed between the two. Similarly, skirmishes between Archdeacon Johnston and Provost Cooper during finance meetings were light-hearted - like the time when it was suggested that the card sent to parishes for display on the porch notice board acknowledging that they had paid their quota, should bear a picture of the bishop. "If they don't pay," threatened the archdeacon, "we'll send them a picture of the provost."

Mrs. Johnston and Mrs. Cooper worked together with a clergy wives group, until Mrs. Cooper's illness and untimely death. Mrs. Johnston continued this work throughout her time in the diocese, visiting tirelessly, often by bus and on foot. It was in 1969, the Golden Jubilee year of the diocese, that this clergy wives group decided there ought to be something special arranged for the clergy and their wives to enjoy together. This was the start of an annual party, with a meal and an entertainment. Sometimes Bishop Parker would write the script for this. It was always hilarious, and one involved curates crawling along the floor with stockings over their heads for a mock hold up. The Vicar of Lidget Green played the part of a porter carrying the bishop's luggage and saying, "What about a tip, bishop?" to which the bishop replied, "Ah yes, the Canterbury Stakes. Put your money on Ramsey." Later in the same play, the curates were in the bishop's study being scolded for preparing such poor sermons. "These would not convert a tomtit," said the bishop, "Now I will show you how to preach a real sermon." He took his text from the Original Book of Nursery Rhymes, "Old Mother Hubbard, she went to the cupboard...." and proceeded to preach a cracking 'sermon' on that text, concluding by thumping his desk so loudly that he woke all the curates who had dozed off with boredom. It brought the house down!

The Jubilee was the undoubted highlight of Bishop Parker's Bradford years, and the way in which it was marked owed much to his emphasis on the spirituality of parochial life. The heart of the Jubilee was an exercise for parishes, based on a booklet prepared by the bishop, called The Consideration. Clergy and laity together were urged to consider the life and work of their parish in relation to:-

1. the Church's ministry to adults, young people and children,

2. the life of the local community,

3. the world-wide mission of the Church.

At the launch of the Jubilee on 3rd September 1969, Bishop Parker's sense of theatre was much in evidence. Models of 149 churches in the diocese were

Bishop Parker, Provost Alan Cooper with verger Brian Boldy receive greetings from Archbishop Coggan brought by Revd. Graham Bettridge

carried in to St. George's Hall by parishioners in costume of the period in which the church was built, together with a representative of the present day congregation. At the bishop's suggestion, several parishes had invited local schools to get the children to make the models, which can still be found on display in some churches. Civic Heads and leaders of other denominations were present, and guests were greeted by Mr. John Foster Beaver who had been a member of the original Bishopric Committee. There were speeches by Mr. Stewart Perowne, son of the first bishop, Mr. David Blunt, son of the second bishop, and by Archbishop and Mrs. Coggan.

Later that month, a Baildon curate, the Revd. Graham Bettridge (now Rector of Kirkby Lonsdale and a Canon of Carlisle Cathedral), travelled from York with a relay of ponies and traps from the Yorkshire Driving Club, bearing a message from the archbishop to be handed to Bishop Parker and Provost Cooper outside Bradford Cathedral. On the way, the cavalcade was enthusiastically received in Dewsbury, the original Mother Church of the area, and the Mayor and Mayoress were present at an open-air service.

Many local Jubilee events took place over the nine month period, which reached a climax on Sunday 28th June 1970 and St. Peter's Day, June 29th. Sunday began with a Diocesan Eucharist in every parish, all using the same readings and hymns. In the evening there were Services of Thanksgiving and Resolve at nineteen centres. Eighteen bishops visited the diocese and one preached at each centre. On Monday evening, in St. George's Hall, in the presence of the Lord Mayor and Lady Mayoress, the coats of arms of Ripon and Wakefield Dioceses were carried in before that of Bradford. Parishes presented their reports on The Consideration, and the Archbishop of Canterbury, the Most Revd. Michael Ramsey, addressed the packed gathering, then all moved across to the cathedral where his sermon was relayed to the crowds overflowing into the grounds.

The Telegraph and Argus, commenting on the events, said: "How many organisations could have filled St. George's Hall and the Cathedral to overflowing on the same night?..... The significance of the evening was not so much whether or not the attendance was large, however, but in the feeling which existed of a large family living in a widely diverse area stretching from south of Bradford to the far north-west. The Bishop of Bradford, the Rt. Revd. Michael Parker, would be the last person to claim any credit for himself, but there is no doubt that since he came to Bradford he has steadily built up parish life and at the same time fostered this diocesan family spirit."

Real research had been undertaken, and valuable insights gained by means of The Consideration, and other bishops asked to see it and made use of Bishop Parker's ideas, but sadly, follow-up waned in Bradford when Bishop Parker retired in 1971, ten years to the day after his Enthronement. Typically, Michael Parker asked that his only farewell gift from the diocese should be a book containing the names of all the clergy and church workers and those he had confirmed.

Lord Mayor, Alderman E. Newby and the Lady Mayoress receive the recently published New English Bibles from Archdeacon Johnston, 1970

CHAPTER 17

O REFORM IT ALTOGETHER

In 1970 the Church of England brought in a synodical system of government and Bradford had to follow the national pattern in implementing this, making some changes to deaneries in order to conform to the standards set by the Synodical Government Measure. The objective was to increase the range of representation on the councils of the church at all levels and bring more democracy to church government. Within the guidelines laid down, Bishop Parker had opted for a large diocesan synod, which, in a small diocese, meant that it was possible for most parishes to be directly represented. The new structures brought with them the need for a more professional approach to administration. In Bradford, Mr. Charles Cockshott was secretary to the Diocesan Board of Finance, and had been since 1954. He was an accountant and kept the accounts, as might be expected, in perfect order in beautiful copperplate handwriting, but he was a churchman of the old school and wanted nothing to do with a new way of going on. It was not until he retired in 1972 and was succeeded by his assistant Mr. David Hennessey, that the role of diocesan secretary began to be developed. Mr. Cockshott's office staff consisted of one typist and David as tea-boy, errand boy and general factotum.

'Wool money' spoke loudly in those days, within the church as well as in the city, and many people, Mr. Cockshott among them, seemed rather in awe of John Foster Beaver, who was one of the city's great textile magnates. He was also a man with a strong sense of responsibility and obligation, playing an active role in the life of Bradford as well as of his home town, Bingley. Among other commitments, he was Chairman of Governors of Bradford Girls' Grammar School, Chairman of Bingley Bench of Magistrates, President of Airedale Agricultural Society, concerned in the establishment of Airedale Hospital, and a benefactor of the Boy Scouts movement. All this was in addition to his long and generous service to the diocese, during which he was chairman of the Board of Finance and of the House of Laity. His public spirited activities in many fields led to the awards of O.B.E. and later C.B.E. He was not, however, held in such awe by the PCC of one small rural parish, which staged a strike when its quota was raised from £7. 4s. 3d to £7. 8s. 0d, and refused to pay anything at all until the powerful chairman of the diocesan board was obliged to re-instate the earlier figure.

A strike was a mild reaction, compared with the opposition Dr. William Scoresby aroused when he was appointed Vicar of Bradford in 1839 and attempted to enforce payment of church rates. A letter he received is quoted in "Celebrated Yorkshire Folk" by J.S. Pattinson:

> "to doctor scorsby V. of B. on his attempting to lay a Ch. rate at a time when the people have been so far enlitened as to know that they have no right to pay it. No Sir if you are determined to have this rate you may get it if you can or if you dare. remember sir you are only a man and you may be in your grave before the rate be collected. the nights are dark guns are plentiful powder is cheap men ARE DETERMINED not to be robbed by parson any longer if you dare either to come yourself or to send collectors you may where you expect to Receive a Shilling, Receive a Bullet; and your head be the Receiver instead of your Pocket. think of the curses in the book of Isaiah Pronounced against those who oppress the poor. But may be you do not believe that part of Skripter be that As it may you may believe that the only way For you to save your life is to be quiet About the Rate."

Even in the second half of the twentieth century, several parishes had important business men as their treasurers, running their finances with benevolent paternalism. In one mill village, all the church's income and bills were put through the mill account for many years, and it was only when the mill owner, who was churchwarden, died, that the PCC discovered how heavily he had been subsidising them.

When David Hennessey became diocesan secretary, he went to as many parishes as possible to explain the quota (or 'share', as it became). He would be allowed his say, but often there would be no questions. The attitude was that he had been given his half hour and had his chance to make his case and cover everything he ought to have covered. All eyes would then turn to the treasurer, who may or may not nod his assent, like a Roman emperor. At St. Wilfrid's, Lidget Green, it was particularly disconcerting when David started his talk and all the ladies on the front row got out their knitting.......

The summer of 1972 saw the arrival of Bradford's fifth bishop. Ross Sydney Hook came to Bradford from Lincoln Diocese, where, as Suffragan Bishop of Grantham, he worked principally with the rural parishes of the southern half of the diocese. Before that, he had been a Residentiary Canon of Rochester Cathedral, Rector of Chelsea and of Chorlton-cum-Hardy in the Manchester Diocese.

Unusually, Ross Hook had become a naval chaplain only two years after ordination. He served with the Royal Marine Commandos in Italy and Yugoslavia and was awarded the Military Cross in 1945, one event in his life about which he was consistently unwilling to talk. The Telegraph and Argus reporter Dudley Akeroyd, in the course of a two hour long interview, only managed to get a rather vague impression that the enemy simply moved on when the commandos arrived. It seems a strange training-ground, but the Times, in March 1972, when the appointment was announced, reported that Bishop Hook was the fifth former naval chaplain on the Episcopal bench, the others being the Rt. Revd. M.A.P. Wood (Norwich), the Rt. Revd. E.B. Henderson (Bath and Wells), the Rt. Revd. G.A. Ellison (Chester) and the Rt. Revd. G.E. Reindorp (Guildford). The Dean of Windsor and former Bishop of Norwich, the Rt. Revd. W.L.S. Flemming, had also been a naval chaplain and the Rt. Revd. J.D. Wakeling (Southwell) had served as a commissioned officer with the commandos before ordination.

Stage and film stereotypes of bishops tend to polarise as either ascetic or bluff, and the new Bishop of Bradford presented superficially as a fine example of the latter, tall, well-built, genial, and a great sports enthusiast. However, in addition to looking the part, he brought with him a wealth of experience in the wider work of the Church of England as well as that gained at parish and diocesan level. He had taken a leading part in diocesan government at Lincoln during the pastoral and administrative changes of the previous two years. His wife, Ruth, almost as tall as her husband, slender, unassuming, brought to the diocese her own deep spiritual and theological insights and was soon warmly appreciated in her own right.

The bishop was enthroned on the fourth of July, in retrospect an appropriate choice for one who was to be instrumental in bringing about close links between Bradford Diocese and the United States of America. In his enthronement sermon, he welcomed Dr. W.G. Wheeler, Roman Catholic Bishop of Leeds, and other members of his Communion, as well as leaders of the Free Churches. He warned that Church divisions cast doubt upon Christian credibility: "Despite the debacle of the proposed Anglican-Methodist scheme, we delay pushing forward toward a new unity at our peril." He also made it clear that he was all in favour of necessary changes in Church life, in words that found a ready echo in the heart of the new, young diocesan secretary: "We are encumbered by an organisation ideally suited to an age that has passed away," he said, and referring to the trail of reports and reforming commissions that had strewn the path of the Church during the last decade, he continued, "These will prove of little importance in the long run unless we offer an attitude of mind and a quality of life that shows itself concerned with living stones, rather than propping up dead ones."

Ross Hook's style was very different from his predecessor, most noticeably in terms of directives to the clergy. In this, he was rather more like Bishop Blunt, seeing his role in respect of the men in the parishes as being an enabling one, and someone who was accessible if needed. He aimed to send out only one letter a year, just before Christmas, but also to meet every clergyman at least once a year, either at a chapter meeting or by calling on him at home. He was too, a much more out-going personality and became a well known speaker at civic events, business and regimental dinners and similar functions. When invitations came in too abundantly, he applied a simple rule-of-thumb in deciding which to accept. If, because of who he was, he was invited to something at which there would otherwise be no church input whatsoever, he would go and provide that dimension. One such event came when, thanks to the Rt. Revd. Eric Treacey, Bishop of Wakefield and former Rector of Keighley, a

Bishop Ross Hook on the Yorkshire Dales Railway

legend had grown up that associated bishops and railways, and Ross Hook found himself on the footplate of a steam engine on the Yorkshire Dales Railway at Embsay, smiling genially, but not inwardly sure that this was quite his scene.

Advised and encouraged by Archdeacon Johnston, the bishop saw the main items on his agenda as central administration, finance and education. He authorised David Hennessey to get on with necessary reforms in the office. This he did by installing modern equipment and increasing the staff to seven, making it possible to provide back-up services to the work of the archdeacons and to diocesan boards in addition to the diocesan board of finance. Even so the North Parade premises still left something to be desired, and one of the secretary's extra duties was to go down and scare the rats away from the ladies' cloakroom.

The arrangement at Church House was rather strange, in that the whole place was run by the Church House Council and was never under the control of the diocese, which had tenant status. Relations between the two bodies were sometimes difficult and by the 1970s the whole place was in a poor state. The council had not enough money, and the diocese had too little to spare to want to pay for the upkeep of a library, restaurant and reading room which it did not particularly want. Eventually the whole place was sold and the diocesan board of finance made an arrangement with the cathedral to refurbish the run-down cathedral hall and make part of that into modern, suitable offices. David Hennessey and his successors found that not only were the premises good, but closeness to the cathedral staff made for a good working relationship. When

David moved to the Diocese of St. Edmundsbury and Ipswich, that contact with the cathedral was something he missed.

When it came to finance, it was clear that a major overhaul was needed. The admirable system introduced by Dr. Perowne had drifted considerably off course over the years, and parishes were again finding a multiplicity of demands on them, with their diocesan quota sometimes being pushed well down the list. There were separate assessments for such things as parsonage repairs, rates, and clergy stipends, with some smaller parishes having to find disproportionately large amounts. In addition, all sorts of groups and causes were demanding support and the bishop determined that during his time there would be no big appeal, and he discouraged appeals in general. He believed that churches should for the most part be able to foresee their needs and budget for them. He commended to parishes the principles of stewardship as an alternative to certain local efforts. One of the more bizarre of these took place in the parish of Clapham with Keasden, when the vicar, the Revd. Peter Winstone, spent twelve hours on a bed of nails, sponsored by the minute. The Bishop of Ripon heard of this, clearly thought it presented an inappropriate image of the Church of England, and tried to get the Bishop of Bradford to intervene; but Bishop Hook supported his man with a letter: "My Dear Peter, I am not sure that I think your idea is a good one, but I would go to any length to preserve to you the right to do it."

WELL, VICAR, LIFE NIVVER WOR A BED O' ROSES AT CLAPHAM!

What the bishop was aiming for was a system where there was one charge only on a parish. Inevitably it would be considerably more than the old quota, in some cases double or treble, but he believed that Yorkshire people would respond, once it had been explained, and if they were convinced that those making the proposals were being honest and straightforward with them. When it came to putting the scheme to diocesan synod, the bishop was confident, but Mrs. Hook spent the afternoon walking up and down in Heaton Woods praying, "Oh do let it be all right." It was all right, with general acceptance that the system was fair, that all parishes were being assessed by the same criteria and that the method of assessment would be regularly reviewed and agreed on. The new name 'share', which replaced 'quota', is much more indicative of the nature and purpose of the giving.

Mr. Foster Beaver's successor as chairman of the board of finance, Mr. Stanley Wilson, contributed to the acceptance of the new system by helping to explain it to parish representatives, and he continued the tradition of dedicated service in carefully managing diocesan finance. The diocese is fortunate too in the chairman since 1982, Mr. Tony Hesselwood, who, with the diocesan secretary, has willingly visited parishes from one end to the other of the diocese to talk to PCCs, incumbents and treasurers, discussing difficulties and ironing out misunderstandings. The goodwill these officials, professional and voluntary, have generated, has contributed to the way the people of the diocese have kept on responding.

There was a spin-off benefit too from the new arrangement. As payment of curates became a diocesan responsibility, it meant that they could be directed to those parishes where extra help was most needed, rather than just to those who could afford them. The bishop could also take into account the quality of training that particular incumbents could offer. Shortages in clerical manpower were beginning to be felt, and this was a useful first step in working out the best deployment of those available. Plans were made too for the creation of more united benefices among the smaller rural parishes, although incumbents' freeholds meant that action could only be taken as vacancies arose.

Increased participation by lay people, whether assisting in parish worship or as members of decision-making boards and committees, brought with it the need for better and more widespread education, on both theological and organisational levels. "Education" in the diocese was the responsibility of Canon John Baker, Rector of Leathley with Farnley, who was wholly concerned with church schools, and retired in 1972. Lincoln was one of the first dioceses to decide that there should be a wider educational brief than this, and building on his experience there, Bishop Hook appointed Frank Sargeant as a residentiary canon to head up a programme of adult Christian education and, acting on recommendations in the Government's Albemarle Report, Bradford Council agreed to finance a youth officer.

There was a great deal of government emphasis in the 1970s on the needs of young people, and many sports and youth centres were built at this time. Not only church youth leaders were funded, but those from other organisations, such as Scouts or the Duke of Edinburgh's Award scheme. The first diocesan youth officer appointed under this arrangement was the Revd. Keith Smalldon, and he was succeeded by the Revd. Roger Wood. It was an unusual situation. The only direct responsibility was to the bishop, as a bishop's officer, and there was no job description or specified allocation of time between church and council. In fact Roger Wood felt that any such division would have been an artificial one and the role was rather that of the Church at work in society.

He was a tutor on the training courses for youth leaders run by Bradford Metropolitan District Council, but also worked with other local authorities into whose territory Bradford Diocese stretches, and was always available to talk to parishes, deaneries or diocese to help with church-based youth work. He also involved himself directly in working with young people aged from 14 to 21, whether it was a weekend programme, a summer camp, or taking a group of teenagers to Taizé or to the U.S.A.

The arrangement was only brought to an end by council spending cuts, and because the diocese was not in a position to take over the full cost of the work, it was necessary to revert to the system of having part-time youth officers who combined the job with a curacy or small parish.

The diocesan camps are a project that began in the early 1960s when the Revd. John Potter, Vicar of Kettlewell, organised a children's camp at Kettlewell using some ex-army tents. Gas cookers made by the local blacksmith out of angle iron and burners salvaged from old cookers became known as 'Potter Ranges', and were in use for many years. Gradually more equipment, including several marquees, was acquired, and as more people became involved the camps were taken further afield. Early leaders included the Revd. Tony Sparham and Mrs. Penny Driver and the children's camps also had a large network of younger helpers who came back year by year. The diocese recognised the value of camping as an activity and began to budget for staff training and additional equipment. Two weeks of children's camps were run, one for 10 to 12-year-olds and one for over 12s. In 1977, family camps were added, and the Revd. Canon Bruce Grainger, who has supplied this information, became an assistant leader.

For a number of years, youth holidays were held in hostel accommodation and in about 1980 it was decided to add a youth week under canvas to the diocesan camping programme. Mr. Tony Hesselwood assumed overall responsibility and Canon Grainger became leader of the family camps when John Potter retired from camping in 1979. The camps continue to attract good numbers - over 100 sometimes - advertising being done through churches and schools. They have become much less spartan in style, though the standard of cuisine has always been good, and camp entertainments of high standard. Richard and Sue Nicholas, who helped with stores and cooking back in 1977, have now taken over the organisation.

The remaining strand in Bishop Hook's education policy was the appointment of Canon David Creaser to look after church schools. The Church in the early 19th century had been among the pioneers in providing general education as well as religious instruction, through Sunday schools, evening classes and weekday schools. Sir Francis Powell had been the most generous benefactor of Bradford Church of England Schools' Society, which was formed in 1881 and continued until 1920, when Dr. Perowne was invited to become its president, and it was felt appropriate to merge the society with the newly formed diocesan education committee. The reactions and decisions of church authorities in response to early Education Acts is well documented in "Education in Bradford, 1870 - 1970," published by the Educational Services Committee of Bradford Corporation.

The 1944 Act brought into being the system whereby voluntary schools, which included Church of England schools, had the choice of becoming 'aided' or 'controlled'. Aided schools retained their right to denominational teaching according to their Trust deeds, and the right of their managers to appoint staff. The managers were responsible for 50% of the cost of improvements to school buildings to bring them up to the Ministry of Education's requirements. Later the financial commitment became 15% of building maintenance costs. This is the responsibility of the parish concerned, with help from the diocesan 'Barchester Fund'.

Those schools which felt they could not afford the necessary building costs had the option of becoming controlled schools. For them, maintenance became the responsibility of local education authorities, but denominational religious education would be allowed for two periods a week and the managers would be consulted about the appointment of a head teacher. This Act laid down for the first time in the country's educational history that religious education must be given in every type of school and that every day should begin with an act of collective worship.

The diocese's schools divided between the two categories according to individual circumstances, and some disappeared completely over the years, just as some of the inner city churches did, for the same reasons of population shift, coupled with increasing provision of local authority school places.

The diocese has never had a secondary school, though the possibility of acquiring one in Skipton was considered in the 1970s, and has only one middle school, with controlled status. Of its primary schools, in 1992, 28 were aided and 34 controlled; 33 are in Bradford Archdeaconry and 29 in Craven, and they are spread throughout the diocese and into the local education authority areas of Bradford, North Yorkshire, Lancashire, Leeds, Cumbria and Calderdale. In 1924, when church schools were first listed in the Diocesan Year Book, there were 42 in Bradford and 62 in Craven, with average attendances ranging from 9 in the smallest rural school to 525 in the city.

Although many rural schools are small, the diocese has always had a policy not to support the closure of any school unless the governors specifically requested it, and the board of education has always fought the local authorities when they have tried to cease to maintain schools, although some have inevitably gone. The tiny school at Stainforth, for example, came to the end of the road when a family with seven children moved out of the village and made it unworkable, literally overnight. Two fine little schools in Hurst Green parish went when neither was big enough for Lancashire to be willing to continue supporting, and an acceptable amalgamation could not be worked out.

By the 1980s, several urban schools had a high proportion of children of other faiths, but only one, St. Paul's Manningham, with a 100% Muslim intake, requested a complete change of status to become a local authority school. The 1988 Education Act affected the teaching of religious education in all schools, reinforcing the requirement for every local education authority to produce an agreed syllabus. The Church of England has a statutory right to be represented on the Agreed Syllabus Conference, which consists of four committees representing: the local authority; teaching representatives; the Church of England; other denominations and faiths. An agreed syllabus requires unanimous agreement between these committees.

Canon Creaser, in 1992, believed the system to be working well on the whole, although religious education was under-funded. He stressed that the emphasis of religious education had changed since the early years of universal education in England, and was no longer a confessional discipline based on Christianity, but concerned with knowledge about religious beliefs; but he still felt that church schools could provide a nuance that could not be found anywhere else. One of their great strengths was their local base. It remained to be seen where the 1992 government's 'opting out' policy would lead.

CHAPTER 18

CHANGES AND CHANCES

Craven by this time had a new archdeacon. archdeacon Sephton died in 1972 and was succeeded by the Ven. Martin Kaye. Regular senior staff meetings, which had not taken place for many years, began again, and Archdeacon Kaye, with Bishop Hook, did much to bring the two archdeaconries back into a whole and wholesome relationship. Later, when Archdeacon Johnston left, Archdeacon Kaye became director of ordinands and responsible for post-ordination training. He is remembered as a man of great spiritual gifts, at his best as a tutor or retreat director, but, unlike William Johnston, he was not able to combine this with a flair for administration and had no parish experience beyond his first curacy. David Hennessey commented that, "In those days, if you didn't understand drains and downpipes, pointing mixes and such things, you were considered very poor beer as an archdeacon."

Martin Kaye had in fact been a tutor and chaplain at Cuddeston Theological College, domestic chaplain to the Archbishop of York, and assistant secretary to the body responsible for selecting candidates for ordination. His appointment in 1977 to be a Canon of St. George's Chapel, Windsor, would have been another appropriate use of his gifts and it was very sad that he died only a few days before he should have taken up this post.

The next archdeacon was deeply rooted in the parishes of Craven Archdeaconry. As Vicar of Sedbergh, Cautley and Garsdale, and Rural Dean of Sedbergh, Canon David Rogers knew rural communities and country ways. It was said that no parish or priest could get away with anything when he was archdeacon because they could not come up with anything he had not already met or thought of when he was an incumbent! Archdeacon Rogers became known for his thorough and painstaking work, and underlying this was a deep pastoral concern for the clergy and people of his archdeaconry. Insistence on proper care of a parish's material assets was but a means of saving a parochial church council or its successors from later burdens that might blight the whole life of a parish by their financial implications. Efficient stewardship at diocesan level would certainly have a bearing on the working and living conditions of the rural clergy under his care. Like Martin Kaye, he was concerned with mergers and unions of parishes, particularly those of Wharfedale. Resistance was sometimes attributed to anxiety at the different churchmanship of a proposed partner, but often the deeper reason was a reluctance to accept that the old order had to change at all.

Two objectives David Rogers set for himself were, firstly, that the country voice should be heard, and the remotest parishes have equal consideration with the rest; secondly, that there should be the best possible balance in terms of age and experience among the country clergy. Bishop Parker, though so careful in placing his junior clergy, had had a tendency to move older men into the country in a rather haphazard manner. Only Sedbergh, Skipton and Barnoldswick had curates, and in order to get more young men into rural areas, the archdeacon persuaded some parishes to accept a young man as priest-in-charge for two or three years, who might then be instituted as vicar if it was working out, or leave without ill-feeling at the end of that time. This was done only where a neighbouring parish had an experienced incumbent to whom the younger man could turn for advice and support, and had the effect of creating much-needed virtually second curacy posts for the diocese.

In 1976, William Johnston became Suffragan Bishop of Dunwich in the Diocese of St. Edmundsbury and Ipswich. Bishop Hook wrote in Bradford Diocesan News: "No better chairman have I ever met - an efficient administrator, knowledgeable in finance and a shrewd judge of affairs, but he has never been content with these things alone. He brought to his work a great pastoral care for the clergy and laity in his Archdeaconry. I was grateful for his shrewdness, and his plain speaking when he thought the bishop was wrong!"

William Johnston newly consecrated Bishop of Dunwich

Canon Sargeant became Archdeacon of Bradford and Kenneth Cook was appointed to the cathedral canonry. Frank Sargeant was a Lincolnshire man, but, according to David Hennessey, could "out-Yorkshire the Yorkshire men - people think Yorkshire folk are blunt, but, when it came to cutting through 'waffle', oblique hints or euphemism, Frank would go straight for the jugular!" It was Archdeacon Sargeant and Canon Cook together who devised the Called of God programme. This was a course of basic Christianity, and if anyone who undertook it felt a call to a specific ministry in the Church, they could be properly directed to explore their vocation. The course was open to men and women, and Canon Cook and the bishop became aware of the high quality of women candidates and began to wonder what the future would hold for those women who went on to theological college. Bradford Diocese was a leader in abolishing the post of a separate adviser for women's ministry. Later, when Canon Grainger was diocesan director of ordinands and the Revd. Ruth Wigram was deputy director, they shared the role in such a way that both were concerned with both male and female candidates.

The two new archdeacons were good friends and quickly developed an amicable and effective style of working together, each with his specific responsibilities for his own archdeaconry, but presenting a united, and sometimes formidable team on diocesan occasions. Together they were to steer the diocese through the seven month gap between the fifth and sixth bishops and during the unexpected vacancy in see that so tragically arose only two years after that. Similar in stature, and only slightly smaller than the bishop, they were in every sense men it was difficult to ignore.

It was with due awareness of his own build that Bishop Hook chose his new registrar when Henry Firth retired, also in 1977. Jeremy Mackrell, he declared, was the only solicitor tall enough to walk behind him in processions! Height, of course, was no more than a bonus point, and Mr. Mackrell proved to be a great asset, not only to Bradford Diocese, but to the Church. He has become a familiar figure at institutions, and takes care to greet new incumbents and encourage them to ask his advice whenever necessary. His active part in the life of the Christian laity includes giving lectures, as part of a diocesan lay training course, on the very relevant and also very difficult theme of "Being a Christian on Monday." In these, he has helped people to explore the issues involved in living out the faith in daily life, where there are complex and sometimes conflicting responsibilities. He also plays a full part in ecclesiastical legal affairs at national level.

It was a remarkable year for the diocese, bringing new appointments in all three senior clerical positions as well as that of registrar. Alan Cooper retired from the cathedral, not to a life of leisure, but, in keeping with his long-standing commitment to the work of the Church overseas, to serve in Karachi, Pakistan. The appointment of a new provost was the responsibility of the Simeon Trustees, who took into account what Bishop Hook had to say about the requirements of the post, although no names were suggested by him. They also consulted with the Lord Mayor and Chief Executive of the city. The outcome of their deliberations was the appointment the warden, Mr. John Cullingworth, announced to the cathedral congregation as "Brandon the firebrand".

Brandon Donald Jackson's ministry in Yorkshire began with a curacy at St. George's, Leeds, working in some of the poorest parts of that city and with the church's centre for the homeless at St. George's crypt. He was actively seeking another inner city post in 1965, when Bishop Parker persuaded him to come to a very different situation at St. Peter's, Shipley. In his twelve years there, he earned a reputation as a vigorous and outspoken leader of a dynamic, growing church, and became widely known through television broadcasts, becoming in 1969 religious adviser to Yorkshire Television. His was the first appointment as Vicar and Provost of Bradford to be made from within the diocese since its inception, and those who knew him, and those who had formed their own picture of him, awaited the outcome with interest!

Alan Cooper's work in developing more of a traditional cathedral style to the worship and general ambience had succeeded, but possibly at the cost of a certain warmth and liveliness; those responsible for the cathedral music had gradually become more dominant until, during the interregnum, a situation had been reached where, as the new provost put it, "the tail was wagging the dog." Before he arrived, members of the choir had been allowed, or led, to believe that Brandon Jackson disliked choral music and intended doing away with the organ, whereas in reality both Brandon and Mary Jackson were lovers of church music and staunch supporters of Church of England musical traditions, where those traditions were used to the glory of God and for the enhancement of worship.

A modest proposal that at one Evensong a month, the congregation should be able to join in the Magnificat and Nunc Dimittis was received as a signal that battle was to be joined, and the ensuing conflict between provost and choir and organist formed an unhappy background to cathedral life for several years. When eventually the provost felt he must insist on the resignation of the organist, it was not simply because of a clash of style or emphasis, or even personalities, although much was made of the latter publicly. Standards of behaviour within the choir had become totally unacceptable to the provost, who became the butt of a campaign in the correspondence columns of the local newspaper. Some choir members also chose to resign and it took several years for new organists to build up a new choir. The contribution made to this by Mr. Alan Horsey FRCO has been outstanding in producing a high standard of music which has become an integral part of the whole worshipping life of the cathedral.

Unhappy though this episode was, and for no one more painful than for the provost and his family, it was no more than one dark patch in an otherwise bright and colourful period in the life of the cathedral. Provost Jackson built on what Provost Cooper had achieved in enhancing its cathedral status, while not losing sight of the parochial needs of its own congregation. The strand he particularly developed was the cathedral's role as the mother church of the diocese.

He saw to it that visitors were made welcome, including groups of children, and soon school parties, of all faiths or none, were being shown round and having the purpose and work of a cathedral explained to them. Drawings, poems, letters and essays produced after such visits were often to be seen displayed in the cathedral. Organisations, whether church based such as Mothers' Unions, or from the city, were encouraged to use the building for special services and were always warmly welcomed from the provost's stall to "your cathedral."

A series of Deanery Evensongs was arranged, when the churches of a deanery would cancel their Sunday evening service and clergy and people would come to Bradford. The Friends of the Cathedral organisation expanded at this time and they would go as a group into parishes to share in a Sunday morning service and take greetings from the cathedral to the parish. On Ascension Day and occasional Sundays, choir, clergy and members of the congregation would all go out to a rural village church for Evensong. Mary Jackson launched a very successful appeal to lay people in the parishes to donate kneelers for the cathedral. Wherever there was a response, she personally took the canvas and wools and explained the work. Many were given and worked in memory of a dearly loved relative or friend, and each has a label on the underneath to tell who gave it, who worked it, and where applicable, in whose memory.

Undoubtedly Provost Jackson could be controversial and did sometimes favour a confrontational approach to issues where others might have chosen a more diplomatic route, but in many respects his ministry, though adapted to the needs of the time, echoed that of Provost Tiarks - his unequivocally expressed evangelical faith, his frequent newsworthiness, his T.V. appearances, and his relationship with civic leaders and the business community. In the latter he was greatly helped by one of his curates, the Revd. Roger Scoones, who regularly visited many of the factories and offices in the city. There was a well supported series of early morning 'Business Men's Breakfasts', mostly at the Bradford Club, at which business people, men and women, could enjoy a simple meal together then listen to a Christian speaker and join in discussion, before going to work. At these meetings, as in the cathedral, the provost was meticulous in greeting and talking to people, acknowledging with a brief pleasantry those he knew, and spending most of his time among those he did not yet know.

A project initiated by Brandon Jackson in the city, and of enormous benefit to Bradford, was the Cathedral Centre. The scheme was sparked off by a gift of £5,000 to the provost by a businessman in the congregation of St. Barnabas, Heaton, for the express purpose of helping unemployed young people in the city. The provost appealed to the cathedral congregation for suggestions as to how best to use the gift, and was approached by two men, both involved with youth training work, and both attending a cathedral service for the first time that day. They begged him not just to use up the money and have done with it, but to start something big and on-going.

The old Cathedral School, which had been leased by Bradford College as an art annexe, had just come vacant, and what was set up there became the biggest Youth Training Scheme project in the voluntary sector in West Yorkshire. Run by a management committee, chaired by a senior member of the cathedral (the provost at first, then leading lay men), with funding from local and national government and the European Community, it provides basic education in English and reading, a wide range of vocational training and a social and advice centre. A modestly priced canteen is run by catering trainees.

The extent of church involvement in social issues has varied over the years. Bishop Blunt was always outspoken on behalf of those with little influence, and the actions of individual Christians have often been effective in great and small ways. Charles and Nora Goodchild were among many church people who have contributed to the social fabric of the community when, within a very short time of their arrival at Tosside, they became probation officers for the court at Bolton-by-Bowland and later served the courts at Ingleton and Settle. Dr.Coggan made Charles Goodchild Director of Social Responsibility while he was at Holme Wood, and in this capacity he was instrumental in setting up the Diocesan Council for Social Aid, whose brief included the promotion of temperance and higher moral standards and the relief of suffering arising from delinquency, intemperance or addiction. The council also provided a management committee for Spooner House probation hostel from 1947 until it closed in 1988, as a result of reorganisation of probation hostel financing by the Home Office.

Other senior clergy and officers of the diocese have taken part at committee level in such projects as the Probation Liaison Committee, Victim Support Scheme, City Farm, and Bradford Day Shelter, which became Horton Housing Association, and there were further responses to social issues during the time of the seventh bishop.

Concern with the Church overseas, though always a prominent part of church work in Bradford Diocese, was not, up to this time, organised at a diocesan level, apart from occasional appeals for funds. Parishes supported various missionary societies and many kept in touch with individual missionaries. Those who had gone out from the diocese to work overseas would have prayer support and correspondence from their home parish, and Bishop Parker often sent a personal gift of a book to those he knew about.

Provost Cooper had kept a noticeboard in the cathedral, with news of those working overseas, and it had been his happy inspiration to ask a member of the cathedral congregation, Mrs. Joan Simms, to be responsible for keeping this up to date. He could not have made a better choice. Mrs. Simms kept conscientiously in touch with all the mission partners (the newer and more expressive term for missionaries), and provided a welcome, and, if necessary, a sympathetic ear, for those who came home on leave.

Eventually Mrs. Simms became chairman of an overseas working party set up by the Diocesan Board of Mission. This group was responsible for a quarterly newsletter about those who were working for the Church overseas, with information out of their letters, and prayer requests. Joan saw to it that a small gift from the diocese as a whole went out to them at Christmas and took upon herself a huge commitment to letter writing. Annual gatherings for parents of mission partners provided a relaxed social atmosphere in which parents could compare notes and share anxieties with others in similar situations. The working party also concerned itself with promoting the work of the missionary societies throughout the diocese, and with the situation of Christians in Iron Curtain countries, through the work of Keston College.

A means of relating to the work of the Church overseas that was totally new to Bradford was brought about almost entirely by the effort and enthusiasm of Bishop Ross Hook. The traditional, western, paternalistic concept of missionary work was changing, and as far back as 1963, the Anglican Communion had adopted a new policy of mutual sharing, recognising that every Province had gifts and insights to share. As part of this concept, partner dioceses were beginning to be set up, rather like an ecclesiastical equivalent of civic twinning.

An American acquaintance asked Bishop Hook whether he would consider his diocese becoming the partner of an American one. He was invited in January 1977 to go over to meet Bishop William Marmion and address the annual council of the Diocese of Southwestern Virginia. This is one of three dioceses in the State of Virginia and not, in spite of its name, to be confused with West Virginia which is another state entirely. The two bishops got on wonderfully well and Bishop Hook saw certain advantages to the scheme. Southwestern Virginia had some similarities with Bradford. It was even founded in the same year, and had industrial centres and miles of glorious country with small towns and villages - but also enough cultural differences to be stimulating. In so many places, he had found, people behave as though the only church is the one where they happen to live, and he saw the partnership as a way of broadening vision.

Paradoxically, he rightly anticipated objections from some of those who were already outward looking, who feared that such a link might be a distraction from the needs of third world countries, not simply for material help, but for friendship, understanding and acceptance as equal partners in the Gospel. So it was decided that, when the two partners had got to know each other, they should consider where else, in a totally different culture, they could reach out, preferably together, to make a three-sided link.

This first stage slowly came into being and groups of people took part in exchange visits. Several Bradford parishes set up one to one links with parishes in

Bishop Hook with Bishop Heath Light, Bishop Marmion's successor in Southwestern Virginia

Southwestern Virginia, and arranged their own levels of communication and exchanges, and lasting individual friendships have been made. Bishop Hook asked the Revd. Keith Potter to be particularly involved in the development of the link in the early years. At diocesan level, both adult and youth visits and programmes of activities have been set up. The link is subject to periodic review, but has been kept up and built on although there have been changes of bishops in both dioceses. The intended incorporation of a third partner was still in the planning stage when Ross Hook left Bradford for Lambeth in 1980 to take up the newly created post of Chief Personal Assistant to the Archbishop of Canterbury.

This demanding new role arose out of the archbishop's increasing work load as Diocesan Bishop of Canterbury, Primate of All England and head of the world-wide Anglican Communion. The personal assistant was to establish and manage relationships between Lambeth and other bodies - the Church of England's bureaucracy at Church House, Westminster, the Church Commissioners, government departments. He was to make any statements or responses needed from Lambeth during the archbishop's absence abroad and to assist with the archbishop's pastoral and advisory role towards the bishops of Canterbury Province. For all this, an experienced diocesan bishop with a gift for administration was needed.

Leaving Bradford, Bishop Hook recalled two things which had given him enormous pleasure. The first was that Bradford University, which prided itself on its secular ethos, had awarded him an honorary degree. A fellow recipient on that occasion was the Bradford-born actress, Billie Whitelaw, and seeing them deep in conversation, the Vice-Chancellor took the opportunity to ask, "Well, what did the bishop say to the actress?", to which Miss Whitelaw promptly replied, "Oh! I see you've been doctored!"

The second delight was a farewell dinner given for the bishop by the Lord Mayor, as keen a supporter of Yorkshire Cricket Club as Bishop Hook had always been of Kent, at which the sweet course was an ice-cream replica of Canterbury cricket ground. The diocese held its farewell events in both Bradford and Skipton, and warm tributes were paid, not only to the bishop, but also to Mrs. Hook, whose capacity for giving wise counsel had become well known and appreciated.

CHAPTER 19

THE WAY OF THE CROSS

At the end of an interregnum under the care of the archdeacons, Bradford welcomed its sixth bishop. Geoffrey John Paul was enthroned on 24th April 1981. It should have been a beautiful spring day, or at worst, one of April showers. Instead, the inhabitants of the north of England awoke to a strangely white light, and found themselves under a deep blanket of snow, through which branches laden with spring blossom protruded incongruously.

Bishop Geoffrey Paul arriving for his enthronement

Many ticket holders for the ceremony were unable to reach Bradford, although one who did was afterwards rather scornful of city and suburban dwellers who failed, having herself arrived on time from Garsdale. Local radio broadcast the news that the enthronement would take place as planned and in the event the cathedral was filled to capacity by those, with or without tickets, who could make their way there.

It is an indication of the seriousness with which the diocese was taking its relationships to other ethnic groups and other faiths within the community that, for the first time, the list of visiting dignitaries included representatives of those communities. They brought greetings to which the new bishop responded in the appropriate language - Hebrew, Arabic, Urdu and Gujerati.

Although Bishop Hook had seen finance and education as the chief platforms of his episcopate, this growing issue of race relations was another field in which he had initiated some vital work. Bishop Coggan had foreseen a need for action by church people and Bishop Parker had personally involved himself deeply and effectively in the mid sixties, when he, along with Monsignor Morgan Sweeney, Mr. Norman Bishop (lay reader and Bradford solicitor) and others, set up a voluntary body, the UK.-Commonwealth Immigrants Liaison Committee. Following the 1968 Immigration Act, this liaison committee was transformed into the Bradford Community Relations Council, which Michael Parker chaired. A former Bradford C.I.D. officer, and lay reader at St. Augustine's, Mr. John Naylor, was appointed as liaison officer for immigrants, only the fourth such appointment in the country.

Bishop Parker had invited the Revd. Peter Hawkins to come from India, where he had served for seven years, to work among the Asian population in Manningham. This bishop did not favour specialist posts and Peter's appointment was as curate at St. Paul's and St. Jude's . It was Bishop Hook who moved him to a curacy at the cathedral combined with a newly created specialist post of Bishop's Chaplain for Community Relations. He was involved with members of the Community Relations Council and others in resettling about 500 Asian refugees from Uganda across the diocese. Part of his work was to visit Asian patients in Bradford's hospitals, regardless of their religious background, and to help to educate hospital staff about such basic matters as the names and cultural backgrounds of these patients.

A curate at All Saints' Little Horton, the Revd. Steven Barton, and his Bengali wife Mukti, worked with women's groups and at St. Luke's Hospital, and the Revd. Colin Judd, a former CMS secretary, and his wife began valuable work in the area around nearby St. Columba's. A small group of brothers from the Somerset based Community of the Glorious Ascension elected to come and work in Bradford, and although they went first to St. Clement's parish, the bishop asked them to move to St. Mary Magdalene's, Manningham, to make a contribution to community relations work there. These and other Christian workers helped to forestall some of the problems that could have arisen, and their activities were taken up, increased and improved, with the benefit of experience, through the ensuing decades. This was work which the new bishop greatly appreciated.

Like Bishop Hook, Geoffrey Paul had experience of wartime service with the Royal Navy, using his linguistic gifts to serve as a liaison officer in French ships under British operational command. With first class honours in Modern Languages and Theology, there were those who predicted an academic career after the war, but he turned instead to the mission field and was in India for fifteen years, much of that time as Principal of Kerala United Theological Seminary at Kannamoola. It was only the illness of a daughter that brought Geoffrey and Pamela Paul and their family back to England, where for five years he was a Canon of Bristol Cathedral and director of ordinands.

In 1971 he became Warden of Lee Abbey, a surprising decision to some of his friends, since the community was regarded as strongly evangelical and Geoffrey Paul was originally of a moderate catholic background. Churchmanship

Archdeacons David Rogers and Frank Sargeant, Bishop Geoffrey and Mrs. Pamela Paul and Provost Brandon Jackson

however, mattered little to him. His priorities were to lead and educate within the context of a Christian community. Dr. Rowan Williams (now Bishop of Monmouth) wrote of those days: "Lee Abbey was not exactly the kind of religious community envisaged by Basil and Benedict, but Geoffrey had all the qualities the great monastic legislators looked for in a superior - the skill of adjusting to the varying needs of individuals, the sense of responsibility to God for those in his care, the willingness to exercise authority for the sake of the whole group. He learned a lot about being a father-in-God here that he had not learned even in India and in Bristol, and his teaching skills had their greatest testing and polishing."

He was appointed Suffragan Bishop of Hull in 1977, succeeding Hubert Higgs, and it was here that his outstanding series of public lectures was given. When a Bible Society survey of religious practice in the United Kingdom designated Humberside a 'Christian blackspot', Bishop Paul determined to take his teaching to a wider public. In Lent 1981, he hired Hull City Hall for six weekly addresses, and filled it week after week with up to 1,200 people. The chairmen he invited were carefully chosen to represent a wide cross-section of the community, emphasising that these expositions of the faith were for all. Later, when Geoffrey Paul was Bishop of Bradford, the BBC invited him to give a shortened version of the course, first on the World Service, then on Radio 4.

At his enthronement in Bradford Cathedral, he began with a deceptively simple statement: "As I see it, being a Christian is a matter of believing, belonging and behaving." Then he went on, in a powerful, deep and clear sermon, in unmistakable Geoffrey Paul style, to spell out the commitment, cost and sheer hard work of Christian profession; of that commitment, he said, "There is no way of belonging to Christ except by belonging, gladly and irrevocably to all that marvellous and extraordinary ragbag of saints and fatheads who make up the one holy, catholic and apostolic Church."

The enthronement sermon and others, and the Hull lectures, are available as a book, "The Pattern of Faith", with an introductory memoir by Dr. Williams.

So that as many church people as possible could meet the bishop, deanery days were arranged soon after the enthronement, a system continued by his successors, when the bishop spent the whole day in a deanery, seeing clergy and other key workers during the day, with a service and reception for representatives of all the parishes in the evening. After one of these, a parish representative went home with the comment, "We're going to know we've got a bishop!"

Some undoubtedly found his style more authoritarian than they had been used to, and some significant changes were made to the diocesan structures of boards and committees, after not very widespread consultation and discussion. On other issues, he did listen to a range of points of view, though this was as likely to be by inviting small groups of people with specific interests and expertise to Bishopscroft as by working through more recognisable routes. Often he spoke and acted with a sense of urgency, and it is tempting in retrospect to see a man who knew he was in a hurry.

Bishop and Mrs. Paul were wonderfully hospitable, and regarded their home as the appropriate venue for all sorts of gatherings, in a manner reminiscent of those other former servants of the Church in India, Alex and Ruth Hardy. Bishop's Council, the standing committee of the diocesan synod, began to meet there, with Evensong in the chapel followed by supper, then down to work over the coffee cups. The family's own lifestyle was very simple, but they loved entertaining and providing good food for their guests, and if Pamela occasionally suggested, on a particularly busy day, that she might provide fruit and cheese for dessert, Geoffrey would be sure to say, "I think they might like a nice pudding."

The bishop drove himself around the diocese, and Mrs Paul went with him whenever possible, giving them extra time to talk and be together in their busy lives. In addition to his programme, his wife accepted every possible engagement to open fairs and speak at events, to increase the opportunities for getting to know people. They even considered taking a caravan on tour to the northern end of the diocese for a few weeks at a time.

The parish of Arncliffe with Halton Gill was at this time part of Canon Maurice Slaughter's charge, as Rural Dean of Skipton, but the bishop's first visit, to a service to mark the centenary of the Revd. W.A. Shuffrey's ministry in the dale, was at the invitation of the "unofficial curate of Littondale". Mr Shuffrey's son was to speak at the service and Bishop Paul's role was "to give a benevolent beam and blessing."

The invitation to beam and bless came from one of the most distinguished scholars to have made a contribution to the life of the Church in Bradford Diocese, the Rt. Revd. John A.T. Robinson, Dean of Trinity College, Cambridge, and former Bishop of Woolwich, author of an impressive number and range of books. The publisher's note on the cover of Eric James' biography of John Robinson tells of "the extraordinary success of his best-selling 'Honest to God': sold out on publication, with sales of over a million, its revolutionary though totally committed view of God helped to change the thinking of a generation." John and Ruth Robinson had bought a house in Arncliffe in 1980, to be their home, in which John would spend as much time as his Cambridge appointment would allow, with the hope of eventual retirement there. They had come to love the limestone dales country during a tour of Trinity livings, of which Bradford Diocese had two - Guiseley with Esholt and Sedbergh, Cautley and Garsdale, with some of the loveliest countryside in the north of England between them.

Bishop Geoffrey Paul delighted in the friendship and stimulating company of the Robinsons and asked John to exercise a part-time ministry as Assistant Bishop of Bradford. Bishop Robinson was not quite the pastor the conservative congregations of the quiet dales had been used to, but he took his local duties as seriously as any other aspect of his life's work, visited conscientiously and tried hard to learn about country ways. A Watch Night Service on the theme of peace, after the Falklands War, was probably his most signal failure to speak on the same wavelength as his hearers, but his ministry, with Ruth, to two young cancer sufferers and their families, in Arncliffe and Linton in Craven, brought real and lasting appreciation.

Bishop Paul, like so many incoming bishops, took a hard look at the state of diocesan finance. He found a degree of order and sense of responsibility that he appreciated, but an actual level of income that was no more than enough for a holding operation. He was concerned that at both diocesan and parish level there should be a much greater sense of moving forward, of furthering the Church's prime task of bringing the Good News to all the world, and a greater impact upon society. The campaign he launched bore the title "Budgets for Opportunity". The object was that church communities, particularly at 'grass roots' parish level, should have clearly defined aims. Rather than a parish programme being determined by what could be afforded, the work should be decided first, followed by whatever financial commitment was needed to carry it out.

An early item of unfinished business from Bishop Hook's episcopate was embraced with great enthusiasm by Geoffrey Paul, and that was the establishment of a third partner diocese. Bishop Heath Light of Southwestern Virginia had met the Archbishop of Sudan and was keen to link with the Episcopal Church of that country. Bradford's overseas group were happy with that suggestion until it was discovered that Salisbury Diocese already had such a link. The Rt. Revd. Simon Barrington-Ward, former General Secretary of the Church Missionary Society, suggested that, rather than duplicating Salisbury's contacts, Bradford might like to link, not with the whole Anglican Province of Sudan, but with Omdurman Diocese (later known as Khartoum Diocese), the only diocese in the mainly Islamic north of the country, rather isolated by distance from its own Provincial Headquarters in southern Sudan as well as from the rest of the Anglican Communion.

It has not been an easy partnership, with language difficulties, and political constraints on exchange visits, but has nevertheless proved very much worthwhile, with many lessons to be learned, for example about spiritual liveliness, giving and receiving, relative definitions of hardship, perceptions and misconceptions about people of another race. Those visits that have taken place have been of great value, with Christians in Khartoum appreciative of Bradford's material help, but above all of the prayers and caring.

In 1986, a young Sudanese priest, the Revd. Sylvester Thomas Kambaya, came to Bradford to live and work as a member of the cathedral staff for nine months as part of his training. It was intended that he would become chaplain to the English-speaking expatriate community in Khartoum, based at the cathedral there. Internal problems in Sudan led to the closure of Khartoum Cathedral for several years and Sylvester was not at first able to exercise this ministry as planned. After a short time back in Sudan he went to America for a year's further theological study at the Virginia Seminary. Here he met Christians from the Diocese of Southwestern Virginia, bringing the three-way nature of the partnership to life, before returning to put his further education to use in the Episcopal Church of Sudan. It was not until November 1992 that the cathedral re-opened and services, including those in English, resumed.

Sylvester was not the first African priest to join the staff of Bradford Cathedral. In December 1946 and January 1947 the Revd. Canon Adelukun Williamson Fowell Olumide Howells, of Lagos Cathedral, became a temporary member of the Bradford team. Provost Tiarks declared, "The Church has a very definite word to say about the colour bar. For an English congregation to hear the Word of God from the lips of an African and to receive the sacrament at the hands of an African will demonstrate in Bradford that we mean exactly what we say about the iniquity of the colour bar." Canon Howells became Bishop of Lagos in 1955. In 1959, the Revd. Canon Erica Sabiti was seconded to Bishop Coggan for a time, before being consecrated as suffragan bishop in Uganda. Later he was elected Metropolitan of the Province of Uganda, Rwanda and Burundi.

These Christian links serve to remind Christians that they are part of a world-wide Communion that is in turn part of a universal Church. Partnership enables knowledge to be developed in a meaningful way, beyond the level of a geography lesson or a tourist experience, and in a sense, each partner is thus to the others a token of the whole wide world. Support of traditional missionary societies and interdenominational contacts with Christians in Europe, whether specifically church-generated or through secular twinning schemes, form other strands of this universality.

A very different project, which had been under way for twelve months before

Way of the Cross — Jesus before Herod

Bishop Paul's arrival, also elicited his keen support. A small group of Christians from all the main denominations were working, under the chairmanship of Canon Ted Roberts of Bradford Cathedral, on a dramatic presentation of the events of the Passion, to be enacted in the streets of Bradford on Good Friday, April 9th 1982.

The Way of the Cross was not planned simply as a pageant, or even a religious drama like the various Mystery Plays, but as an act of worship and witness to the relevance of the death and resurrection of Jesus, in and for the city of Bradford in the twentieth century. Historical as well as practical considerations determined the choice of sites used, and although the idea was based on productions Canon Roberts had known in his previous parish in Stepney, the script and route were prepared specifically for Bradford. Civic authorities, police and the electricity board all co-operated with the organising group, and companies and individuals were generous with donations of money, material for costumes, props and expertise.

Of the two hundred performers involved, only the Revd. Arthur Wilson, Vicar of St. Clement's and a member of the steering committee, had any professional theatrical experience - he played Herod, whose palace was sited on the steps of City Hall. St. Sitha's Christian centre and coffee shop, opened in 1981 in Ivegate, had a large upstairs room which became the rehearsal centre. Ivegate itself, site of Bradford's Hall of Pleas in medieval times, and the dungeon where John Wesley's friend John Nelson was imprisoned for preaching in 1744, became the Via Dolorosa. Some authorities also believe it to be on the line of an old Roman way from the iron workings at Bierley out towards Elslack. Most of the set-piece scenes took place outside the Law Courts, Provincial House and City Hall, with theology student Andy Davey as Christ, taking his last steps to the crucifixion site near the old Exchange railway station along the road that used to be called Goodman's End.

"Call to Worship" was a regular feature in the Telegraph and Argus on Saturdays, and on April 3rd 1982, Canon Roberts wrote of the coming event, concluding: "Perhaps the portrayal of this redemptive act in the centre of our city, using its main buildings - Provincial House, the City Hall and its streets - as stages, will bring home to us all, and into the heart of the city, the meaning of that redemption. The last few years have not been happy ones for Bradford. Violence, conflict, murder and economic decline have all left a mark on the city. Violence, conflict and murder are also at the heart of the story of the Cross, but the death of Christ is the seed of hope; it is a seed which could be planted in the lives of many people in Bradford next Friday evening."

At 7 pm on Good Friday, the drama began with Bishop Paul's prayer for grace to "help us walk beside this Prisoner and turn weakness and shame into blessing", and in the pelting rain an estimated 8,000 people did indeed walk the streets alongside the Prisoner and, three hours later, joined in the great climax as the resurrection hope was portrayed in light and music and voices in over a score of languages, all recorded among Bradford's population, proclaiming the empty tomb -"He is not there, He is alive!"

Early in 1983 Bishop Paul appeared tired and unwell, and plans were made for him to go into hospital for the removal of a small growth, although he insisted it should be delayed until after he had preached the University Sermon in Cambridge in late May. He also produced a statement, featured in the Bradford Telegraph and Argus, concerning the forthcoming parliamentary election, not telling anyone who to vote for, but what questions to ask and what policies were compatible with Christian beliefs. Dr. Williams describes it as "a fine and forthright piece, not designed to give much comfort to the government of the day." He challenged the acceptance of mass unemployment and of standards only concerned with self-concern and self-improvement.

The operation, in June, was successful, the growth non-malignant, and it was a bitter irony that the patient contracted a post-operative infection which resisted all attempts at treatment. The Pauls had only been in Bradford for two years, but those who got to know them learned to love and respect them, and it was with a numbing sense of bereavement that the diocese learned of the death of its father-in-God on July 10th 1983.

John Robinson by this time knew of the seriousness of his own illness, and in a tribute to Geoffrey Paul in the September Bradford Diocesan News, he wrote:

> "I last met Geoffrey on Whit Sunday, when I sat under him preaching the University Sermon at Cambridge, since reproduced in the Bradford Diocesan News. As I had no idea he was already under the doctors, or that I was threatened with anything serious, we did not talk about ourselves but about his excellent sermon. Only a week or two later I learned about his first operation, and wrote to tell him that I too had to go into hospital. Characteristically, he wrote back a marvellous letter, in which he said: 'You are quite right. Sometime the four of us must sit down and really share the deep spiritualities of this experience. Meanwhile, I pray that all the sort of things that God means when you are faced with nothing but God may come home to you in real joy and triumph. I hope that we shall have the opportunity for a good, long conversation as soon as I am restored.' Alas, it was never to be; and I have never felt more keenly that there but for the grace of God go I, especially as his trouble, unlike mine, was benign. When we came to make our home in the dales I had no idea what diocese I should find myself in. Imagine my delight when, shortly afterwards, I heard that my old friend, Geoffrey Paul, was to be appointed Bishop of Bradford, and I immediately offered to do what I could as assistant bishop when I was not tied up being Dean of Trinity College. It was a personal privilege too having a diocesan with whom one could discuss New Testament scholarship, especially since he had written in South India a commentary on St. John's Gospel, the subject on which I have been working for the Bampton Lectures at Oxford next year. I only wish we had been able to see more of each other, but whenever his car drew up, usually unannounced, outside our house, I knew I was in for a session with a man whom it made you feel better simply to be with, for however short a time. He was an affectionate, amusing, great-hearted and deeply encouraging saint."

John Robinson's final act for Bradford Diocese was to take a confirmation in Bolton Priory Church. In his sermon he referred to his imminent death, and then he said, "All I've ever tried to do in my ministry is to extend the frontiers of Christian thinking. I've never doubted the essential heart of the Gospel." He died at home in Arncliffe on December 5th.

A simple slab in the floor of the south ambulatory of the cathedral marks the grave of Geoffrey Paul, the only Bishop of Bradford to die in office. Thirty five miles away, in a country churchyard beside the river Skirfare, an equally simple piece of limestone rock from a nearby hillside bears the inscription "John Arthur Thomas Robinson. Born 15 June 1919. Died 5 December 1983."

It is a remarkable thing that this little, unlikely, north-country diocese should have enjoyed the riches of two such men of vision and intellect at the same time, and almost unbelievable to have lost them both within a few short months.

CHAPTER 20

IN THE NEWS

So once again Bradford was without a bishop, and the archdeacons resumed the leadership role they had so recently laid down. This was no easy task. The post of administrative assistant to the bishop was not created until well into the next episcopate, and even straightforward secretarial help was barely adequate at this time.

While Bishop Paul was in hospital, Archdeacon Sargeant had been invited to move to Chester Diocese as Suffragan Bishop of Stockport. His inclination was to refuse, in the circumstances, but the bishop, who confidently expected soon to be back at work, urged him to accept, and so in early January 1984, Frank Sargeant left Bradford. Among gifts from various groups throughout the diocese was a cope made from fine wool cloth produced in Bradford, which the Telegraph and Argus claimed, slightly surprisingly, was the first all-wool cope to be worn by a bishop in England.

Bishop Paul's alterations to diocesan structures had brought many strands of work together under two big boards, and he had appointed an executive officer for each. Canon Christopher Hayward, whom the bishop had known in his Lee Abbey days, came to the Board of Mission and Social Responsibility, and Canon Martin Wharton to the Board of Ministry and Training. These officers, with the one remaining archdeacon, tried to operate the new structures and to promote Budgets for Opportunity in a diocese in which bereavement and bewilderment were the dominating emotions, together with a certain amount of irritation at imperfectly understood concepts that simply did not take off when deprived of the vision of their initiator.

Into this unhappy situation there came, like a breath of fresh air, a small Irishman with wavy hair and square-rimmed glasses. The press made much of the notion of Robert Kerr Williamson as "the people's bishop", although Bradford has

Bishop Robert Williamson and his wife Anne

never had a bishop who was anything else, albeit each in his own style and in the context of his time. But it is easy to see why Robert Williamson's background caught the imagination. The youngest of fourteen children of a Belfast ship yard worker, he left school at fourteen, and only later set out and obtained the necessary qualifications to enter theological college. His earliest Christian ministry was as a lay worker in some of the toughest parts of London and later he was vicar of inner city parishes in Nottingham before moving to Bramcote, and shortly after that, in 1979, becoming Archdeacon of Nottingham.

No one could long remain in ignorance of the new bishop's Celtic roots, with his accent and a sense of humour that led a child to write, after an episcopal visit to a school, "If our bishop is ever out of a job, he can get a job as a stand up comic." The BBC was not long in discovering him, and he became a frequent broadcaster, though not primarily as a comedian! He was often on Radio 2's 'Pause for Thought', giving a clear cut Christian message, not esoteric, not pious, and yes, often with humour, and always relevant to the day to day life of 'ordinary' people. In January 1993, by this time Bishop of Southwark, he was appointed Chairman of the Central Religious Advisory Committee, which advises the BBC and the Independent Television Commission on religious matters.

'St. Patrick's Breastplate' was sung at his consecration in York Minster, and the hymn 'Be thou my vision', to the lovely Irish tune 'Slane', at his enthronement in Bradford Cathedral on 14 April 1984. Again there were representatives of other faiths as well as other Christian denominations, and representatives of the partner dioceses. Bishop Heath Light of Southwestern Virginia was represented by the Revd. Robert Thacker from Lynchburg and there were a number of Virginian lay people in the congregation. For Khartoum, the Revd. Butrus Kowa Kori, later to be Area Bishop for Port Sudan, was present, and Bishop Butrus Tia Shukai was represented by the Rt. Revd. Oliver Allison, last expatriate Bishop of Sudan before it became an autonomous province of the Anglican Communion in 1976. As well as the more usual Mayors, Chairmen and Lords Lieutenant, the service was attended by the much more exciting-sounding Sheriff of Nottingham.

Sensitive to the love and respect his predecessor had engendered, and the feelings of loss that still prevailed, the new bishop intended a low-key approach and a very gradual introduction of his own style, but a number of circumstances conspired to thrust him into the public eye.

The first, most dramatic and most tragic event was the fire at Bradford's Valley Parade football ground in May 1985, in which 56 people died. Bradford City had just won promotion to the Second Division of the Football League and the fire was all the more horrendous in contrast to the jubilant atmosphere with which the afternoon had started. Bradford's emergency services and countless numbers of individuals responded wonderfully and selflessly to the needs of that day, and the Church added its own much needed dimension.

No effective ecumenical network then existed and the Bishop of Bradford was the only leader of a Christian denomination actually to live in Bradford. In a situation like this, an immediate response was needed, and Bishop Williamson and Provost Jackson took the decision to make the cathedral a focal point for the city's shock and pain. An announcement was made on local radio on Sunday morning, and at 3 pm, just 24 hours after kick-off, the cathedral was filled to overflowing, the altar and chancel steps covered with flowers, rosettes and Bradford City scarves. Stafford Heginbotham, chairman of the football club, was invited to read a Bible passage, but was too overcome and his place was taken by the former chief executive of Bradford, Gordon Moore. The bishop preached and the cathedral was left open for a stream of people, mostly young, to come in and write in the fire disaster book provided, or just to kneel in silent grief. Cathedral clergy were present all day to comfort and pray with many of those who came. The eyes of national and international media were on Bradford that weekend, with CBS News, and Kate Adie for the BBC, and a spotlight was turned on the 7th Bishop of Bradford.

Just over a year later, when the Valley Parade ground was ready to be re-opened, bishop and provost were again instrumental in arranging for a memorial service to be held there. This time there was time to plan, and the event had ecumenical and inter-faith dimensions. Bradford's Asian community, many of whom had been foremost among the helpers on the day of the fire, wanted to be associated with the memorial and Bishop Williamson, with his community relations chaplain Peter Hawkins, the provost and Roman Catholic and Free Church representatives, went to great lengths to produce a service that would be acceptable to all, without compromising its essentially Christian nature.

The growing importance of inter-faith issues in all but the outer fringes of Bradford Metropolitan District was the second major factor bringing the bishop into the realm of community activity. Asian, and more specifically Muslim, affairs first came into general prominence in Bradford with the halal meat controversy in 1982-3, and again with what became known as the Honeyford affair, when a Bradford headteacher challenged the growth of multi-culturalism in his school which had a high proportion of Muslim children.

It became clear that if church leaders were to respond meaningfully to these sorts of issues, they must be properly informed. Bishop Williamson found Peter Hawkins immensely helpful, but he was by this time Vicar of Allerton, and others with some expertise like the Revd. Colin Judd and the Revd. Bill Holliday, were working hard in their own areas. There was now a need for more work than could be carried out by part time chaplains with parish duties.

Philip Lewis had spent six years in Pakistan at an ecumenical Christian Study Centre devoted to research and resource Christian-Muslim relations. He came as a full time lay chaplain and he and his family lived in the predominantly Asian district of Manningham. Later, Bishop Williamson felt this work merited a much higher profile, and created for him the senior diocesan post of Bishop's Adviser on Inter-Faith Issues.

In 1992 Philip Lewis was honoured to be asked to deliver the Eighth Lambeth Inter-Faith Lecture at Lambeth Palace which he entitled 'Beyond Babel: an Anglican Perspective on Bradford'. This was an acknowledgement of the

Clockwise: Bishop Williamson with Govinder Dhaliwal, Sher Azam, Counc. Mohammed Ajeeb, Fazlul Haq, Philip Lewis and Mohammed Naeem

contribution made by the Diocese of Bradford to the national debates and issues generated by Faith communities living side by side.

Another interesting appointment to Manningham came in the middle of 1992 when the Revd. Geoffrey Peters became Team Vicar. Mr. Peters was the first Pakistani Church of England clergyman to be ordained in England. A former member of the diplomatic service, and fluent in ten languages, he said on his appointment, "I see my main role as acting as a bridge between my faith and different religions. I know Manningham has many Pakistanis living there but it is also a multi-cultural community. It is a place where a pastor priest would be an example for different faiths and different communities. I hope to work as a pastor, as a community leader. I see myself as a helpline for every nationality and faith."

Philip Lewis's role has been a vital one in enabling the bishop to work as a bridge-builder, representing both the host community to the Asian leaders, and the Asian community to the host community and local authority officials. Bradford's civic leaders were, on the whole, still demonstrating that forward-looking acceptance that had for so long been a hallmark of Bradford's attitude to immigrants, and in 1985 Councillor Mohammed Ajeeb became Bradford's first Muslim Lord Mayor. It is interesting to note that Bradford's first Jewish Mayor was Charles Semon in 1864, and the first Jewish Lord Mayor after city status was conferred, was Jacob Moser in 1910, several decades before neighbouring Leeds, with its strong Jewish community, made such an appointment.

There were still tests ahead, and it is likely that Bishop Williamson's bridge building work saved Bradford from the worst of the disturbances some other multi-racial areas have suffered. Even the potentially explosive incident when Salman Rushdie's 'Satanic Verses' was publicly burnt in Bradford provoked less reaction and counter-reaction than might have been. ("The Satanic Verses: Bradford Responds", a collection of essays edited by David G. Bowen and produced by Bradford and Ilkley Community College, is helpful to anyone seeking to understand this issue. It includes essays by Philip Lewis and Dr. Neal Robinson, former chaplain to the students at Bradford University). Simon Lee and Peter Stanford, in their book "Believing Bishops" published in 1990, pay tribute to the Bishop of Bradford, contrasting his actions with the picture the media expected to find of "Anglican bishops sitting on the nearest available fence with their gaitered legs dangling on either side." They outline the actions he took in urging both sides to examine their consciences, and conclude, "Bishop Williamson did at least try to bring the communities together, as a reconciler or pastor. His example, of action on the ground, is worth a dozen abstract reports. If we are to believe bishops when they seek to inform our consciences, they must show us that informed consciences lead to more Christ-like behaviour. They can only do that through the witness of their lives."

The bishop's fairness and genuineness were so much appreciated by the Asian communities that some of their leaders began to refer to him as "our bishop". His unequivocal stance on his own Christian faith was an essential part of earning their respect, but he sometimes found it harder to have his actions accepted by some of his own church people. There were those in areas unaffected by the problems who could not see why their bishop was involving himself in what they saw as purely political matters. Interestingly, this attitude did not come from the furthest rural depths of the diocese, where he received sympathy and an understanding that he needed to be involved, even if the issues themselves were imperfectly understood.

In December 1985, the report commissioned by the General Synod of the Church of England, "Faith in the City", was published. Much of its content came as no surprise in Bradford, since an extensive study within the diocese had already been carried out by a group set up by the diocesan pastoral committee, and a report published early in 1984 identifying urban areas of particular need (Urban Priority Areas), and beginning to formulate a strategy for supporting the work of the church in these areas.

Thanks to national publicity generated by "Faith in the City" and the government's prickly reaction to it, Bradford became an immediate beneficiary in two interesting ways. Firstly, the Mothers' Union Central Council decided to fund some community work in urban dioceses, and in 1987 they provided the salary for Mrs. Elaine Appelbee to work part-time as a community development worker in the Little Horton team. This was an informal arrangement between the parishes concerned, which was set up in line with the pastoral committee's recommendation for the development of collaborative rather than lone ministries in difficult inner city areas. Mrs. Appelbee's work was concerned with creating a sense of community where little or none existed, by helping local people to become more confident, more self-reliant and able to do something for themselves about their quality of life .

A celebration at the Hutson Street project

It is not, by its nature, rapid or spectacular work, but one project did take off so well that it became one of the 'flagships' used by the national Church Urban Fund in its publicity. This was the Hutson Street project, in which the local authority and the church co-operated to convert a disused launderette into a thriving community centre, in which a playgroup, craft group and tenants' association are among a range of activities to have developed. Once under way, the project attracted further funding from trusts and national government so that it could expand. The rural parish of Bolton Abbey has also contributed to the running costs as part of its response to the needs of the diocesan family as a whole. Other rural or suburban parishes have involved themselves in other ways with UPA projects.

Secondly, two parishes in the south of England sent money to the Bishop of Bradford to assist in urban work in the diocese, with the expressed hope that it would be used for people and not for buildings. The bishop decided this would best be used in a way which would help a large number of parishes, rather than just one or two, and Mr. Jim Heaton was appointed to work three days a week as Urban Officer. One aspect of his job not anticipated even in the wide job description he was given, was the use of urban Bradford as a resource for church groups in other parts of England wanting to learn more about UPA problems. Truro Diocese in particular sent a team to Bradford and hosted a return visit. This led to holidays in Cornwall for some of Bradford's less privileged children, as well as helping Truro to identify and respond to some of its internal needs.

Mrs. Appelbee later became Bishop's Officer for the Church in Society, a full-time role in which the Urban Officer's brief was incorporated.

Following on the publication of "Faith in the City", the Archbishop of Canterbury launched the Church Urban Fund in April 1988. Target figures were produced for each diocese to raise, ranging from £50,000 for Sodor and Man to £1,500,000 for Oxford, Bradford's being a relatively modest £200,000. UPA parishes could apply for grants from the fund, and Bradford has been a recipient, not only for Hutson Street, but a whole range of other work, including provision of a Church Army evangelist to live on the Ravenscliffe housing estate in north Bradford and work there with an ecumenical group, and youth workers for Holme Wood and Thornbury.

At the same time, the bishop was aware of the need for money actually to be spent on church buildings, again mostly in the city areas where the Victorian buildings were even less suitable for local needs in the 1990s than they had been at the time of Bishop Coggan's survey. One, St. Augustine's in Otley Road, had been brilliantly re-ordered, with the old building partially demolished. At the west end, the porch and tower remain; at the east, the chancel is open to the sky, providing a quiet garden, and a mixture of old and new building houses meeting rooms, coffee shop and an exciting new church. St. Columba's, Great Horton, had undergone a slightly less radical change, with no demolition, but the interior divided into a full-scale restaurant, rooms for all manner of community activity and a worship area for the very small Christian community

St. Augustine's Otley Road, Bradford during reconstruction

now living in that part of Bradford. The church there, under Colin Judd's leadership, developed a range of outreach appropriate to the local situation, with playgroups, literacy work, a luncheon club and shopping trips by minibus for the elderly.

Because it was clear that some of the other older churches were becoming a real burden to the poorer parishes, the Diocese of Bradford Church Building Appeal was launched, and the hope was that this would bring in enough to meet Bradford's obligation to the Church Urban Fund as well as money to help with building repairs and alterations. The outcome of this appeal could only be described as disappointing. There was confusion between this and the nationally publicised CUF, there were international appeals for victims of famine, war and natural disasters, and in an extraordinary re-run of Bradford diocesan history, Provost Jackson's appeal for a major re-ordering of the cathedral had the same effect as Provost Tiarks' cathedral appeal had had on Bishop Blunt's 'Forward Movement'.

The re-ordering of the cathedral was concerned with making a better use of the interior space, and although the plans were inevitably controversial, particularly when it came to removing all the pews and the nave organ designed by Sir Edward Maufe, which had dominated the west end, the result was accepted by most people as a success. The rows of upholstered chairs are dignified, comfortable, and above all versatile, and being lower and lighter than the pews, give an impression of greater spaciousness. A small kitchen with serving hatch, discreetly incorporated, and the opened-up west crossing have made it possible for refreshments to be served and people to mix informally after services, lectures and concerts.

Bradford's contribution to the Archbishop's fund was embarrassingly low in the first year, and when it was plain that the Building Appeal was not going to provide the solution, the bishop, members of the appeal committee and trustees took the decision to bring it to a close. A new initiative was launched under the title 'Committed to Caring', and this was clearly presented as being first of all to fulfil Bradford's contribution to the Church Urban Fund, and then to raise as much again for use within the diocese in a variety of ways including rural work and other needs which did not qualify for CUF grants. In launching 'Committed to Caring', the bishop stressed that the work should be underpinned by prayer and a proper thanksgiving for all we had and had received as a diocese. The £200,000 was raised on target and Bradford's obligation fulfilled, and at the time of writing, the second half is still coming in.

In the late 1980s, finance was not only a problem for the church. Nationally, recession was beginning to bite, and locally Bradford Metropolitan District Council announced a package of spending cuts. Parish clergy were foremost among those who appreciated the potential harm to those least able to fend for themselves, and some were prepared to take part in demonstrations and to provide a voice for the voiceless. The church leaders listened to their men and women on the spot and looked carefully at the proposals. The Bishop of Bradford met with the Leader of the Council, Councillor Eric Pickles, and his Deputy, and a joint statement was issued by the bishop and the leaders of the Roman Catholics, Methodists, Baptists, United Reformed Church and Salvation Army. The statement backed local actions already taken by clergy, and warned: "We wish to make it quite clear that we have no desire to see the Church leading any kind of organised opposition to the elected Council. We believe though, that it is a legitimate function of the Church to ask questions, and this we have endeavoured to do, and will continue to do." The full text of the statement is to be found in Appendix III.

Early in his episcopate, Bishop Williamson had realised he was to be the target of a good deal of media attention. It was partly because pronouncements, both theological and political, by the new Bishop of Durham, the Right Revd. David Jenkins, had suddenly made bishops in general more newsworthy, and partly that events were unfolding in Bradford itself that called for an on-the-spot response from the only church leader immediately available. With this in mind, the bishop appointed as his press officer, the Revd. Robert Marshall, Curate of Otley and later to become Priest-in-Charge of Embsay with Eastby and Diocesan Communications Officer. In addition to his work for the bishop, Robert Marshall was responsible for the introduction of a diocesan newspaper, 'Newsround', first intended as a 'one off' to share news from one end of the diocese to the other in more depth than the monthly 'Bradford Diocesan News' which includes the bishop's letter and is used as an insert in most parish magazines. 'Newsround', with its tabloid format, good photographs and generally lively appearance, was so well received that it has become a regular publication and the envy of many another diocese. Its creator was later enticed to a similar post in London, but the good work he started in Bradford carries on.

Chapter 21

Desormais

An early appointment when Bishop Williamson arrived was of the Vicar of Eccleshill and Rural Dean of Calverley, Canon David Herbert Shreeve, as Archdeacon of Bradford. David Shreeve's first curacy had been at that same St. Andrew's, Plymouth, which had already provided Bradford with a bishop, provost and cathedral organist. David Hennessey's successor as diocesan secretary, Ray Anderton, was on the point of moving to become diocesan secretary of Gloucester, and Archdeacon Rogers' retirement was less than two years away. Feeling he ought to get to know his diocese better before the need to make new appointments arose, the bishop embarked on an early primary visitation, spending time in every parish. This incidentally fulfilled Bishop Paul's intention that there should be just such a visitation, forestalled by his illness. In the twelve months from October 1985, Bishop Williamson travelled 27,500 miles within the diocese, interviewed 155 clergy and lay-workers and 400 churchwardens and studied the returns from his comprehensive Articles of Enquiry. His conclusions and hopes for the future were published as a Primary Visitation Charge to the Clergy and Laity of the Diocese, full of detail for consideration and action by individuals and groups throughout the diocese, and with a strong underlying theology of mission.

The bishop followed this marathon undertaking with a visit to every church school in the diocese, spending half a day in each, affirming the work of the teachers and talking to the children, often having lunch with them, sometimes meeting parents who might be invited to the morning assembly on these occasions. He was on the whole impressed with what he found, and particularly the sensitive way in which assemblies and religious education were handled in multi-faith situations. The bishop did not believe schools were an appropriate place for proselytising, but was equally clear that their Christian foundation should not be played down. This programme of visits culminated in one of the happiest events of the episcopacy - a huge party at Bolton Abbey for all the children.

Part way through this round of visits, while attending a meeting of General Synod in London in February 1987, Bishop Williamson suffered a serious heart attack, which kept him out of action for several months, and added new urgency to discussions that were already going on in the diocese about the need for more assistance for the bishop. By this time there was no chaplain, but Bishopscroft had an excellent secretarial staff and the diocesan office was headed by Malcolm

Archdeacon Shreeve and Rev. Robin Gamble inside the completed St. Augustine's

Halliday as diocesan secretary, with Alex McLelland as assistant. It was at a very senior level, directly relating to the work of the bishop, that help seemed to be needed, particularly when the bishop was away at General Synod or one of its committees (he chaired that on stewardship), or attending the House of Lords.

The feeling among senior staff and bishop's council was that a personal assistant to the Bishop of Bradford was needed irrespective of the bishop's state of health, and that some episcopal assistance was also desirable, and so the Revd. Malcolm Goldsmith, an old colleague from Nottingham, was appointed as Personal Executive Assistant, with an office in Bishopscroft. Episcopal assistance was provided in 1988 when the Rt. Revd. David Richard John Evans returned to England after ten years as Bishop of Peru, and was licensed as the first full-time Assistant Bishop of Bradford. He lived in Shipley, to be convenient for Bishopscroft and to avoid any suggestion of his being an area bishop for a particular part of the diocese.

Bishop Evans' role has included conducting many confirmation services, presiding at various meetings in Bishop Williamson's absence, and heading

Bishop David Evans at an International Year service in St. Paul's Shipley

specific pieces of work, such as the diocese's response to the Decade of Evangelism proclaimed at the 1988 Lambeth Conference. Mrs. Dorothy Evans brought great practical experience and wisdom to many aspects of Bradford's involvement with the Church overseas.

Bradford again took the opportunity Lambeth provided, of inviting overseas bishops into the diocese. A day arranged at Bolton Abbey gave people from all over the diocese chance to meet and listen to bishops from Australia, Egypt, Tanzania and Sudan, including the new Bishop of Khartoum, the Rt. Revd. Bulus Idris Tia. Next day, the Archbishop of Capetown, the Most Revd. Desmond Tutu, preached at St. Margaret's, Ilkley, and at Bradford Cathedral, and addressed a huge crowd in the Valley Parade stadium.

Two other changes in senior clergy posts took place during Bishop Williamson's time. In 1986, Archdeacon Rogers retired and was created Archdeacon Emeritus. He and Mrs. Rogers moved from the house provided for the Archdeacons of Craven at Long Preston to Leck, at the most northern tip of Blackburn Diocese, sandwiched between the dioceses of Carlisle and Bradford but still more than ten miles south of his former parish of Sedbergh.

The new Archdeacon of Craven, the Ven. Brian Arthur Smith, though a Scot in origin, came to Bradford from Wakefield Diocese where he had been director of training, and before that, a senior tutor at Cuddeston Theological College. As might be expected from these previous roles, Archdeacon Smith brought aspects of teaching to his ministry in Bradford, including making theological

Archbishop Desmond Tutu at The Valley Parade ground

concepts accessible in his lectures to lay people. He had a keen intellectual wit and his discourses were entertaining as well as informative – with entertainment occasionally prevailing over information. A memorable slide presentation of his visit to Sudan began with the archdeacon arriving with everything he needed except the slides and continued, when this was remedied, with pictures shown with a blithe disregard for 'view from this side' or 'this way up'.

In fact a sometimes vague and bemused air masked a shrewd mind, and it was he who undertook for Bishop Williamson a thorough and searching review of the diocesan infrastructure of boards and committees. He interviewed leaders and members of the various groups, probing always for reasons behind procedures, so that nothing survived without justification, or simply because it had always been done that way. It was with regret as well as congratulations that the diocese said goodbye to Brian and Lissa Smith when the archdeacon was appointed Suffragan Bishop of Tonbridge in Rochester Diocese in 1993.

The next change was at the cathedral, where Brandon Jackson, instead of settling down to enjoy the peaceful progress that should have followed his early difficulties and the upheaval of re-ordering, accepted the position of Dean of Lincoln. Lincoln Cathedral had its own problems, rooted in its ancient constitution, and, among other things, a recent episode involving taking Lincoln's copy of Magna Carta to Australia which had resulted in a serious financial deficit. So Brandon and Mary Jackson left the Bradford stage, only to step into the glare of another spotlight; but that is another story.

The new Provost of Bradford, the Very Revd. John Stephen Richardson, had been one of Bishop Williamson's curates in the Southwell days, and came to Bradford from the Diocese of Bath and Wells where he was Vicar of Christ Church, Nailsea, and diocesan adviser on evangelism. He was installed in Bradford Cathedral on 31 March 1990. Within three years, he too was launching a financial appeal for the cathedral, primarily for urgent repairs to the walls, roof and tower. English Heritage promised £100,000, but for the bulk of the money needed, the provost appealed to the people of Bradford "to join us in working to preserve and restore one of Bradford's oldest buildings so that we, in our generation may be able to pass on our heritage of faith as a light of Christian witness to all who come and visit."

A stage in the rural pilgrimage

Although, specially in the early years of his episcopacy, Bradford-centred events generated so much publicity, Bishop Williamson was concerned to be seen as the bishop of the whole diocese, and to this end asked that in 1991 the whole diocese should focus its attention on rural issues, following the publication of the General Synod report "Faith in the Countryside". He personally undertook a 'rural pilgrimage', spending many weeks walking in the dales from parish to parish, often accompanied by groups of local people who would hand him on at their boundaries. All the churches he visited received a porch card with a message from the bishop and a picture of the wooden cross he wore, which had been specially made for his pilgrimage. He visited farms and local industries, spent time in people's homes, and generally tried to get the feel of a place before preaching in its church. He calculated that by the end of his episcopate, 60% of his time had been spent in the countryside, and certainly no previous Bishop of Bradford had become so well known in so many parts of his diocese.

This rural year was part of a five year plan first proposed by the bishop in his Primary Visitation Charge. He was feeling that his ministry, and to some extent diocesan policy, were being dominated by a series of almost disconnected responses to external events, and wanted to see an ongoing policy of looking in depth at a range of issues. Parishes were free to be involved in the year's theme to whatever extent they chose, and whatever way seemed appropriate locally, but the themes did succeed in directing the thoughts, prayer and work of much of the diocesan family towards the same objectives. The focal points for the five years were: 1990 urban, 1991 rural, 1992 overseas, 1993 youth and education, with 1994 as a year of thanksgiving as the 75th anniversary of the diocese was celebrated.

Bishop Williamson, however, was not destined to guide the diocese through the whole of the programme, and in July 1991 the announcement came that he was to be the next Bishop of Southwark. Roy and Anne Williamson were both happy and fulfilled in Bradford Diocese. Anne had found her role, not only in the more usual work with clergy wives and the Mothers' Union, but also as a magistrate, a regular helper at Manorlands, the Cheshire Home at Oxenhope, and with the church's ministry to the deaf. She had learned to sign and was often to be found assisting at the Deaf Centre (formerly known as the Deaf Institute) in Hallfield Road, Bradford, including helping to cook and serve their Christmas dinners.

The 'Deaf Church' is a chapel within the Deaf Centre. It was originally a Methodist chapel, used for Anglican worship in Bishop Blunt's time and licensed and dedicated to St James by Bishop Williamson after refurbishment. Although an Anglican place of worship, it functions ecumenically, with a Roman Catholic Mass held once a month. The diocese has provided many chaplains to the deaf, a role usually combined with parish work or hospital chaplaincy, or exercised as a retirement ministry. As well as conducting signed services, the work is largely pastoral, with much visiting to individual homes and hospitals. This is especially so in the Craven Archdeaconry where there is no specific 'Deaf Church' and the people are widely scattered. The Revd. Herbert Watkins, having retired to

Silsden, was licensed as chaplain for this part of the diocese in 1988. One of the best known of Bradford's workers in this field was Mr. Christmas James, Principal of the Deaf Institute, who was persuaded by the Revd. E.O. Williams at St. Jude's to take Holy Orders, was ordained in 1951, and for many years gave loyal service both to the Institute and the parish. The churchmanship at St. Jude's was such that this well loved priest was able to rejoice in the title of Father Christmas.

Bishop Williamson's opening paragraph in the Primary Visitation Charge reads: "I have already gone on record as stating that the Diocese of Bradford is one of the most beautiful in the Church of England and my travels during the past twelve months have served to confirm me in that viewpoint. At the same time it is one of the most friendly and interesting – containing a splendid balance between urban, suburban and rural society with all the attendant problems and privileges, challenges and opportunities presented by this rich diversity." He and Mrs. Williamson had assumed, and indeed hoped, that they were settled in Yorkshire for the rest of their lives.

For many people of the diocese, the loss of a bishop who had just completed his rural pilgrimage, and whose eight years seemed to have slipped by so fast, came as a blow, but turning down the call to serve in Southwark was never a serious option, as the bishop made clear in his farewell service in the cathedral on 30th November 1991. It was St. Andrew's day, and the collect for the day spoke of the saint's obedience to the Lord, and continued: "Give us, who are called by your holy Word, grace to follow without delay and to tell the good news of your kingdom." – a message not only to clergy moving on, but to all Christian people wherever they are called to live out their faith.

Malcolm Goldsmith's contract came to an end and the choice of another personal assistant was left for the next bishop to make. Bishop David Evans had been appointed for the duration of Bishop Williamson's episcopacy, which both men had expected to be for considerably longer than proved the case. Fortunately for the diocese, the Church Commissioners agreed that Bishop Evans should stay a little longer, to provide episcopal oversight during the vacancy and to give continuity in the first few months of the next episcopate. His kindly and familiar presence made for a very different transition period than the painful days of 1983, and must have also made life a good deal easier for the archdeacons. At Easter 1993 it was announced that he was to be General Secretary of the South American Missionary Society.

The new diocesan system of councils and committees, brought in just before Bishop Williamson left, but fortunately planned as an infrastructure which was independent of any one bishop's personal policies, had led to some new appointments and some moves within the diocese. Canon Hayward's job as executive secretary to the Board of Mission no longer existed and he left the cathedral to become Rector of Linton. He had taken a keen interest in the link with Khartoum and now became chairman of the diocesan group responsible

Bishop David Smith at his enthronement with Provost John Richardson

for this, in succession to Astrid Hansen. Joan Simms by this time chaired the corresponding body in respect of Southwestern Virginia.

Canon Wharton kept almost his previous brief, becoming Bishop's Officer for Ministry and Training, and moved to the vacant residentiary canonry. Unpacking at no. 2 Cathedral Close proved hardly worth the effort, since before the year was out, Martin Wharton was whisked off to become Suffragan Bishop of Kingston upon Thames in the Diocese of Southwark. This was no doubt a source of pleasure to Southwark's new diocesan bishop, but a disappointment to many in Bradford where many clergy had benefited from his oversight of post-ordination training. He was also very much involved, with the Revd. Paul Slater, in setting up a diocesan course for laity. This was designed to lead on to further vocational training, or equally for those who wanted to develop their own spiritual life and to understand more about the Church of England to which they belonged.

The name of the eighth Bishop of Bradford was announced in April 1992. The Rt. Revd. David James Smith, Suffragan Bishop of Maidstone, was ordained in the Diocese of Newcastle and spent more than twenty years as a parish priest in a wide variety of parishes there before becoming Archdeacon of Lindisfarne from 1981 to 1987.

He was enthroned in Bradford Cathedral on 26 September 1992 in the presence of the Bishops of Southwestern Virginia and Khartoum, representatives of the city, other Christian denominations and other faiths. There were too, many

Ordination in Sedbergh. Left to right: Revd. Alan Fell, Canon Bruce Grainger,
Revd. Ruth Wigram, the Bishop, Revd. Mark I'Anson, Mr. Jeremy Mackrell,
Bishop of Khartoum Rt. Revd. Bulus Idris Tia and Archdeacon Brian Smith

friends from Maidstone and Newcastle and a number of high ranking members of the Armed Forces. David Smith had been, for the past eighteen months, Bishop to H. M. Forces, in which capacity he travelled extensively, visiting members of the Services in Hong Kong, Cyprus, Gibraltar, Germany and Northern Ireland. Partly as a result of this, he came to Bradford with a great enthusiasm for furthering diocesan contacts throughout the world, not only the partnership with Southwestern Virginia and Khartoum, but also closer links with the rest of Europe. The diocesan links committee, successor to the overseas working party, was already looking at ways of promoting this, through local Christian involvement in town twinning schemes and through ecumenical contacts with churches in Europe, and members of this group were much heartened by the new bishop's interest.

Ecumenical work within the area covered by Bradford Diocese has not been spectacular, but the formation of the West Yorkshire Ecumenical Council has helped. Something of this sort was needed to become the Sponsoring Body to deal with and validate local ecumenical projects, but Bishop Williamson's main desire was to have a forum in which he could meet other Christian leaders having responsibility in the Bradford area so that they could be in touch over areas of common concern. To this end he took the initiative by inviting other Church leaders to Bishopscroft in January 1985. A working group was formed, on which the Anglican representative was Archdeacon Shreeve, and from this the plans for forming WYEC emerged.

Local co-operation in some aspects of church work has taken place through various local councils of churches, later known as "churches together", and clergy fraternal meetings. A romantic "one-off" ecumenical gesture occurred in 1968, when St. Wilfrid's, Lidget Green, was loaned to the Russian Orthodox Church for the religious ceremony to mark the wedding of a princess, whose family had fled from their Russian estates in 1918, to a local young man. The ceremony was performed by the Most Revd. Archbishop Anthony, Metropolitan of Sourozh. A few parishes have forged closer and more specific ties, such as the use of Anglican buildings by Roman Catholic congregations in Sedbergh and Wilsden, the Anglican/Methodist sharing at St. Andrew's Keighley, the arrangement for the Methodist circuit to use the parish church at Kettlewell once a month and the Byelorussian Orthodox Church to use St Chad's. There is a more closely knit arrangement between Cononley's Anglican and Methodist congregations, with its shared ministry. A wider than national setting may help to nurture the growing belief that Christians ought not to be pursuing separately those aspects of Christian mission that they could be undertaking together.

Among the appointments made early in Bishop Smith's episcopacy were the Revd. Paul Slater's move from Cullingworth to Bishopscroft to become the new personal assistant and the arrival of Canon Christopher Lewis as Bishop's Officer for Ministry and Training. Canon Lewis came from Canterbury Diocese where he was Team Rector of Whitstable, Rural Dean of Reculver and an

Honorary Canon of Canterbury Cathedral, a welcome reversal of losses of Bradford's key personnel to the southern province!

In late 1993, changes to the cathedral statutes led to the first appointments for Bradford of six honorary lay canons, to serve for a period of five years. These appointments, announced early in the 75th anniversary year, were intended to mark "clear and substantial contribution to the life of the diocese over a number of years", and were seen by the surprised recipients as a very great honour. This was followed in 1994 by the announcement that the new Archdeacon of Craven was to be Canon Malcolm Leslie Grundy from the Diocese of Ely. Canon Grundy was Team Rector of Huntingdon, and before that served for six years as Director of Education in London Diocese.

The Anniversary itself came as the conclusion of Bishop Williamson's five year plan. It had been his stated intention that the emphasis should be on quiet thanksgiving for the blessings of the last three quarters of a century and for the lives and contributions of the diocese's many personalities and many more unsung but devoted and committed Christians throughout its parishes. This intention was appreciated and supported by Bishop Smith. As a focal point for the whole diocese, a special service was planned to take place at the cathedral on 6th October, 1994, with the Archbishop of York, the Rt. Revd. John Hapgood, as preacher. For November 20th, the Sunday before the foundation date, forms of service have been prepared and made available to all parishes so that congregations throughout the diocese can take part in a symbolic act of family unity.

It would be inappropriate to assess the style and impact of those leading the work of the Church in Bradford Diocese who are only part way through their ministry here at the time of writing, but Bishop Smith's stance on one of the most widely ever publicised issues in the Church of England is a matter of record. Less than two months after his enthronement, the bishop was in London for the General Synod's historic vote on the ordination of women to the priesthood.

Like his predecessor, and the majority of clergy in the diocese and lay people on the electoral rolls of its parishes, Bishop Smith was in favour of the motion, while expressing understanding and pastoral concern for those who did not share his view. Before the vote, he said that he had enormous respect for the arguments of those who disagreed with him. "There is no way I can be dismissive of them or their views. I hold them in high regard and want them to remain part of the Church of England. I want to put a lot of my energy, time and prayer into helping people live, work and minister together, in whatever the circumstances might be, as part of the same Church."

In 1981, Provost Jackson had appointed Deaconess Judith Rose to be the cathedral's first woman chaplain to the congregation, and many women deacons, and, before 1987, deaconesses, have served throughout the diocese. Bishop Blunt always appreciated the contribution of women working professionally within the Church. Back in 1930, Bishop Perowne told the diocesan conference that he could see no fundamental objection in principle to admitting women to the priesthood and he advocated giving greater prominence to the role of women in the Church.

Changes, whether as radical as the ordination of women, or simply the introduction of a new translation of the Bible, use of alternative services, or modern music, are disturbing, and opponents of change often warn of the effect they might have on closer relationships with other Christian traditions. Arthur Perowne had something to say about this in December 1928, in a conference address provoked by reaction to the proposed new prayer book: Looking further ahead to a re-united Christendom, he wondered, was it conceivable that they would ever have reunion on the basis of uniformity, either in doctrine or in worship? Truth was far too big to be tied down to a simple or single formula. Worship was largely a matter of temperament, and so long as they kept to the ultimate standard of Scripture, they must be ready and willing to allow varieties of interpretation in the value of doctrine, and much greater variety in the order of worship. Their first duty was to rise above the present controversies and set them in their right proportion from the height of God's purpose.

A message, perhaps, from the days of Bradford Diocese's infancy for its present and its future?

THE TEN CHURCHES AND CHURCH CLOSURES

Bradford Church Building Society – the Ten Churches

St. Stephen Bowling	1860	All Saints Little Horton Green	1863
St. Philip Girlington	1860	Holy Trinity Leeds Road	1864
St. Mary Laisterdyke	1861	St. Barnabas Heaton	1864
St. Thomas Wigan Street	1861	St. Michael & All Angels City Road	1867
St. Luke Broomfields	1862	St. Bartholomew Bowling	1872

The Society was aided by the Ripon Church Building Society and the Incorporated Church Building Society.

Churches which have closed.

Mission or daughter churches in parentheses; no doubt there are others which are not recorded and some which were the forerunners of parish churches.

Barnoldswick	St. James		1842 – 1960
Bingley	Holy Trinity	rebuilt 1974	1868 – 1974
Bradford	Christ Church	Darley Street	1815 – 1878
		Eldon Place	1879 – 1940
	Holy Trinity	Leeds Road	1864 – 1966
	(St. Alban	Bowling Back Lane	1883 – 1960)
	St. Andrew	Legrams Lane, Listerhills	1853 – 1966
	(St. Peter	Princeville	1877 – 1950)
	St. Bartholomew	Hall Lane, Bowling	1872 – 1962
	St. Chrysostom	Bolton Road	1890 – 1966
	St. James	Manchester Road/Nelson St.	1838 – 1965
	St. John	Little Horton Lane	1871 – 1965
	St. John	Manchester Road (bottom)	1839 – 1870
	St. John	Tong Street	1860 – 1970
	St. Jude	Lumb Lane	1843 – 1966
	(St. Aidan	Cornwall Terrace	1896 – 1960)
	St. Luke	Chandos St. Broomfields	1862 – 1940

	St. Luke	Victor Road Manningham	1881 – 1984
	(St. Silas	Fairfield Road	1912 – 1958)
	St. Margaret	Thornbury	1909 – 1990
	St. Mark	Grosvenor Road Manningham	1874 – 1959
	St. Michael and All Angels	City Road	1867 – 1958
	St. Thomas	Wigan Street Westgate	1862 – 1935
	(St. Edmund	Bingley Street, Brownroyd	1876 – 1955)
	(St. George	Lidget Green	1880 – 1909)
	(St. Hilda	off Little Horton Lane	1896 –)
	(St. Lawrence	Bolton Woods	1880 – 1985)
	(St. Peter	Toftshaw	1924 – 1950)
	(St. Saviour	Jesse Street, Thornton Rd.	1883 – 1966)
	(St. Thomas of Canterbury	Beacon Road	1944 – 1959)
Cottingley	St. Michael and All Angels	relocated 1968	1886 – 1968
Dale Head	St. James	relocated Stocks	1852 – 1936
Earby	The Iron Church		1889 – 1916
Halton Gill	St. John the Baptist	ancient, rebuilt	1626 – 1976
Idle	Chapel of Ease	Towngate (consec. 1694)	1630 – 1828
	St. John	Cavendish Road relocated Thorpe Edge	1874 – 1962 1963 –
Keighley	Holy Trinity	Lawkholme Lane	1882 – 1972
	St. Mary Virgin	Eastwood	1855 – 1954
	St. Peter	Halifax Road Holycroft then in hall until	1882 – 1954 1975
	(St. Matthew	Braithwaite	1854 – 1975)
	(St. Michael	Bracken Bank	1958 – 1983)
	(St. Paul	Parkwood	1884 – 1966)
Pudsey	St. Paul		1846 – 1982
Vale of Lune	St. Gregory the Great (consec. 1918)		1862 – 1984
Wilsden	St. Matthew	Laneside (relocated)	1826 – 1957

Breakaway Churches:

Laisterdyke	St. Paul	Free Church of England	1883 – 1895
Wilsden	St. James	Free Church of England	1869 – 1894

BRADFORD DIOCESE – MOTHERS' UNION

Bradford Diocese – Mothers' Union
(from information supplied by Mrs. Audrey Waterhouse)

Diocesan Presidents

1919 - 1922	Mrs. Helena Frances Perowne	1961 - 1963	Mrs. Elizabeth Higgs
1922 - 1928	Mrs. Stanton Jones	1963 - 1966	Mrs. Olga Leach
1928 - 1940	Mrs. Herbert Mitchell	1966 - 1973	Mrs. Sheila Sheppard
1940 - 1943	Mrs. Watson	1973 - 1976	Mrs. Rosemary White
1943 - 1952	Mrs. Winifred Pedley	1976 - 1982	Mrs. Maisie Hibbert
1952 - 1961	Mrs. Gwyneth Tiarks	1982 - 1988	Mrs. Jane Parkinson
		1988 - 1994	Mrs. Audrey Waterhouse

A Selection From Minute Books, 1928 Onwards.

1928   Mrs. Herbert Mitchell protested via Mary Sumner House about Gretna Green Weddings.

1935   Became 'Friends of Cathedral', charge of £5 p.a., giving free use of cathedral.

1937   10/6d. sent to Public Morality Council towards fighting Contraceptive Bill. Balance in M.U. Diocesan Account £157.

1939   All members agreed to knit for the troops.

1945   City of Bradford has adopted Borough of Coulsden in the south of England which had suffered terribly in the war, M.U. asked to contribute goods and clothing.

1948   Moral Welfare Council set up, M.U. to have representative, gave £10 to help this venture. Collection for destitute children of the world.

1949   M.U. office opened in Church House, North Parade.

1950   Priest's desk given to M.S. House Chapel, London, in memory of Mrs. Perowne by Bradford and Worcester Dioceses not now needed. Suggest it go to a church bombed during the war.

1957   Overseas meeting, speaker Miss Elder from our linked diocese of St. John's Transkei.

1959   St. John's Transkei sent £1.18.4d as gift. Used for material for tablecloth for diocesan meetings. Mrs. Pedley embroidered MU emblem.

1964   Miss Marjorie Wilson, M.U. worker in Transkei, visited. Lady Day service at Holy Trinity Skipton for first time. Help offered to families of men in prison.

1970   Golden Jubilee of diocese. M.U. celebrations at St. Margaret's Ilkley.

1972   Triennial Festival speaker Mrs. Susan Varah, Central President. We raise £350 to bring member from Transkei to attend Central Council.

1973   Bradford to provide Wool Stall at Central Overseas Sale in London. 'Thursday Listening Post' counselling sessions begun. Office in Church House to close.

1976   Centenary of World Wide M.U. Bradford had floral clock in Lister Park. Mrs. Nontobica Mafika came to Bradford from Transkei and took part in Centenary celebrations in London.

1978   Tuesday Listening Post opens in Keighley. Busoga Diocese in Uganda becomes our second link.

1980   Four branches closed, Keighley Listening Post closed.

1982   M.U. diocesan prayer chain started. Banner sent to Transkei, money raised for bicycles for leaders in Busoga.

1987   Community worker Mrs. Elaine Applebee appointed to work at Hutson St. Mrs. S. Sheppard visited Busoga. Media Awareness Project founded.

1991   Mrs. Applebee completed term of office at Hutson St. Decade of Evangelism - Mrs. Mavis Bromley appointed Decade Officer.

1992   International year - Dr Cyril Okeroche from Nigeria spoke at Cathedral gathering. Teddy bears knitted by members, in bags made by prisoners in Armley gaol sent with clothes and bedding to Busoga. Thank-you visit to gaol by M.U. officers. Mrs Audrey Waterhouse visited Bradford Diocesan link Diocese of Southwestern Virginia.

1993   Mrs Audrey Waterhouse spoke at AGM of Union of Catholic Mothers, Leeds Roman Catholic Diocese.

1994   Anniversary Year - MU Central President to attend Rejoice and Celebrate, a pageant and Eucharist in Bradford Cathedral.

STATEMENT ISSUED BY CHURCH LEADERS

Introduction

1. We, the leaders of various Christian traditions and churches in this area, met together in Bradford on November 4th 1988 to discuss the implications of the policies outlined by the Bradford Metropolitan District Council and passed at the Council Meeting on October 25th. We have listened with interest to the Bishop of Bradford's report of his meeting with the Leader and Deputy Leader of the Council earlier today, and we make these comments in the light of that conversation.

2. We support and welcome the initiatives already taken by some of our number to draw attention to areas of concern which seem to emerge from a consideration of these policies. In particular, we welcome the stress which has been placed on our need to care for those who are most at risk and vulnerable in our society.

3. As leaders of the various churches we believe that we are in exceptionally good positions to gain understanding of what is going on in the community. We have clergy working in all areas who keep us well informed, and we are also briefed by extremely competent professionals from a variety of disciplines.

4. We wish to make it quite clear that we have no desire to see the Church leading any kind of organised opposition to the elected Council. We believe though, that it is a legitimate function of the Church to ask questions, and this we have endeavoured to do, and will continue to do.

5. Our Christian tradition is one of identification with the poor, and of seeking justice and peace in the structures of society. We share a common commitment to the One who laid down his life for others, and who taught that we are to care for one another in the same way that God cares for each one of us. Having said that, we would not wish to imply that we believe that Christians have a monopoly of care, and we readily acknowledge that many others, including Civic, community and other Faith groups, are also committed to caring.

6. We believe Britain to be a rich nation, and the signs of prosperity and affluence are all around us for everyone to see. We are therefore disturbed by the fact that the gap between the rich and the poor in our society is growing, and that the wealth of creation is not shared in a way which honours and brings dignity to all members of our community.

7. The overall effect of the policies to be pursued by the Council, in our view, despite assurances to the contrary, may well accentuate and accelerate the divisions we see within society rather than reduce the ever-widening gap.

Present Concerns

8. We are particularly concerned about:
   i. measures affecting the poor, especially those with young children.
   ii. measures affecting the elderly, which may increase their vulnerability and anxiety.
   iii. the decision to close down the Benefits Shops, which have brought so much help to so many, and have at the same time brought a considerable amount of money into the community.
   iv. measures affecting education, particularly those with special needs, disabilities, and whose mother-tongue is not English; also the reduced commitment to community education issues.
   v. measures which we believe will increase anxiety within the Asian community. Bradford has a good track record in race relations, and we fear that many of the good things that have been achieved could be jeopardised.

vi. the number of people who are likely to lose their jobs. We are also concerned lest the burden is borne disproportionately by the Asian community, thus undermining some of the gains made within the Equal Opportunities policy during the last few years.

vii. measures affecting the morale of very many people working within the Voluntary Sector who are deeply anxious about their future role. We note with interest the Council's plans for a Community Trust but believe that insufficient care has been taken, and insufficient information given to the Voluntary Sector to assuage their fears.

9. In conclusion we wish to voice three further anxieties:

i. the apparent shift in emphasis by the Council from services and caring, to financial targets and efficiency, important though these undoubtedly are.

ii. the way in which the package was presented to the people of Bradford, giving little opportunity for reflection and understanding. This itself has certainly been the cause of much confusion. It may well be that some of the fears are groundless, and not all are directly related to the activities of the Council - nevertheless, an atmosphere of uncertainty and apprehension has been generated.

iii. in particular we note that a considerable number of these measures seem to affect those who are least able to speak for themselves.

Future Plans

10. i. We commit ourselves to continue to listen to the voices of the poor and to do whatever we are able in order to stand alongside them, and to ensure that their voice is heard by others.

ii. We will ask our clergy, who live and work in every area of the District, to monitor the effects of the proposed cuts, and to set them alongside the assurances that have been given to us that the least well off in our society will be protected.

iii. We will look again at what we ourselves do in the community, scrutinise our priorities, and see if we are able to continue any of the work that may be stopped as a result of the proposed cuts.

iv. We recognise the invidious position that the Lord Mayor finds himself in; and we shall continue to give him our respect as the Senior and Representative Citizen of the whole community.

v. We shall continue our dialogue with representatives of the other World Faiths who are part of our community, and do all in our power to ensure that those who are of other cultures can live a full life, free from fear, with respect for their cultural identity, and with open and equal access to the opportunities that our society affords.

vi. We call upon our churches to remember the Council, its Members and employees, in their prayers. That those whom the community have elected to represent them may find strength, courage and vision to work for the good of all.

vii. We commit ourselves to work for a situation of creative dialogue with the Council; each recognising the rights of the other, and to work for the health of our community with honesty and integrity. We appreciate the willingness expressed by the Leader of the Council to meet us, and to remain in conversation with us. We have valued the real efforts to get Bradford 'bouncing back' again, and we would wish to affirm the richness and the many positive and creative aspects of Bradford, emphasising that for the vast majority of people, this is a good place to be.

Conclusion

11. We accept that our calling as Christians, and the responsibilities placed upon us as leaders, means that we recognise the priority which must be given to the needs of the poor and the vulnerable in our society.

Signed:

The Rt. Rev. Robert K. Williamson, Bishop of Bradford
The Rt. Rev. David Konstant, Bishop of Leeds
The Rev. Mrs. Kathleen Richardson, Methodist Chairman
The Rev. John Nicholson, N.E. Superintendent, Baptist Union
The Rev. Donald Hilton, Moderator, United Reformed Church
Major Douglas Rayner, Salvation Army.

Bradford Cathedral, the High Altar

SENIOR CLERGY

Bishops of Bradford

Arthur William Thomson Perowne	1920-1931	Bishop of Worcester	1931
Alfred Walter Frank Blunt	1931-1955	retired	
Frederick Donald Coggan	1956-1961	Archbishop of York	1961
		Archbishop of Canterbury	1974
Clement George St. Michael Parker	1961-1971	retired	
Ross Sydney Hook	1972-1980	Chief of Staff to Archbishop of Canterbury	1980
Geoffrey John Paul	1981-1983	died in office	
Robert Kerr Williamson	1984-1991	Bishop of Southwark	1992
David James Smith	1992-		

Vicars and Provosts of Bradford concerned in this history
(the list in the cathedral dates back to 1293)

Frank Theodore Woods	1912-1916	Bishop of Peterborough	1916
		Bishop of Winchester	1924
Frederic Sumpter Guy Warman	1916-1919	Bishop of Truro	1919
		Bishop of Chelmsford	1923
		Bishop of Manchester	1929
William Stanton Jones	1919-1928	Bishop of Sodor and Man	1928
Cecil Wilfred Wilson (Provost from 1931)	1928-1932	Bishop of Middleton	1932
Edward Worsfold Mowll	1933-1943	Bishop of Middleton	1943
John Gerhard Tiarks	1944-1962	Bishop of Chelmsford	1962
William Hugh Alan Cooper	1962-1977		
Brandon Donald Jackson	1977-1989	Dean of Lincoln	1989
John Stephen Richardson	1990-		

Archdeacons of Bradford

William Stanton Jones	1921-1928		
Cecil Wilfred Wilson	1928-1932		
Frederick George Ackerley	1932-1934		
Sidney Edward Lowe	1934-1953		
Kenneth Kay	1953-1957		
Hubert Lawrence Higgs	1957-1965	Bishop of Hull	1965
William Johnston	1965-1976	Bishop of Dunwich	1976
Frank Pilkington Sargeant	1977-1984	Bishop of Stockport	1984
David Herbert Shreeve	1984-		

Archdeacons of Craven

in Ripon:		in Bradford:	
Charles Musgrave	1836-1875	Henry Lucas Cook	1920-1928
Vincent William Ryan	1875-1894	James Francis Howson	1928-1934
Joseph Bardsley	1894-1896	Frederick George Ackerley	1934-1949
Francis Charles Kilner	1896-1913	Thomas John Williams	1950-1956
Henry Lucas Cook	1913-1920	Arthur Sephton	1956-1972
		Martin Kaye	1973-1977
		David Arthur Rogers	1977-1986
		Brian Arthur Smith Bishop of Tonbridge	1987-1993 1993
		Malcolm Leslie Grundy	1994-

Other Clergy who have served in Bradford and become Bishops

George Frederick Townley	Bishop of Hull	1957
Bernard Markham	Bishop of Nassau	1962
Eric Treacey	Bishop of Wakefield	1968
Alan Smithson	Bishop of Jarrow	1990
John Martin Wharton	Bishop of Kingston-upon-Thames	1992

BRADFORD DIOCESAN PARISH LISTS
1920 AND 1993

1920 Original Title *Parish Names in bold type*		1993 Current Title
Addingham	St. Peter 15c/18c	**Addingham**
Allerton	St. Peter 1879 consecrated 1884	**Allerton** with St. Francis of Assisi: 1982
(Appletreewick St. John the Baptist 16c, see Burnsall)		
Arncliffe with **Halton Gill**	St. Oswald: Ancient rebuilt 1841 St. John the Baptist Ancient rebuilt 1626 and 1848, closed 1976	Kettlewell-with-Conistone, Hubberholme and **Arncliffe**-with-**Halton Gill** 1984
Austwick	Church of the Epiphany 1841	Clapham with Keasden and Austwick 1985 with Eldroth Church 1627 restored 1983
Baildon	St. John the Evangelist 1848 Ancient: rebuilt St. Hugh, Coach Road,1963 St. James, Otley Road, 1904	**Baildon**
Bankfoot Bradford	St. Matthew 1849	**Bankfoot**
Barnoldswick or Gill Kirk	St. Mary le Gill 1174/16c with St. James 1842–1960 Holy Trinity 1960	**Barnoldswick** with **Bracewell** 1960
Ben Rhydding	St. John the Evangelist 1905	**Ben Rhydding**
Bentham (Low)	St. John the Baptist Ancient rebuilt 1340, 1822, 1877	**Bentham St. John**
Bentham (High)	St. Margaret 1837	**Bentham St. Margaret**
Bierley	St. John the Evangelist 1766 (with St. Peter Toftshaw 1924–1950)	**Bierley**
Bingley with Harden	All Saints Ancient St. Saviour 1892	**Bingley All Saints** with Crossflatts, St. Aidan 1969 and Eldwick, St. Lawrence 1893

Bingley   Holy Trinity 1868-1974   **Bingley Holy Trinity**
                     rebuilt 1974   with Gilstead, St. Wilfrid 1905

(Blubberhouses St. Andrew 1851 see Leathley)

Bolton   St. James the Apostle 1877   **Bolton St. James** with
                     (with St. Lawrence Bolton Woods **St. Chyrsostom 1966**
                     1880 - 1985)

Bolton Abbey   St. Mary and St. Cuthbert 12c   **Bolton Abbey**
with **Barden**   parish formed 1864

Bolton by Bowland St. Peter and St. Paul 15c   **Bolton by Bowland** with
(or **Bolland**)   **Grindleton** 1982

Bowling   St. Bartholomew 1872-1962   merged with St. John Bowling
                     Hall Lane   1962 later with Bierley

Bowling   St. John the Evangelist 1842   **Bowling St. John**
                     re-ordered 1992

Bowling   St. Stephen 1860   **Bowling St. Stephen**

Bracewell   St. Michael 12c   **Barndoldswick** with
                                                      Bracewell 1960

Bradford – see Bankfoot, Bolton, Bowling, Buttershaw, Eccleshill, Fairweather Green, Girlington, Heaton, Horton, Holme Wood, Laisterdyke, Lidget Green, Listerhills, Manningham, Thorpe Edge.

Bradford   Cathedral Church of St. Peter   **Bradford St. Peter**
                     Ancient

Bradford   St. Augustine 1872-1986   **Bradford St. Augustine**
                     Otley Road consecrated 1877
                     rebuilt 1988

Bradford   Christ Church
                     Darley Street 1815-1878
                     Manningham/Eldon Place 1879-1940

Bradford   St. Chrysostom 1890-1966   merged with Bolton St.James
                     Bolton Road

Bradford   St. Clement 1894   **Bradford St. Clement**
                     Barkerend Road

Bradford   Holy Trinity 1864-1966
                     Leeds Road
                     with St. Albans Mission 1883-1960
                     Bowling Back Lane

Bradford   St. James the Great 1838-1965   merged with Horton All Saints
                     Manchester Road

Bradford   St. Luke 1862 -1940   merged with Bowling
                     Chandos Street, Broomfields   St. Bartholomew 1940

Bradford   St. Michael & All Angels 1867-1958 merged with St. Mary
                     City Road   Magdalene Manningham 1956

1920 Original Title *Parish Names in bold type*		1993 Current Title
Bradford	**St. Thomas** 1862 - 1935 Wigan Street, Westgate	merged with Christ Church 1935
(Bradley St. Mary see Cononley)		
Broughton-in- Airedale	**All Saints** 1132	**Broughton, Marton and Thornton** 1977
(Buckden see Hubberholme)		
Burley-in-Wharfedale	**St. Mary the Blessed Virgin** 1843	**Burley-in-Wharfedale**
Burnsall	**St. Wilfrid** 12c/1612	**Burnsall** with **Rylstone 1989** (with Parcevall Hall) and Appletreewick St. John the Baptist
Burton-in-Lonsdale	**All Saints** 1870	**Thornton-in-Lonsdale** with **Burton-in-Lonsdale** 1975
Buttershaw	**St.Paul** 1842	**Buttershaw St. Paul**
	St. Aidan 1959 St. Thomas of Canterbury 1944-1959 Beacon Road	**Buttershaw St. Aidan**
Calverley	**St. Wilfrid** Ancient	**Calverley**
(Carlton St. Bartholomew see Guiseley)		
Carleton-in-Craven	**St. Mary the Virgin** Ancient	**Carleton** and **Lothersdale** 1978
Cautley with **Dowbiggin**	**St. Mark** 1847	**Sedbergh, Cautley & Garsdale** 1974
Chapel-le-Dale	**St. Leonard** 17c restored 1869	**Ingleton** with **Chapel-le-Dale** 1968
Clapham with **Keasden**	**St. James** Ancient rebuilt 1814 **St. Matthew** 1873	**Clapham** with **Keasden** and **Austwick** 1985
Clayton	**St. John the Baptist** 1851 consecrated 1856 parish formed 1857	**Clayton**
Coniston Cold	**St. Peter** 1846	**Kirkby in Malhamdale** with **Coniston Cold** 1987
(Conistone St. Mary see Rylstone and Kettlewell)		
Cononley with **Bradley**	**St. John the Evangelist** 1864 **St. Mary** 1914 relocated 1963	**Cononley** with **Bradley**
Cottingley	**St. Michael & All Angels** 1886-1968 relocated 1968	**Cottingley**
Cowgill	**St. John the Evangelist** 1837	**Dent** with **Cowgill** 1974
Cowling	**Holy Trinity** 1845	**Cowling**

(Crossflatts St. Aidan see Bingley All Saints)

Cross Roads-cum-Lees	**St. James** 1910 – Parish formed 1911 Iron Mission Church dedicated 1887	**Cross Roads-cum-Lees**
Cullingworth	**St. John the Evangelist** 1847	**Cullingworth**
Dale Head	**St. James** 1852-1936 relocated in 1938	**Long Preston w Tosside** 1984 Stocks in Bowland
Denholme Gate	**St. Paul** 1846	**Denholme Gate**
Dent	**St. Andrew** 11c	**Dent** with **Cowgill** 1974
Denton	**St. Helen** 1776 Dedicated to St. Helen 1890	**Weston** with **Denton** 1969

(Draughton St. Augustine see Skipton Holy Trinity)

(Dunsop Bridge St. George see Slaidburn)

(Earby formerly with Thornton-in-Craven)

	All Saints 1909 Original Iron Church 1889-1916	**Earby** 1923
Eccleshill	**St. Luke** 1848	**Eccleshill**

(Eldroth 1627 see Austwick)

(Eldwick St. Lawrence see Bingley All Saints)

Embsay with **Eastby**	**St. Mary the Virgin** 1853	**Embsay** with **Eastby**
Esholt with **Hawkesworth**	**St. Paul** 1837	**Guiseley** with **Esholt** 1983 (with Hawkesworth C of E School)
Fairweather Green	Conventional District **St. Saviour** 1966 Jesse Street Mission 1883-1966 parish formed 1924	**Fairweather Green**
Farnley	**All Saints** 1851 originally 1215	**Leathley** with **Farnley, Fewstone** and **Blubberhouses** 1984
Farsley	**St. John the Evangelist** 1843	**Farsley**
Fewston with **Blubberhouses**	**St. Michael & St. Lawrence** Ancient **St. Andrew** 1856	**Leathley** with **Farnley Fewston** and **Blubberhouses** 1984

(Firbank became part of diocese in 1925)

Firbank	**St. John the Evangelist** 1842	**Firbank Howgill** and **Killington** 1977
Frizinghall	**St. Margaret** 1896	**Shipley St. Paul** and **Frizinghall St. Margaret** 1983

Gargrave	**St. Andrew** Ancient rebuilt 1852	**Gargrave**
Garsdale	**St. John the Baptist** 1860 Earlier Church ?	**Sedbergh Cautley** and **Garsdale** 1974
Giggleswick	**St. Alkelda** 10c rebuilt 15c	**Giggleswick** and **Rathmell** with **Wigglesworth** 1982

(Gilstead St. Wilfrid see Bingley Holy Trinity)

Girlington	**St. Philip** 1860 St. Edmund Brownroyd 1876 -1905 (transfered to St. Chad)	**Girlington**
Gisburn	**St. Mary** 13c-15c	**Gisburn**

(Glusburn All Saints see Sutton-in-Craven)

(Grassington Schoolhouse see Linton)

Greengates	**St. John the Evangelist** Consecrated 1893 Parish 1911	**Greengates**
Grindleton	**St. Ambrose** 1805	**Bolton by Bowland** with **Grindleton** 1982
Guiseley	**St. Oswald** Ancient	**Guiseley** with **Esholt** 1983 Carlton St. Bartholomew 1824 Esholt St. Paul 1837 Tranmere Park St. Peter 1957

(Hainworth see Keighley Ingrow)

(Halton Gill see Arncliffe and Kettlewell)

(Halton West see Hellifield)

(Harden see Bingley All Saints)	**St. Saviour** 1892 Parish formed 1930	**Harden** and **Wilsden** 1960

(Hawksworth see Esholt)

Haworth	**St. Michael & All Angels** 1881 1317 rebuilt 1590, 1755 and 1881	**Haworth** (with Stanbury 1848)
Heaton	**St. Barnabas** 1864	**Heaton St. Barnabas**
	St. Martin 1959 Mission Church 1933	**Heaton St. Martin**

(Hebden St. Peter see Linton)

Hellifield	**St. Aidan** 1905	**Hellifield**

(Holme Wood St. Christopher 1968 temporary building 1958, see Tong)

Horton, Great	**St. John the Evangelist** 1874 formerly Bell Chapel 1806	**Great Horton**
Horton, Little	**All Saints** 1864 Bramley Street Mission 1871-1935	**Horton All Saints** (with Michael Ramsey House)

Horton, Little	**St. Columba** 1902	**Bradford St. Columba** with **St. Andrew** 1966
Horton, Little	**St. John** 1871-1965 Little Horton Lane	
Horton, Little	**St. Oswald** 1902	**Bradford St. Oswald**
Horton-in-Ribblesdale	**St. Oswald** 12c-14c	**Langcliffe** with **Stainforth** and **Horton-in-Ribblesdale** 1985
Howgill	**Holy Trinity** 1838	**Firbank Howgill** and **Killington** 1977
Hubberholme	**St. Michael & All Angels** Ancient parish formed 1765	**Kettlewell-with-Conistone Hubberholme** and **Arncliffe-with-Halton Gill** 1984
Hurst Green	**St. John the Evangelist** 1848	**Hurst Green & Mitton** 1982
Idle	**Holy Trinity** 1830 with St. John The Divine 1874-1962 Cavendish Road, became parish 1924 (see Thorpe Edge)	**Idle**
Ilkley	**All Saints** Ancient	**Ilkley All Saints**
Ilkley	**St. Margaret** 1879	**Ilkley St. Margaret**
Ingleton	**St. Mary** 13c rebuilt 1887	**Ingleton** with **Chapel-le-Dale** 1968

(Ingrow St. John see Keighley)

(Keasden St. Matthew see Clapham)

Keighley see also Thwaites Brow and Utley

Keighley	**St. Andrew** 1848 Ancient: rebuilt 1710, 1805 and 1848	Keighley St. Andrew
Keighley	**All Saints** 1908 in Schoolbuilding 1879	**Keighley All Saints**
Keighley	**St. John the Evangelist** 1843 Ingrow St. Michael 1856-1983 Gospel Lane, Bracken Bank	**Ingrow** with **Hainworth**
Keighley	**Holy Trinity** 1882-1972 Lawkholme Lane	
Keighley	**St. Mary the Virgin** 1855-1954 Dalton Lane, Eastwood	
Keighley	**St. Matthew** 1854-1975 Braithwaite	

Keighley	**St. Paul** 1884 – 1966 Parkwood wooden building 1864–1885	
Keighley	**St. Peter** 1882 – 1954 Holycroft continued in hall to 1975	merged with St.Andrew 1950
Kelbrook	**St. Mary** 1839	**Kelbrook St. Mary**
Kettlewell	**St. Mary** 12c rebuilt 1820	**Kettlewell-**with**-Conistone Hubberholme** and **Arncliffe-**with**-Halton Gill** 1984
Kildwick	**St. Andrew** Ancient rebuilt 1320 restored 1901	**Kildwick St. Andrew**

(Killington All Saints 14c, part of diocese in 1951, see Firbank Howgill & Killington)

Kirkby Malham	**St. Michael the Archangel** 15c	**Kirkby in Malhamdale** with **Coniston Cold** 1987
Laisterdyke	**St. Mary** 1861 re-ordered 1987	**Laisterdyke St. Mary**
Langcliffe	**St. John the Evangelist** 1851	**Langcliffe** with **Stainforth** and **Horton-in-Ribblesdale** 1985
Leathley	**St. Oswald** Ancient	**Leathley** with **Farnley Fewston** and **Blubberhouses** 1984
Linton with Hebden	**St. Michael** 14c **St. Peter** 1841	**Linton** Hebden (with Grassington Church House)
Lidget Green	**St. Wilfrid** 1905	**Bradford St. Wilfrid**
Listerhills	**St. Andrew** 1853-1966 St. Peter Princeville 1877-1950	with Bradford St. Columba
Long Preston	**St. Mary the Virgin** 12c-17c	**Long Preston** with **Tosside** 1984
Lothersdale	**Christ Church** 1838	**Carleton** and **Lothersdale** 1978
Low Moor	**St. Mark** 1857	**Low Moor St. Mark**
	Holy Trinity 1836 formerly 1606	**Low Moor Holy Trinity** (see Wibsey)
Manningham	**St. Chad** 1913 St. Edmund Brownroyd 1905-1955 (transferred from St. Philip)	**Manningham St. Chad**
Manningham	**St. Mark** 1874-1959 Grosvenor Road	merged with St. Jude 1958

1920 **Original Title** *Parish Names in bold type*		1993 **Current Title**
Manningham	**St. Jude** 1843-1966 Lumb Lane St. Aidan, Cornwall Terrace 1896-1960	United with St. Paul
Manningham	**St. Luke** 1881-1984 Victor Road St. Silas Mission 1912-1958	merged with St. Paul 1984
Manningham	**St. Paul** 1848 restored 1971 and 1991	**Manningham** 1984 Sts. Paul, and Mary Magdalene
Manningham	**St. Mary Magdalene** 1878	
Marton-in-Craven	**St. Peter** 12c/19c	**Broughton Marton & Thornton** 1977
Menston with Woodhead	**St. John the Divine** 1871	**Menston** with **Woodhead**
Morton	**St. Luke** 1851	**Morton**
Mytton	**All Hallows** 13c/15c	**Hurst Green** and **Mitton** 1982

(Newall see Otley)

(Newsholme St. John, formerly under Keighley St. Andrew, see Oakworth)

Oakenshaw cum Woodlands	**St. Andrew** 1889	**Oakenshaw** cum **Woodlands**
Oakworth	**Christ Church** 1846	**Oakworth** Newsholme St. John 1844
Otley	**All Saints** Ancient	**Otley** Newall and Weston Estate
Oxenhope	**St. Mary the Virgin** 1848	**Oxenhope**

(Parcevall Hall see Burnsall)

Pudsey	**St. Lawrence** 1821	**Pudsey St. Lawrence & St. Paul** 1982
Pudsey	**St. Paul** 1846 -1982	
Queensbury (or Queenshead)	**Holy Trinity** 1845	**Queensbury**
Rathmell	**Holy Trinity** 1842	**Giggleswick** and **Rathmell** with **Wigglesworth** 1982
Rawdon	**St. Peter** 1864 formerly 1684	**Rawdon**
Riddlesden	**St. Mary the Virgin** 1848 Parish formed 1875	**Riddlesden**
Rylstone with Conistone	**St. Peter** 1853 St. Mary 11c now with Kettlewell	**Burnsall** with **Rylstone** 1989

1920 Original Title *Parish Names in bold type*		1993 Current Title
Sedbergh	**St. Andrew** Ancient	**Sedbergh Cautley &** **Garsdale** 1974
Settle	**Holy Ascension** 1838	**Settle**
Shelf	**St. Michael & All Angels** 1850	**Shelf** (with Woodside Church Centre)
Shipley	**St. Paul** 1826	**Shipley St. Paul &** **Frizinghall St. Margaret** 1983
Shipley	**St. Peter** 1909	**Shipley St. Peter**
Silsden	**St. James** 1712 3rd restoration 1967	**Silsden**
Skipton	**Christ Church** 1839	**Skipton Christ Church**
Skipton	**Holy Trinity** 12c/15c	**Skipton Holy Trinity** with Draughton St. Augustine 1897
Slaidburn	**St. Andrew** 16c/18c	**Slaidburn** with Dunsop Bridge St. George
Stainforth	**St. Peter** 1842	**Langcliffe** with **Stainforth** and **Horton-in-Ribblesdale** 1985

(Stanbury see Haworth)

Steeton	**St. Stephen** 1881	**Steeton**

(Stocks-in-Bowland St. James see Dale Head and Long Preston with Tosside)

Sutton-in-Craven	**St. Thomas** 1869	**Sutton-in-Craven** with Glusburn All Saints
Thornbury	**St. Margaret** 1909-1990 Mission Church opened 1896 Parish formed 1912 Temporary premises 1990	**Thornbury**
Thornton	**St. James** 1872 formerly 1612	**Thornton**
Thornton-in-Craven and **Earby**	**St. Mary** 1461 **All Saints** 1909	**Broughton Marton** and **Thornton** 1977
Thornton-in- **Lonsdale**	**St. Oswald** Ancient rebuilt 1870/1933	**Thornton-in-Lonsdale** with **Burton-in-Lonsdale** 1975
	St. John the Divine 1963	**Thorpe Edge** Bradford
(Thwaites Brow part of Keighley)	**St. Barnabas** 1971 parish 1974 originally 1885	**Thwaites Brow** Keighley
Tong with **Tong Street**	**St. James** 1727 originally 1170 **St. John** 1860 - 1970	**Tong** with Holme Wood St. Christopher 1968

Tosside	St. Bartholomew 18c	**Long Preston** with **Tosside** 1984

(Tranmere Park St. Peter see Guisley)

(Utley part of Keighley)	**St. Mark** – 1888 parish formed 1981	Utley

(Vale of Lune Chapel/St. Gregory the Great built 1862 consec. 1918 part of Sedbergh redundant 1984)

Waddington	**St. Helen** 14c/15c rebuilt 1900	**Waddington** with West Bradford St. Catherine 1897

(West Bradford St. Catherine see Waddington)

Weston	**All Saints** Ancient repaired and amended 1686	**Weston** with **Denton** 1969

(Weston Estate see Otley)

Wibsey	Holy Trinity 1836 formerly 1606	**Low Moor Holy Trinity**

(Wigglesworth see Rathmell)

Wilsden	**St. Matthew** 1826 – 1957 temporary 1957 – 1975 relocated 1975	**Harden** and **Wilsden** 1960
Windhill	**Christ Church** 1869	**Windhill**
	St. James the Great 1959	**Woodhall**
	St. Cuthbert 1959	**Wrose**
Wyke	**St. Mary the Virgin** 1847	**Wyke**
Yeadon	**St. Andrew** 1895	**Yeadon St. Andrew**
Yeadon	St. John 1844	**Yeadon St. John**

Sources

Bradford Diocesan year books and the minutes of conferences, synods, boards and committees, correspondence, reports and addresses from the registrar's and Bishopscroft archives have provided much of my information. Much more has come from the following, who kindly agreed to be interviewed by me and in several cases lent me family scrap-books, (where possible, newspaper cuttings from these have been attributed in the text, but not all have been identifiable):

Mr. John S. Bailey (nephew of the second Mrs. Perowne)

Mrs. Molly Bailey (Hurst Green, memories of Archdeacon Ackerley)

Revd. Dr. and Mrs. Stanley Bennett

Revd. Ernest Blanchard

Mr. David Blunt

Mrs. Amy Bond (née Blunt)

Miss Pam Bradley (Parcevall Hall)

Revd. Canon John Clayton

The Rt. Revd. Lord and Lady Coggan

Revd. Canon David Creaser

Mr. John Cullingworth (cathedral warden)

Miss Elsie Cunliffe (moral welfare)

Rt. Revd. David Evans

Mr. Edward Garnett (stewardship)

Revd. Norman Goodacre

Mrs. Nora Goodchild

Revd. Canon Bruce Grainger

Dr. Ruth Hardy

Mrs. Kitty Hartley (provost's and bishops' secretary)

Revd. Canon Christopher Hayward

Revd. David Hennessey

Rt. Revd. and Mrs. Ross Hook

Very Revd. and Mrs. Brandon Jackson

Mrs. Marguerite Johnston

Miss Beatrice Kennedy (cathedral lady worker)

Miss Margaret Leach (Scargill)

Mr. Philip Lewis (race relations)

Mrs. Caroline Moore (The Way of the Cross)

Revd. Canon and Mrs. Eric Murgatroyd

Mrs Pamela Paul

Mr. Leslie Perowne

Miss Irene Price (Scargill)

Miss N. Pullan (Shipley, memories of Canon Perrett)

Mrs. Ann Remfry (née Tiarks)

Mrs. Ida Roberts (St. Mary Magdalene's)

Mrs. Ruth Robinson

Ven. David Rogers

Rt. Revd. Frank Sargeant

Revd. Preb. and Mrs. Robert Sharp

Mr. and Mrs. John Thornhill (Thornbury, memories of Revd. Norman Goodacre)

Mr. Derrick Watson (Gargrave, memories of Bishop Hardy)

Rt. Revd. Martin Wharton

Miss Audrey Wignall (memories of Mr. Henry Firth)

Rt. Revd. Robert Williamson

Revd. Roger Wood

Miss Irene Yarborough (memories of Mr. John Foster Beaver)

(In some instances I have used the Christian names of married women for clarity of identification).

In addition, my husband recorded a conversation with a truly remarkable lady, the 102 year old Deaconess F.M.(Prudence) Bullock, and the following responded by letter:

Miss Dorothy Bulman

Very Revd. Alan Cooper

Miss Stella Drew (cathedral lady worker)

Ven. Charles Forder

Revd. Peter Hawkins (race relations)

Revd. John Mowll

Mrs. Joy Smithells (née Beaver)

Revd. Canon Edward Richardson

Revd. Canon John Towell

Revd. John Winder

Published biographical material on some of Bradford's former bishops and priests has provided enjoyable and valuable background reading: 'History of the Diocese of Chelmsford' by Canon Gordon Hewitt (for Guy Warman and John Tiarks). 'Blunt' by John S. Peart-Binns 1969. 'Donald Coggan, Servant of Christ' by Margaret Pawley 1987. 'A Life of Bishop John A.T. Robinson' by Eric James 1987. 'A Pattern of Faith' by Geoffrey Paul, Introductory Memoir by Rowan Williams 1986.

Much of the material, particularly from the interviews, is wide-ranging, and has been used throughout the book, but where possible the main sources are listed chapter by chapter.

Chapter 1. Dr. Owen Chadwick's lecture on the occasion of the centenary of St. Albans' Diocese 1977. 'How a City Grows' by Horace Hird 1966. 'History of the Diocese of Chelmsford' by Canon Gordon Hewitt. Bradford Bishopric Committee minutes and correspondence. Bradford Diocesan twenty first anniversary booklet. Press cuttings in cathedral library. Mr. Mossman's press cuttings in the registrar's archives. Bradford Diocesan year books. Bradford Diocesan Conference minutes and Bishop's Letters.

Chapter 2. Bradford Bishopric Committee minutes and correspondence. Press cuttings and correspondence in registrar's archives. Press cuttings in cathedral library. Sedbergh, Howgill and Cautley Parish Magazine Nov. 1919. Bolton-by-Bolland Church Magazine Dec. 1918.

Chapter 3. Bradford Bishopric Committee minutes and correspondence. Press cuttings in cathedral library. Mr. Leslie Perowne, Bishop Perowne's family album and scrap-book.

Chapter 4. 'The History and Topography of Bradford' by John James 1841. 'Continuation and Additions to the History of Bradford and its Parish' by John James 1866. 'Round about Bradford' by William Cudworth 1876. 'History of the Parish of St. John's, Bierley' by Wilfrid Hiles. St. Luke's Manningham, jubilee and 75th anniversary histories. 'One Hundred Years 1848 - 1948' by Harry Bancroft (St. Andrew's, Keighley). Unpublished continuation of the history of Keighley Parish by Sidney Park.

Chapter 5. Diocesan year books. Ven. David Rogers. Revd. Ernest Blanchard. 'Bolton Priory and its Church' by Peter Watkins 1989. 'Outstanding Churches in the Yorkshire Dales' by Val Leigh 1983. 'Outstanding Churches in Craven' by Val Leigh and Brian Podmore 1985. Church magazines and guidebooks from Barnoldswick, Grindleton, Haworth, Mitton, Waddington.

Chapter 6. Press cuttings and correspondence in registrar's archives. Conference minutes. Diocesan Acts Book. Miss Dorothy Bulman's notes on the Girls' Friendly Society. Report of the Bishop's Commission on the Needs of the Diocese 1928. Bradford Cathedral Grand Bazaar programme. Mr. Leslie Perowne, Bishop Perowne's family album and scrap-book. St. Matthew's, Wilsden, parish scrap-book. Mr. John Bailey, the Bailey family album.

Chapter 7. Mr. David Blunt, Mrs Blunt's scrap-books. Mrs. Amy Bond. 'Blunt' by John S. Peart-Binns 1969. Diocesan year books. Conference minutes. Report of the Bishop's Commission on the Needs of the Diocese 1928. Issues of the 'Bishop's Messenger'. Historical Pageant of Bradford Souvenir Book.

Chapter 8. Mr. David Blunt, Mrs. Blunt's scrap-books. Registrar's archives. Episcopal Visitation Returns, Diocese of Ripon 1836 - 1856, quoted by J.M. Cunningham. Deaconess Bullock. 'Bishop Blunt and the Abdication Crisis' by Mary Lister, Bradford Antiquarian 1986. Conference minutes. Bishopscroft archives.

Chapter 9. Mr. David Blunt, Mrs. Blunt's scrap-books. Conference minutes. Guiseley church magazines. St. Jude's and St. Aidan's magazine. Parish histories of St.Luke's, Manningham, and Keighley. Revd. John Winder, Revd. Canon John Towell, Ven. Charles Forder.

Chapter 10. Conference minutes. Diocesan Board of Finance minutes. Ven. Charles Forder. Mrs. Ann Remfry, Tiarks' family scrap-book. Miss Elsie Cunliffe.

Chapter 11. Conference minutes. Mr. Derrick Watson. Dr. Ruth Hardy, press cuttings. Mrs. Nora Goodchild. Revd. Norman Goodacre. Mr. David Blunt.

Chapter 12. 'Donald Coggan' by Margaret Pawley 1987. Lord and Lady Coggan. 'Convictions' by Donald Coggan 1975. Tiarks' family scrap-book. Conference minutes. Mrs. Kitty Hartley. Revd. Canon John Clayton. 'Cowling, a Moorland Parish' edited by Alec Wood - Chapter 8. 'Religion' by Revd. Robert Carter. Rt. Revd. and Mrs. H. Higgs.

Chapter 13. Miss Beatrice Kennedy. Mrs. Kitty Hartley. Conference minutes. Mrs. Nora Goodchild. St. Christopher's, Holme Wood, tenth anniversary booklet. 'Donald Coggan' by Margaret Pawley 1987. Lord Coggan. Miss Margaret Leach. Miss Irene Price. 'My Name Shall be There' by Margaret Leach. Revd. Canon John Clayton.

Chapter 14. Miss Audrey Wignall. Conference minutes. Mr. Edward Garnett.

Chapter 15. Conference minutes. Revd. Canons Bruce Grainger, Eric Murgatroyd and John Clayton. Revd. Prebendary Robert Sharp. Mr. John Foster Beaver's Memoirs, courtesy of Mrs. Joy Smithells. 'Decently and in Order' by Michael Parker. 'Diocese of Bradford Constitution and Regulations' by Michael Parker. Report of the Bishop's Commission 1963. Mrs. Marguerite Johnston, Mrs. Johnston's scrap-book. Pastoral committee minutes. Bishop's Commission on Keighley 1967 (The Watson Commission).Bishopscroft archives. Miss Pam Bradley. Parcevall Hall Silver Jubilee booklet.

Chapter 16. Conference minutes. 'History of the Diocese of Chelmsford' by Canon Gordon Hewitt. Mrs. Ann Remfry, the Tiarks' scrap-books. Very Revd. Alan Cooper. Mrs. Marguerite Johnston, Mrs. Johnston's scrap-book. Revd. Prebendary Robert Sharp. 'The Consideration'. Jubilee issue, Bradford Diocesan News.

Chapter 17. Revd. David Hennessey. Bishop Hook's memorial tribute to Mr. John Foster Beaver. 'Celebrated Yorkshire Folk' by J.S. Pattinson. Rt. Revd. and Mrs. Hook, their scrap-book. Bishopscroft archives. Revd. Roger Wood. Rt. Revd. Frank Sargeant. Revd. Canon Bruce Grainger, Revd. Canon David Creaser.

Chapter 18. Revd. David Hennessey. Ven. David Rogers. Bradford Diocesan news. Rt. Revd. Frank Sargeant. Rt. Revd. and Mrs. Hook, their scrap-book. Very Revd. and Mrs. Brandon Jackson. Mrs. Nora Goodchild.

Chapter 19. Revd. Peter Hawkins. 'Community Building and Interfaith Relations' by Richard Wallace. Rt. Revd. Frank Sargeant. 'A Pattern of Faith' - introduction by Rowan Williams 1986. Mrs. Pamela Paul. 'A Life of Bishop John A.T. Robinson' by Eric James 1987. Bradford Diocesan News. Diocesan synod minutes. 'Links. A Short History of the Partnerships and an Introduction to the Diocese of Khartoum' by Astrid Hansen 1989. Mrs. Caroline Moore, 'The Way of the Cross' cuttings.

Chapter 20. Rt. Revd. Frank Sargeant. Rt. Revd. Martin Wharton. Revd. Canon Christopher Hayward. Rt. Revd. Robert Williamson. Very Revd. Brandon Jackson. Bishopscroft archives. Mr. Philip Lewis. 'The Satanic Verses - Bradford Responds' (Bradford & Ilkley Community College) 1992. 'Believing Bishops' by Simon Lee and Peter Stanford 1990. 'Faith in the City'. Pastoral committee report on Urban Priority Areas. 'Committed to Caring' literature. Synod minutes.

Chapter 21. Rt. Revd. Robert Williamson. Primary Visitation Charge 1986. Synod minutes. Conference minutes.

ACKNOWLEDGEMENTS FOR ILLUSTRATIONS

The author and the Diocese of Bradford are most grateful for permission to reproduce photographs and drawings from personal family albums and the following

The Telegraph and Argus (and Yorkshire Observer): pages 32 78 122 134 163 166 168 173 175 176 179

The Yorkshire Evening Post: pages 104 120 130 140 154 174

The Westmorland Gazette: page 180

Bassano Studios London (Elliott & Fry): page 69

C. H. Wood (Bradford) Ltd.: back cover

Bradford Economic Development Unit: frontispiece

Bradford Cathedral: pages 34 92 190

Gordon Bastow: page 56

J. Barrie Birch: page 43

Nigel Cottam: page 9

Canon Ralph Crowe: pages 58 95 141

John F. Hansen: pages 47 75 147 170

David Hyde (Skipton): page 14

Mary McMahon: page 129

Mike Peak: pages frontcover 45 114

Ronald G. Sims: page 126

Peter Watkins: page 48

Gill Wood: page 53

INDEX

Bold number indicates illustration